CW01660304

Raspberry Pi Pico Essentials

Program, build, and master over 50 projects with MicroPython and the RP2040 microprocessor

Dogan Ibrahim

elektor
design > share > sell

This is an Elektor Publication. Elektor is the media brand of
Elektor International Media B.V.
PO Box 11, NL-6114-ZG Susteren, The Netherlands
Phone: +31 46 4389444

Declaration

The Author and the Publisher have used their best efforts in ensuring the correctness of the information contained in this book. They do not assume, and hereby disclaim, any liability to any party for any loss or damage caused by errors or omissions in this book, whether such errors or omissions result from negligence, accident or any other cause.

British Library Cataloguing in Publication Data
A catalogue record for this book is available from the British Library

ISBN 978-3-89576-427-1 Print
ISBN 978-3-89576-428-8 eBook
ISBN 978-3-89576-429-5 ePub

Prepress Production: D-Vision, Julian van den Berg

Preface

Traditionally, a computer was built using a microprocessor chip and many external support chips. A microprocessor includes a Central Processing Unit (CPU), an Arithmetic and Logic Unit (ALU), and timing and control circuitry — and as such it is not particularly useful on its own. A microprocessor must be supported by many external chips such as memory, input/output, timers, interrupt circuits etcetera, before it becomes a useful computer. The disadvantage of this type of design was that the chip count was large, resulting in complex design and wiring, and high power consumption.

A microcontroller on the other hand is basically a single chip computer including a CPU, memory, input/output circuitry, timers, interrupt circuitry, clock circuitry, and several other circuits and modules, all housed in a single silicon chip. Early microcontrollers were limited in their capacities and speed and they consumed considerably more power. Most of the early microcontrollers were 8-bit processors with clock speeds in the region of several MHz and offered only hundreds of bytes of program and data memories. These microcontrollers were traditionally programmed using the assembly languages of the target processors. 8-bit microcontrollers are still in common use, especially in small projects where large amounts of memory or high speed are not the main requirements. With the advancement of chip technology we now have 32-bit and 64-bit microcontrollers with speeds in the region of several GHz and offering several GB of memory space. Microcontrollers are nowadays programmed using a high-level language such as C, C#, BASIC, PASCAL, JAVA, etc.

The Raspberry Pi Pico is a high-performance microcontroller, designed especially for physical computing. Readers should realize that microcontrollers are very different from single-board computers like the Raspberry Pi 4 (and other family members of the Raspberry Pi). There is no operating system on the Raspberry Pi Pico. Microcontrollers like the Raspberry Pi Pico can be programmed to run a single task and they can be used in fast real-time control and monitoring applications.

The Raspberry Pi Pico is based on the fast and very efficient dual-core ARM Cortex-M0+ RP2040 microcontroller chip running at up to 133 MHz. The chip incorporates 264 KB of SRAM and 2 MB of Flash memory. What makes the Raspberry Pi Pico very attractive is its large number of GPIO pins, and commonly used peripheral interface modules, such as SPI, I^2C, UART, PWM, plus fast and accurate timing modules.

Perhaps the biggest advantage of the Raspberry Pi Pico compared to other many microcontrollers in the marketplace is its very low cost, large memory, and fast and accurate timing modules. At the time of writing this book the cost of a single unit was around $6.

Raspberry Pi Pico can easily be programmed using some of the popular high-level languages such as MicroPython, or C/C++. There are many application notes, tutorials, and datasheets available on the Internet covering the use of the Raspberry Pi Pico.

This book is an introduction to using the Raspberry Pi Pico microcontroller with the MicroPython programming language. The Thonny development environment (IDE) is used in all the projects in the book, and readers are recommended to use this IDE. There are over 50 working and tested projects in the book, covering almost all aspects of the Raspberry Pi Pico.

The following sub-headings are given for each project to make it easy to follow:

- Title
- Brief Description
- Aim
- Block Diagram
- Circuit Diagram
- Program Listing with full description

I hope your next microcontroller-based projects make use of the Raspberry Pi Pico, and this book becomes useful in the development of your projects.

Dr Dogan Ibrahim
London, February, 2021

Chapter 1 • Raspberry Pi Pico Hardware

1.1 Overview

The Raspberry Pi Pico is a single-board microcontroller module developed by the Raspberry Pi Foundation. This module is based on the RP2040 microcontroller chip. In this Chapter we will be looking at the hardware details of the Raspberry Pi Pico microcontroller module in some detail. From here on, we will be calling this microcontroller module "Pico" for short, in for appreciation and recognition though of its official name: Raspberry Pi Pico.

1.2 Pico hardware module

The "Pico" is a very low-cost, $4 microcontroller module based on the RP2040 microcontroller chip having a dual Cortex-M0+ processor. Figure 1.1 shows the front view of the Pico hardware module which is basically a small board. At the centre of the board is the tiny, 7×7 mm RP2040 microcontroller chip housed in a QFN-56 package. At the two edges of the board there are 40 gold-coloured metal GPIO (General-Input-Output) pins with holes. Soldering pins to these holes enables external connections to be easily made to the board. The holes are marked starting with number 1 at the top left corner of the board and the numbers increase downwards up to number 40 which is at the top right-hand corner of the board. The board is breadboard-compatible (i.e. 0.1-inch pin spacing), and after soldering the pins, the board can be plugged on a breadboard for easy connection to the GPIO pins using jumper wires. Next to these holes you will see bumpy circular cut-outs which can be plugged in on top of other modules without having any physical pins fitted.

Figure 1.1: Front view of the Pico hardware module.

At one edge of the board there is the micro-USB B port for supplying power to the board as well as for programming it. Next to the USB port there is an on-board user LED that can be used during program development. Next to this LED sits a button named as BOOTSEL that is used during programming of the microcontroller as we will see in next Chapters. At the other edge of the board, next to the Raspberry Pi logo, there are 3 connectors that can be used for debugging your programs.

Figure 1.2 shows the back view of the Pico hardware module. Here, all the GPIO pins are identified with letters and numbers. You will notice the following types of letters and numbers:

GND	-	power supply ground (digital ground)
AGND	-	power supply ground (analogue ground)
3V3	-	+3.3 V power supply (output)
GP0 – GP22	-	digital GPIO
GP26_A0 – GP28_A2	-	analogue inputs
ADC_VREF	-	ADC reference voltage
TP1 – TP6	-	test points
SWDIO, GND, SWCLK	-	debug interface
RUN	-	default RUN pin. Connect LOW to reset the RP2040.
3V3_EN	-	this pin by default enables the +3.3V power supply. +3.3 V can be disabled by connecting this pin LOW.
VSYS	-	system input voltage (1.8 V to 5.5 V) used by the on-board SMPS to generate +3.3 V supply for the board.
VBUS	-	micro-USB input voltage (+5 V)

Figure 1.2: Back view of the Pico hardware module.

Some of the GPIO pins are used for internal board functions. These are:

GP29 (input)	-	used in ADC mode (ADC3) to measure VSYS/3
GP25 (output)	-	connected to on-board user LED
GP24 (input)	-	VBUS sense - HIGH if VBUS is present, else LOW
GP23 (output)	-	Controls the on-board SMPS Power Save pin

The specifications of the Pico hardware module are as follows:

- 32-bit RP2040 Cortex-M0+ dual core processor operating at 133 MHz
- 2 Mbyte Q-SPI Flash memory
- 264 Kbyte SRAM memory
- 26 GPIO (+3.3V compatible)
- 3× 12-bit ADC pins
- Serial Wire Debug (SWD) port
- Micro-USB port (USB 1.1) for power (+5V) and data (programming)
- 2× UART, 2 x I^2C, 2 x SPI bus interface
- 16× PWM channels
- 1× Timer (with 4 alarms), 1× Real-Time Counter
- On-board temperature sensor

- On-board LED (on port GP25)
- MicroPython, C, C++ programming
- Drag & drop programming using mass storage over USB

The Pico's GPIO hardware is +3.3 V compatible and it is therefore important to be careful not to exceed this voltage when interfacing external input devices to the GPIO pins. +5 V to +3.3 V logic converter circuits or resistive potential divider circuits must be used if it is required to interface devices with +5 V outputs to the Pico GPIO pins.
Figure 1.3 shows a resistive potential divider circuit that can be used to lower +5 V to +3.3 V.

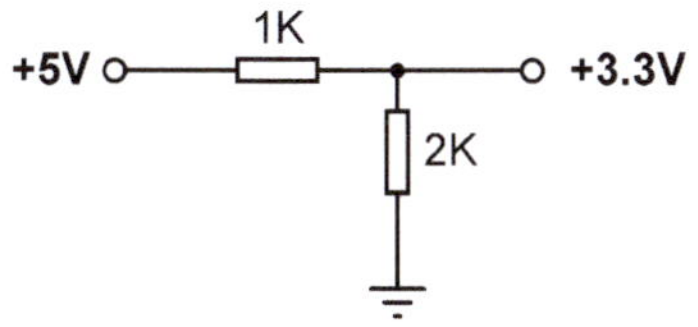

Figure 1.3: resistive potential divider circuit.

1.3 Comparison with the Arduino UNO

The Arduino UNO is one of the most popular microcontroller development boards used by students, practicing engineers, and hobbyists. Table 1.1 shows a comparison of the Raspberry Pi Pico with the Arduino UNO. It is clear from this table that the Pico is much faster than the Arduino UNO, having larger flash and data memories, providing more digital input/output pins, and sporting an on-board temperature sensor. The Arduino UNO operates at +5 V and its GPIO pins are +5 V compatible. Perhaps some advantages of the Arduino UNO include having a built-in EEPROM memory, and having a 6-channel ADC rather than a 3-channel.

Feature	Raspberry Pi Pico	Arduino UNO
Microcontroller	RP2040	Atmega328P
Core and bits	Dual core, 32-bit, Cortex-M0+	Single-core 8-bit
RAM	264 Kbytes	2 Kbytes
Flash	2 Mbytes	32 Kbytes
CPU speed	48 MHz to 133 MHz	16 MHz
EEPROM	None	1 KByte
Power input	+5 V through USB port	+5V through USB port
Alternative power	2–5 V via VSYS pin	7–12 V
MCU operating voltage	+3.3 V	+5 V
GPIO count	26	20
ADC count	3	6
Hardware UART	2	1
Hardware I2C	2	1
Hardware SPI	2	1
Hardware PWM	16	6
Programming languages	MicroPython, C, C++	C (Arduino IDE)
On-board LED	1	1
Cost	$4	$20

Table 1.1: Comparison of Raspberry Pi Pico and Arduino UNO.

1.4 Operating conditions and powering the Pico

The recommended operating conditions for the Pico are:

- Operating temperature: –20ºC to +85ºC
- VBUS voltage: +5 V ±10%
- VSYS voltage: +1.8 V to +5.5 V

An on-board SMPS is used to generate the +3.3 V to power the RP2040 from a range of input voltages from 1.8 V to +5.5 V. For example, 3 alkaline size-AA batteries can be used to provide +4.5 V to power the Pico.
The Pico can be powered in several ways. The simplest method is to plug the micro-USB port into a +5 V power source, such as the USB port of a computer or a +5 V power adapter. This will provide power to the VSYS input (see Figure 1.4) through a Schottky diode. The voltage at the VSYS input is therefore VBUS voltage minus the voltage drop of the Schottky diode (about +0.7 V). VBUS and VSYS pins can be shorted if the board is powered from an external +5 V USB port. This will increase the voltage input slightly and hence reduce ripples on VSYS. VSYS voltage is fed to the SMPS through the RT6150 which generates fixed +3.3 V for the MCU and other parts of the board. VSYS is divided by 3, and is available at analogue input port GPIO29 (ADC3) which can easily be monitored. GPIO24 checks the existence of VBUS voltage and is at logic HIGH if VBUS is present.
Another method to power the Pico is by applying external voltage (+1.8 V to +5.5 V) to the VSYS input directly (e.g., using batteries or external power supply). We can also use the USB input and VSYS inputs together to supply power to Pico, for example to operate with both batteries and the USB port. If this method is used, then a Schottky diode should be used at the VSYS input to prevent the supplies from interfering with each other. The higher of the voltages will power VSYS.

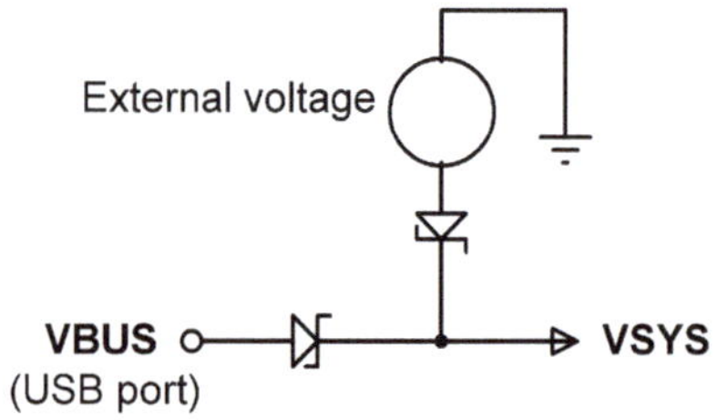

Figure 1.4: Powering the Pico.

1.5 Pinout of the RP2040 microcontroller and Pico module

Figure 1.5 shows the RP2040 microcontroller pinout, which is housed in a 56-pin package. The Pico module pinout is shown in Figure 1.6 in detail. As you can see from the illustration, most pins have multiple functions. For example, GPIO0 (pin 1) doubles as the UART0 TX, I2C0 SDA, and the SPI0 RX pin.

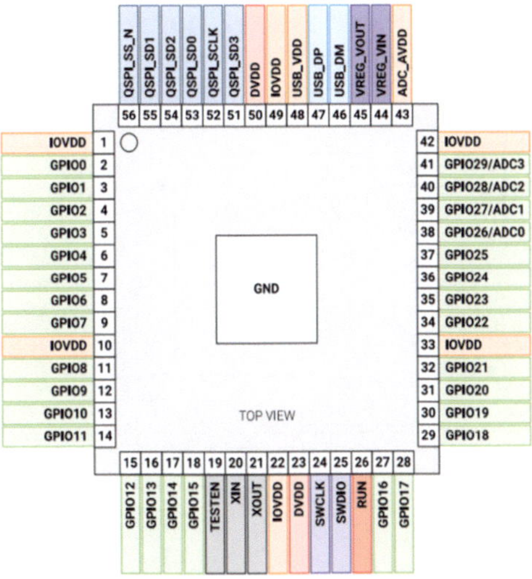

Figure 1.5: RP2040 microcontroller pinout.

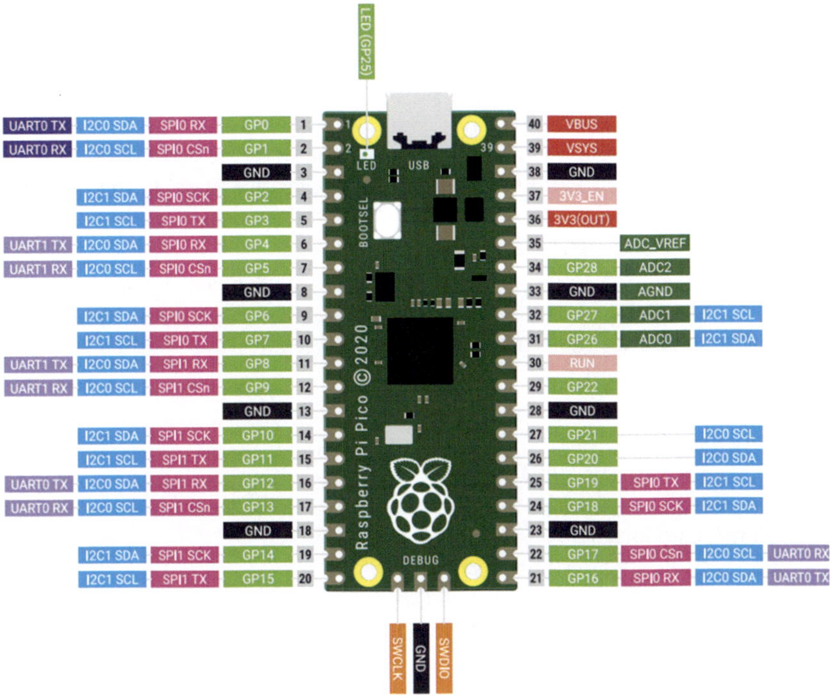

Figure 1.6: Raspberry Pi Pico pinout.

Figure 1.7 shows a simplified block diagram of the Pico hardware module. Notice that the GPIO pins are directly connected from the microcontroller chip to the GPIO connector. GPIO nos. 26-28 can be used either as digital GPIO or as ADC inputs. ADC inputs GPIO26-29 have reverse-biased diodes to 3 V and therefore the input voltage must not exceed 3V3 +

300 mV. Another point to note is that if the RP2040 is not powered, applying voltages to GPIO26-29 pins may leak through the diode to the power supply (there is no problem with the other GPIO pins and voltage can be applied when the RP2040 is not powered).

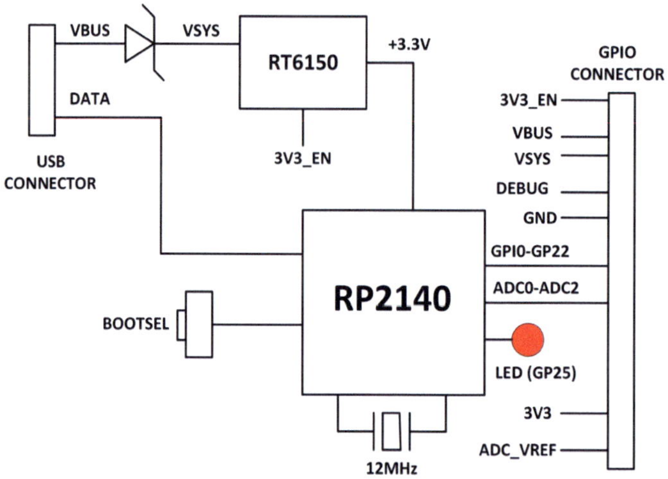

Figure 1.7: Simplified block diagram.

1.6 Other RP2040 microcontroller-based boards

During the writing of this book, some third-party manufacturers have been developing microcontrollers based on the RP2040 chip. Some examples are given in this section.

1.6.1 Adafruit Feather RP2040

This microcontroller board (Figure 1.8) has the following basic specifications:

- RP2040 32-bit Cortex-M0+ running at 125 MHz
- 4 MB Flash memory
- 264 KB RAM
- 4× 12-bit ADC
- 2× I^{2}C, 2× SPI, 2× UART
- 16× PWM
- 200 mA LiPo charger
- Reset and Bootloader buttons
- 24 MHz crystal
- +3.3 V regulator with 500 mA current output
- USB type-C connector
- on-board red LED
- RGB NeoPixel
- on-board STEMMA QT connector with optional SWD debug port

Figure 1.8: Adafruit Feather Rp2040.

1.6.2 Adafruit ItsyBitsy RP2040

The ItsyBitsy RP2040 (Figure 1.9) is another RP2040-based microcontroller board from Adafruit. Its basic features are very similar to Feather RP2040. It has USB-micro B connector and provides +5 V output.

Figure 1.9: Adafruit ItsyBitsy RP2040.

1.6.3 Pimoroni PicoSystem

This is a miniature gaming board (Figure 1.10) developed around the RP2040 microcontroller. Its basic features are:

- 133 MHz clock
- 264 KB SRAM
- LCD screen
- joypad
- buttons
- LiPo battery
- USB-C power connector

Figure 1.10: Pimoroni PicoSystem.

1.6.4 Arduino Nano RP2040 Connect

This board (Figure 1.11) offers 16 MB flash, 9-axis IMU, and a microphone. It has a very efficient power supply section equipped with Wi-Fi/Bluetooth.

Figure 1.11: Arduino Nano RP2040 Connect.

1.6.5 SparkFun Thing Plus RP2040

This development platform (Figure 1.12) provides an SD card slot, 16 MB flash memory, a JST single-cell battery connector, a WS2812 RGB LED, JTAG pins, and Qwiic connector. Its basic features are:

- 133 MHz speed
- 264 KB SRAM
- 4× 12-bit ADC
- 2× UART, 2× I^2C, 2× SPI
- 16× PWM
- 1× timer with 4 alarms

Figure 1.12: SparkFun Thing Plus RP2040.

1.6.6 Pimoroni Pico Explorer Base

This development board (Figure 1.13) includes a small breadboard and a 240 × 240 IPS LC display with 4 tactile buttons. A socket is provided on the board to plug-in a Raspberry Pi Pico board. The basic features of this development board are:

- piezo speaker
- 1.54-inch IPS LCD
- 4× buttons
- 2× half-bridge motor drives
- two breakout I^2C sockets
- easy access to GPIO and ADC pins
- mini breadboard
- no soldering required
- Raspberry Pi Pico not supplied

Figure 1.13: Pimoroni Pico Explorer Base.

1.6.7 SparkFun MicroMod RP2040 Processor

This board (Figure 1.14) includes a MicroMod M.2 connector for access to the GPIO pins.

Figure 1.14: SparkFun MicroMod RP 2040 Processor.

1.6.8 SparkFun Pro Micro RP2040

This board (Figure 1.15) includes a ES2812B addressable LED, boot button, reset button, Qwiic connector, USB-C power interface, PTC fuse, and castellated GPIO pads.

Figure 1.15: SparkFun Pro Micro RP2040.

1.6.9 Pico RGB Keypad Base

This board is equipped with 4×4 rainbow-illuminated keypad (Figure 1.16) with APA102 LEDs. The basic features are:

- 4×4 keypad
- 16× APA102 RGB LEDs
- keypad connected via I^{2}C I/O expander
- GPIO pins labelled

Figure 1.16 Pico RGB Keypad Base.

1.6.10 Pico Omnibus

This is an expansion board (Figure 1.17) for the Pico. The basic features of this board include:

- GPIO pins labelled
- two landing areas with labelled (mirrored) male headers for attaching add-ons
- 4× rubber feet
- compatible with Raspberry Pi Pico
- fully assembled
- dimensions approx. 94 × 52 × 12 mm

Figure 1.17: Pico Omnibus.

1.6.11 Pimoroni Pico VGA Demo Base

This board (Figure 1.18) has VGA output and SD card slot. The basic features are:

- powered by Raspberry Pi Pico
- 15-pin VGA connector
- I^2S DAC for line out audio

- PWM audio output
- SD card slot
- Reset button
- headers to install your Raspberry Pi Pico
- three user switches
- no soldering required

Figure 1.18: Pimoroni Pico VGA Demo Base.

Chapter 2 • Raspberry Pi Pico Programming

2.1 Overview

At the time of writing this book, the Raspberry Pi Pico accepts programming with the following programming languages:

- C/C++
- MicroPython
- assembly language

Although the Pico by default is set up for use with the powerful and popular C/C++ language, many beginners find it easier to use MicroPython, which is a version of the Python programming language developed specifically for microcontrollers.
In this Chapter we will learn how to install and use the MicroPython programming language. We will be using the Thonny text editor which has been developed specifically for Python programs.
Many working and fully tested projects will be given in the next Chapters using MicroPython with our Pico. Use of the C language will also be discussed in later Chapters with some projects.

2.2 Installing MicroPython on the Pico

MicroPython must be installed on the Pico before the board can be used. Once installed, MicroPython stays on your Pico, unless it is overwritten with something else. Installing MicroPython requires an Internet connection, and this is required only once. Since the Pico has no Wi-Fi connectivity, we will need to use a computer with Internet access. This can be done either by using a Raspberry Pi (e.g. Raspberry Pi 4), or by using a PC. In this section we will see how to install using both methods.

2.2.1 Using a Raspberry Pi 4 to aid installing MicroPython on the Pico

The steps are as follows.

- Boot your Raspberry Pi 4 and log in to Desktop.
- Make sure your Raspberry Pi is connected to the Internet.
- Hold down the **BOOTSEL** button on your Pico.
- Connect your Pico to one of the USB ports of the Raspberry Pi 4 using a micro-USB cable while holding down the button.
- Wait a few seconds and release the **BOOTSEL** button.
- You should see the Pico appear as a removable drive. Click **OK** in the **Removable medium is inserted** window (Figure 2.1).

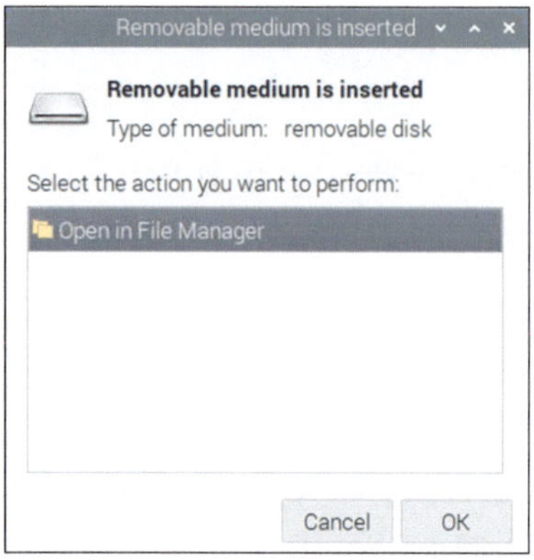

Figure 2.1: Click OK.

- In the **File Manager** window, you will see two files with the names **INDEX.HTM** and **INFO_UF2.TXT** (Figure 2.2).

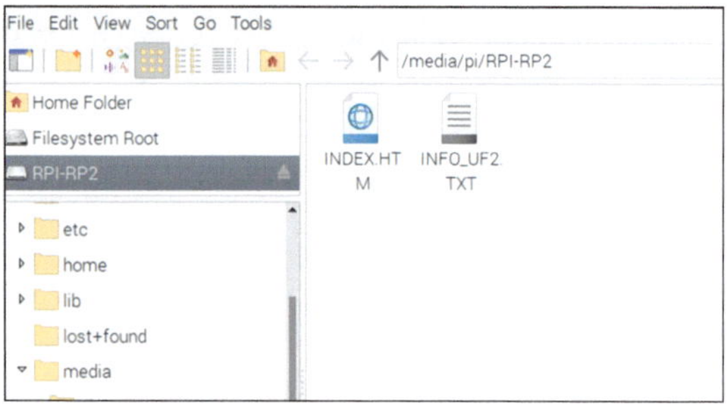

Figure 2.2: Notice two files.

- Double-click on file **INDEX.HTM** and scroll down.
- You should see the message **Welcome to your Raspberry Pi Pico** displayed in a web page (Figure 2.3).

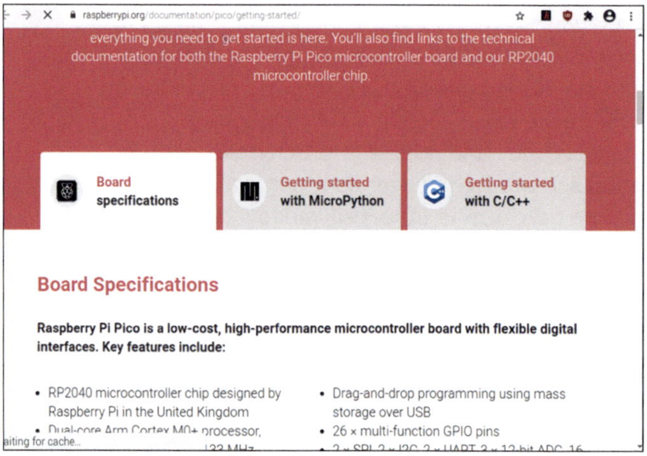

Figure 2.3: Displayed message.

- Click on the **Getting started with MicroPython** tab and click **Download UF2 file** to download the **MicroPython** firmware. You should see the downloaded file at the bottom of the screen. This will take only a few seconds (Figure 2.4).

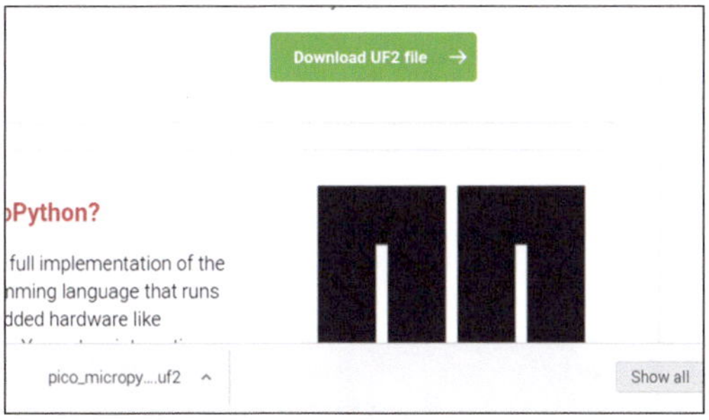

Figure 2.4: Download the UF2 file.

- Close your browser window by clicking on the cross icon located at the top right corner.
- Open the **File Manager** by clicking on menu, followed by **Accessories**.
- Open the **Downloads** folder (under **/home/pi**) and locate the file with the extension: **.uf2**. This file will have a name similar to: **micropython-20-Jan-2021.uf2** (Figure 2.5)

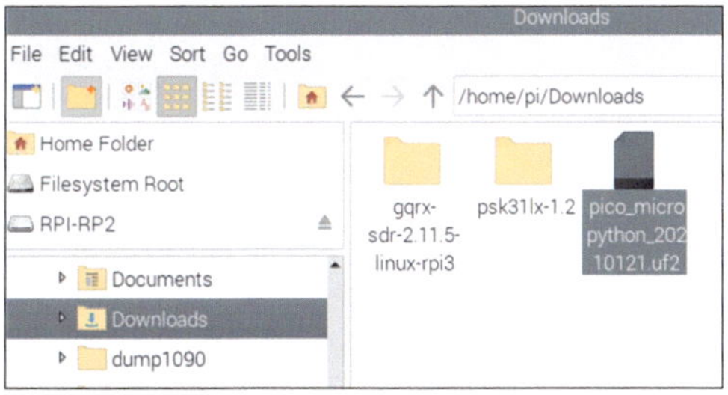

Figure 2.5: Locate the file with extension: ".uf2".

- Drag and drop this file to Raspberry Pi Pico's removable drive which is named: **RPI-RP2** (at the top left side of the screen – see Figure 2.5).
- After a while, the **MicroPython** firmware will be installed onto the internal storage of Pico and the drive will disappear.
- Your Pico is now running **MicroPython**.
- Powering-down the Pico will not erase MicroPython from its memory.

Using the Thonny text editor from Raspberry Pi

Thonny is a free Python Integrated Development Environment (IDE) developed specifically for Python. It has built-in text editor and debugger and a number of other utilities that can be useful during program development.

In this section we will learn how to use Thonny by invoking it from Raspberry Pi. You should leave your Pico connected to Raspberry Pi. We will create a one-line program to display the message **Hello from Raspberry Pi Pico**.

The steps are given below.

- Click Menu, followed by **Programming** on your Raspberry Pi Desktop and then click **Thonny Python IDE** (see Figure 2.6). The author had version 3.3.3 of Thonny installed on his Raspberry Pi 4.

Figure 2.6: Start Thonny on your Raspberry Pi.

- Click on the label **Python** at the bottom right-hand corner of Thonny (Figure 2.7).

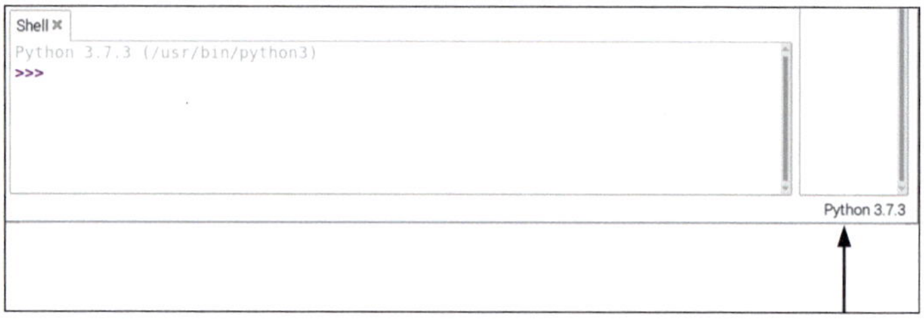

Figure 2.7: Click on Python in the bottom right-hand corner.

- Click to select **MicroPython (Raspberry Pi Pico)** as shown in Figure 2.8.

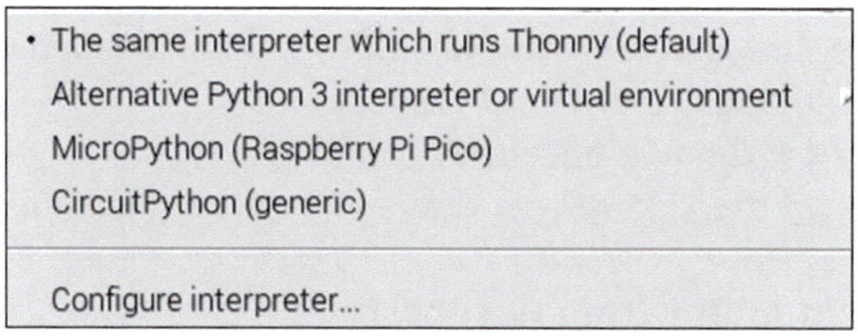

Figure 2.8: Select: Raspberry Pi Pico.

- You should see the version number of your MicroPython displayed in the bottom part of the screen where Shell is located (Figure 2.9).

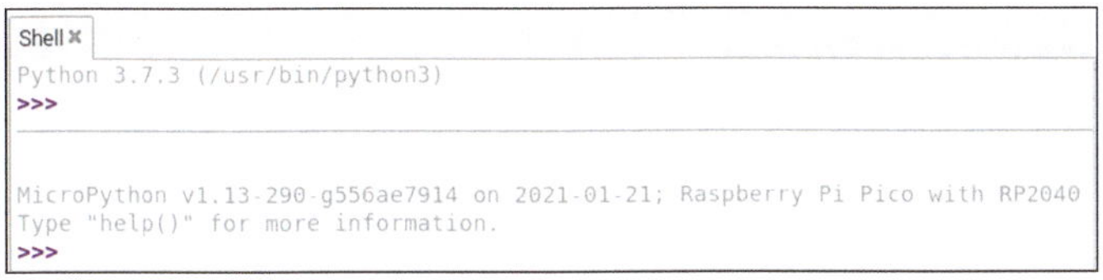

Figure 2.9: Version number of MicroPython is displayed.

- We are now ready to write our simple program. Enter the following line in the lower part of the screen where **Shell** sits. Program statements written in this part of Thonny are executed online and immediately. This part is normally used to test parts of a program. Enter:

```
print("Hello from Raspberry Pi Pico")
```

you should see message **Hello from Raspberry Pi Pico** displayed as shown in Figure 2.10.

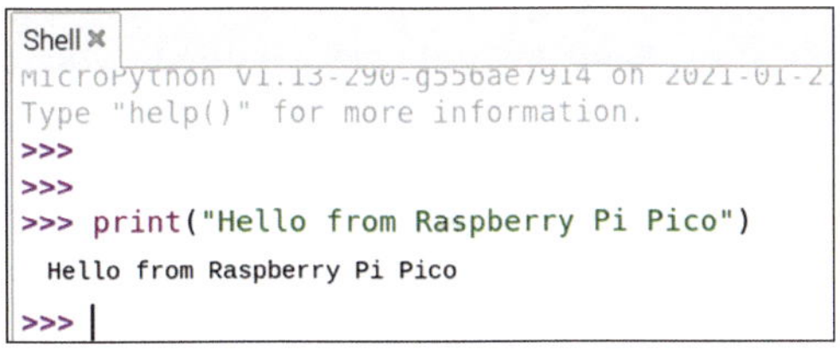

Figure 2.10: Displaying a message.

Thonny's icons

At the top of the Thonny screen you will see a number of icons as shown in Figure 2.11. The functions of these icons are described in this section (notice that plain letters are used to identify the icons).

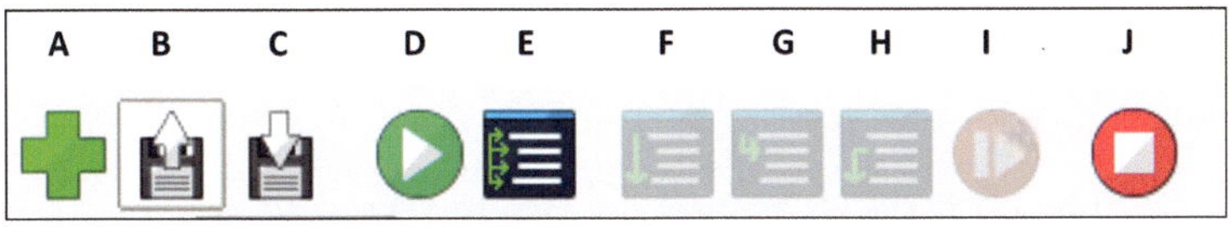

Figure 2.11: Icons presented by Thonny.

A: NEW. Create a new file.
B: Open. Open an existing file
C: Save. Save a file
D: Run. Run the current program
E: Debug. Debug the current program
F: Step Over. Step over a function when in Debug mode
G: Step Into. Step into a function in Debug mode
H: Step Out. Step out of a function in Debug mode
I: Resume. Resume a stopped session
J: Stop/Restart. Stop/restart a session

Writing a program using Thonny

In an earlier section we have seen how to execute a statement online using the Thonny **Shell**. In almost all applications we have to write programs. As an example, the steps to write and run a very simple one-line program to display message **Hello from program...** are given below.

- Enter the program statements at the upper part of the screen as shown in Figure 2.12.

Figure 2.12: Write the program at upper part of the screen.

- Click **File** followed by **Save As** and give a name to your program. e.g. **FirstProg.** You have the option of storing the program either on your Raspberry Pi or on the Pico. Click **Raspberry Pi Pico** to save it on the Pico (Figure 2.13). Enter the name of your program (**FirstProg**) and click **OK** (notice that the file is saved with the extension **.py**).

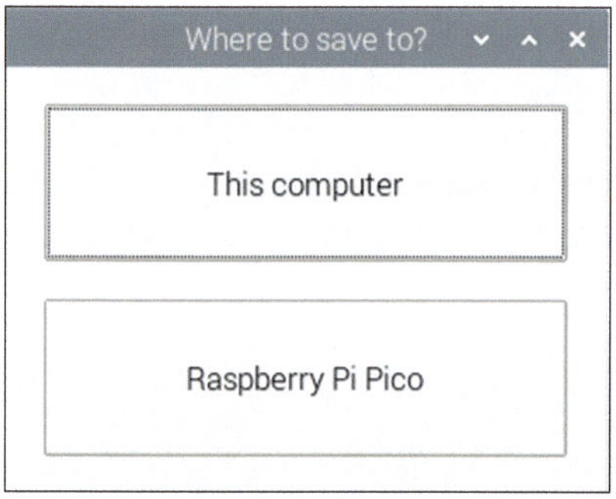

Figure 2.13: Click Raspberry Pi Pico to save your program.

- Click the green arrow icon at the top of the screen (under **Run**) to run your program. The output of the program will be displayed in the lower **Shell** part of the screen as shown in Figure 2.14.

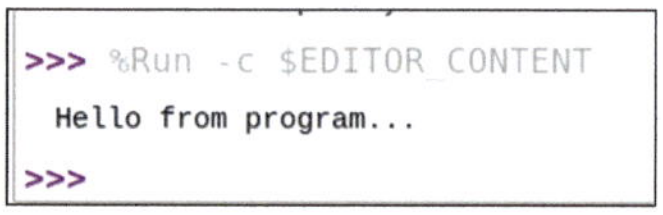

Figure 2.14: Output of the program.

2.2.2 Using a PC (Windows 10) to help install MicroPython on Pico

In Section 2.2.1 we have learned how to install **MicroPython** on Pico using a Raspberry Pi 4. In this section we will see how to install **MicroPython** using only a PC running the Windows 10 operating system. This is the option the readers should choose if they do not have access to a Raspberry Pi.
The steps are as follows.

- Make sure your PC is connected to the Internet.
- Hold down the **BOOTSEL** button on your Pico.
- Connect your Pico to the USB port of your PC using a micro-USB cable while holding down the button.
- Wait a few seconds and let go the **BOOTSEL** button.
- You should see the Pico appear as a removable drive with the name **RPI-RP2** as shown in Figure 2.15 (drive **E:** in this case).

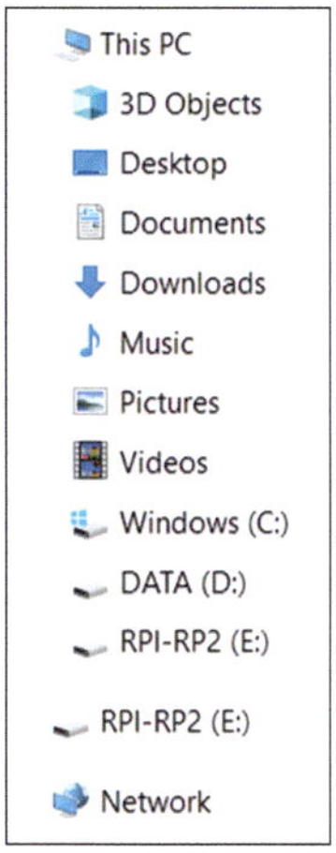

Figure 2.15: Pico as a removable drive RPI-RP2.

- Click on drive RPI-RP2. You will see two files with the names **INDEX.HTM** and **INFO_UF2.TXT** (see Figure 2.16).

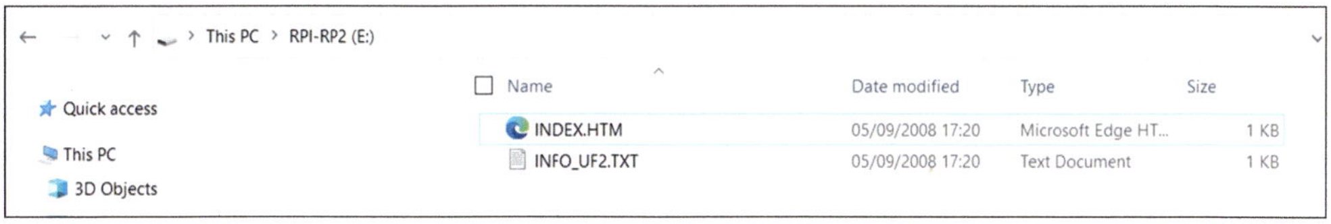

Figure 2.16: You will see two files.

- Double-click on file **INDEX.HTM** and scroll down.
- You should see the message **Welcome to your Raspberry Pi Pico** displayed in a web page (Figure 2.17)

Figure 2.17: Displayed message.

- Click on the **Getting started with MicroPython** tab and click **Download UF2 file** to download the **MicroPython** firmware. You should see the downloaded file at the bottom of the screen. This will take only a few seconds (Figure 2.18).

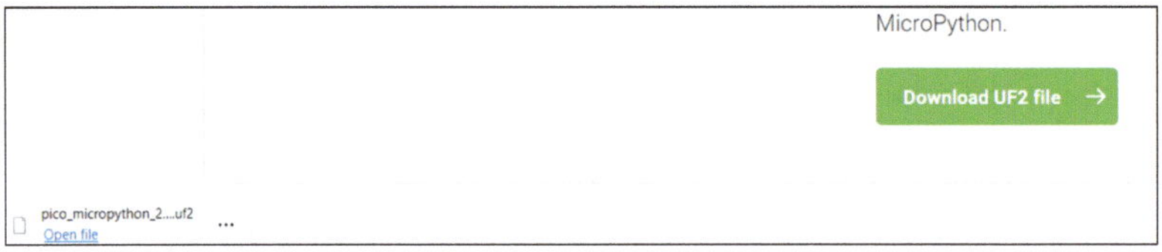

Figure 2.18. Download the "UF2" file.

- Close your browser window.
- Open the **File Explorer** on your PC.
- Open the **Downloads** folder and locate the file with the extension: **.uf2**. This file will have the name similar to: **micropython-20-Jan-2021.uf2** (Figure 2.19).

Figure 2.19: Locate file with extension ".uf2".

- Drag and drop this file to Raspberry Pi Pico's removable drive named: **RPI-RP2**.
- After a while, the **MicroPython** firmware will be installed onto the internal storage of Pico and the drive RPI-RP2 will disappear.
- Your Pico is now running **MicroPython**.
- Powering down the Pico will not erase **MicroPython** from its memory.

Using the Thonny text editor from the PC

In the previous section we have learned how to use the Thonny on Raspberry Pi and develop, save, and run programs on the Pico.

In this section we will be using Thonny on the PC so that a Raspberry Pi is not needed to develop and run our programs. First of all, we have to install Thonny on our PC (if it is not already installed). The steps are given below.

- Go to the Thonny.org web site: https://thonny.org/ .
- Click on the link at the top right-hand side of the screen to install Thonny (see Figure 2.20).

Figure 2.20: Click to install Thonny.

- You should see an icon on the Desktop (Figure 2.21) of your PC. Double-click to start Thonny.

Figure 2.21: Thonny icon on the PC Desktop.

- The startup screen of Thonny on your PC is shown in Figure 2.22.

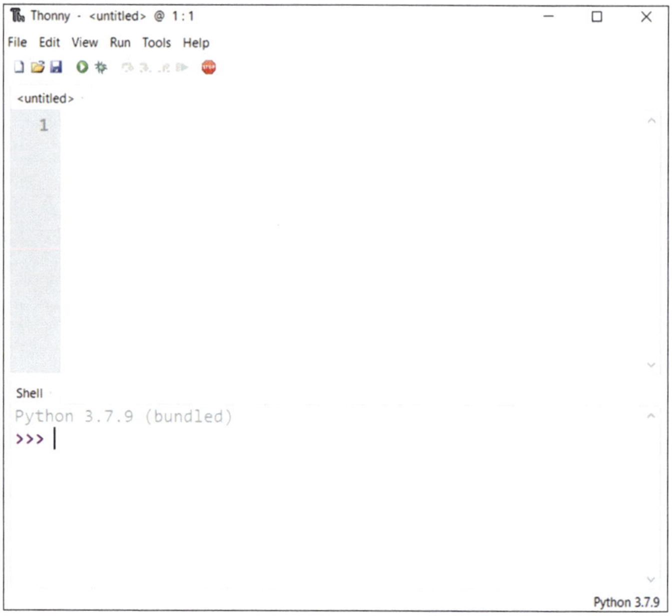

Figure 2.22: Thonny startup screen on the PC.

- Click on the label **Python** at the bottom right-hand corner of the screen and click to select **MicroPyhton (Raspberry Pi Pico).**
- You are now ready to write your programs.
- Enter the following statement at the lower part of the screen (in Shell):

```
print("hello from Thonny on PC")
```

- You should the message hello from Thonny on PC is displayed as shown in Figure 2.24.

Figure 2.24: Displaying the message.

In this book we will be using Thonny on the PC to write programs and to execute them on the Raspberry Pi Pico.
Simple example programs are given in the remainder sections of this Chapter. The aim here has been to review the basic Python programming concepts. However, this book does not aim to teach Python programming. There are many books and tutorials on the Internet for learning Python.

Example 1 — Average of two numbers read from the keyboard

In this example, two numbers are read from the keyboard and their average is displayed. The aim of this example is to show how data can be read from the keyboard.

Solution 1

The program is named **Average** and the program listing and an example run of the program are shown in Figure 2.25. Function **input** is used to read the numbers in the form of strings from the keyboard. These strings are then converted into floating point numbers and stored in variables **n1** and **n2**. The average is calculated by adding and then dividing the numbers by two. The result is displayed on the screen.

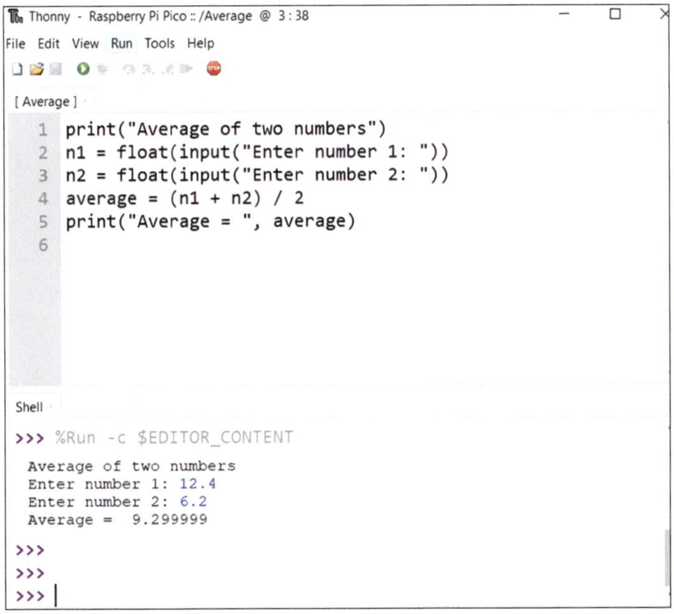

Figure 2.25: Program: Average and a sample run.

Example 2 — Average of 10 numbers read from the keyboard

In this example, 10 numbers are read from the keyboard and their average is displayed. The aim of this example is to show how a loop can be constructed in Python.

Solution 2

The program is named **Average10** and the program listing and an example run of the program are shown in Figure 2.26. In this program a loop is constructed which runs from 0 to 9 (i.e. 10 times). Inside this loop the numbers are read from the keyboard, added to each other, and stored in variable **sum**. The average is then calculated and displayed by dividing **sum** by 10. Notice that a new-line is not printed after the print statements since the option **end = ' '** is used inside the print statement.

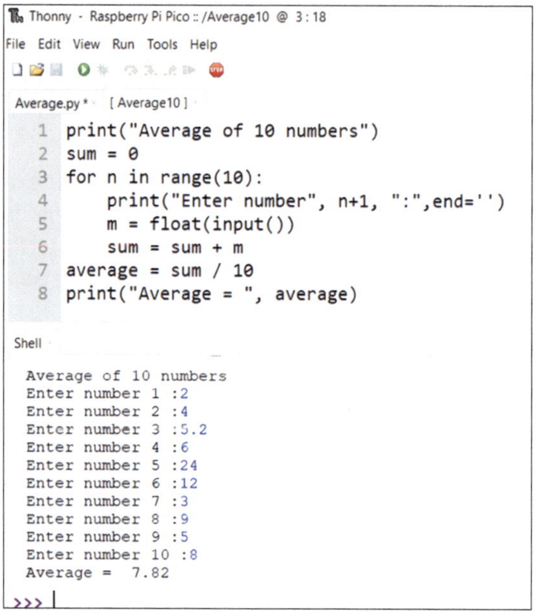

Figure 2.26 Program: Average10, and a sample run.

Example 3 — Surface area of a cylinder

In this example the radius and height of a cylinder are read from the keyboard and its surface area is displayed on the screen.

Solution 3

The program is named **CylArea**, and the program listing and an example run of the program are shown in Figure 2.27. The surface area of a cylinder is given by:

```
Surface area = 2 × π × r × h
```

Where **r** and **h** are the radius and height of the cylinder respectively. In this program the **math** library is imported so that function **Pi** can be used in the program. The surface area of the cylinder is displayed after reading its radius and height.

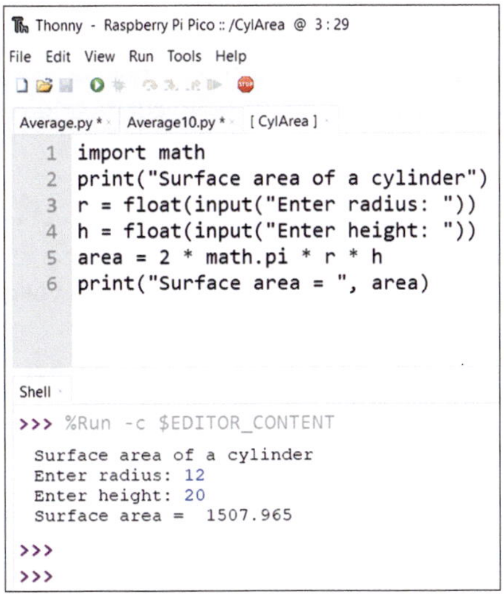

Figure 2.27: Program: CylArea, and a sample run.

Example 4 — ºC to ºF conversion
In this example the program reads degrees Celsius from the keyboard and converts and displays the equivalent degrees Fahrenheit.

Solution 4
The program is named **CtoF** and the program listing and an example run of the program are shown in Figure 2.28. The formula to convert ºC to ºF is:

$$F = 1.8 \times C + 32$$

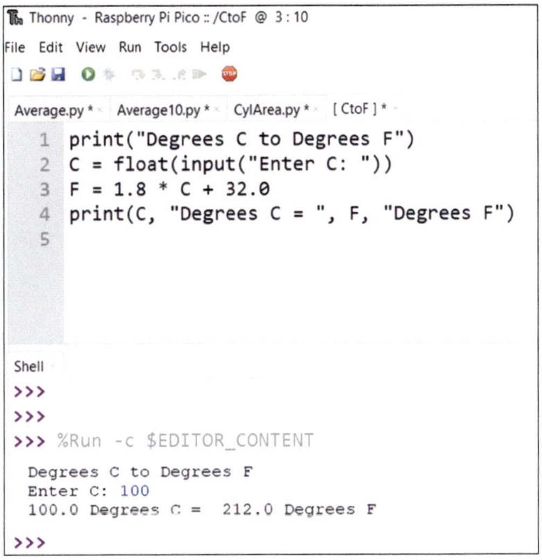

Figure 2.28: Program: CtoF, and a sample run.

Example 5 — Surface area and volume of a cylinder (user function)

In this example, the surface area and volume of a cylinder are calculated whose radius and height are given. The program uses a function to calculate and return the surface area and the volume.

Solution 5

The program is named **CylAreaSurf** and the program listing, and an example run of the program are shown in Figure 2.29. The surface area and the volume of a cylinder are given by:

Surface area = $2 \times \pi \times r \times h$
Volume = $\pi \times r^2 \times h$

Where **r** and **h** are the radius and height of the cylinder respectively. Function **Calc** is used to get the radius and height of the cylinder. The function returns the surface area and volume to the main program which are displayed on the screen.

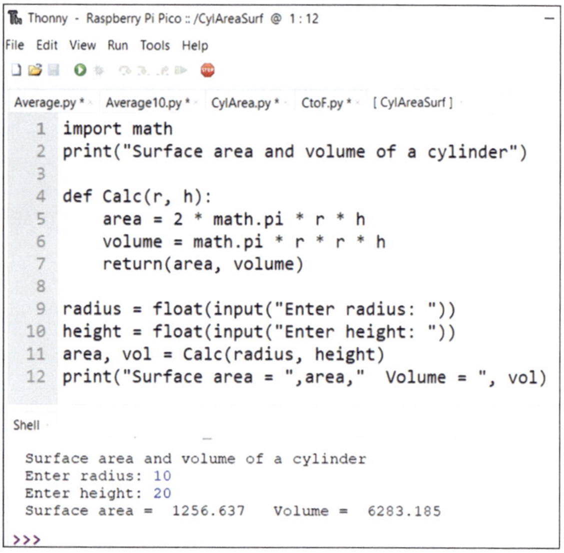

Figure 2.29: Program CylAreaSurf, and a sample run.

Example 6 — Table of squares of numbers

In this example the squares of numbers from 1 to 10 are calculated and tabulated.

Solution 6

The program is named **Squares**, and the program listing and an example run of the program are shown in Figure 2.30. Notice that **\t** prints a tab so that the data can be tabulated nicely.

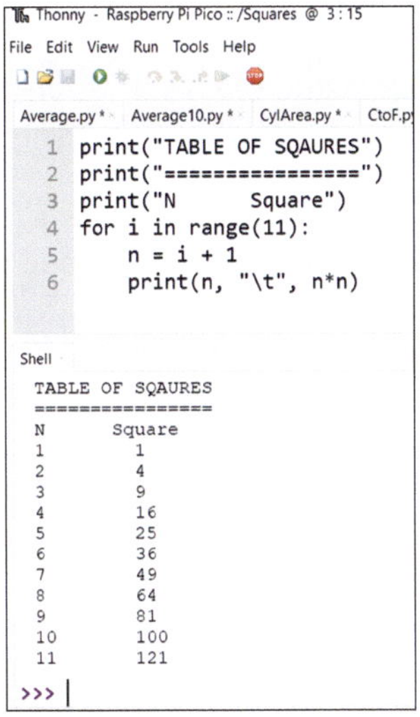

Figure 2.30 Program: Squared numbers, and a sample run.

Example 7 — Table of trigonometric sine

In this example, the trigonometric sine is tabulated from 0 to 45 degrees in steps of 5 degrees.

Solution 7

The program is named **Sines**, and the program listing and an example run of the program are shown in Figure 2.31. It is important to notice that the arguments of the trigonometric functions must be in radians and not in degrees.

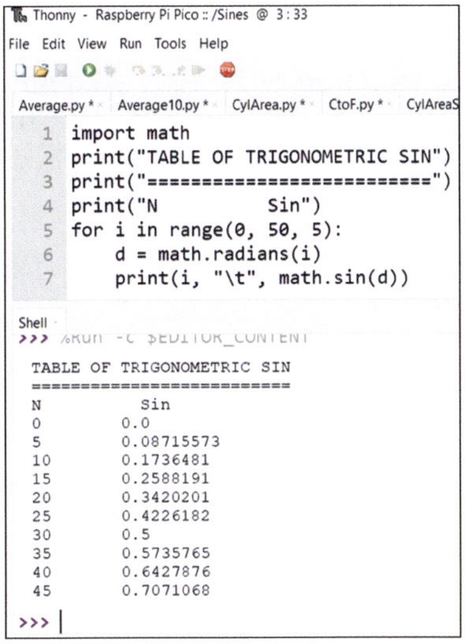

Figure 2.31: Program: Sines, and a sample output.

Example 8 — Table of trigonometric sine, cosine and tangent

In this example, the trigonometric sine, cosine, and tangent are tabulated from 0 to 45 degrees in steps of 5 degrees.

Solution 8

The program is named **Trig**, and the program listing and an example run of the program are shown in Figure 2.32.

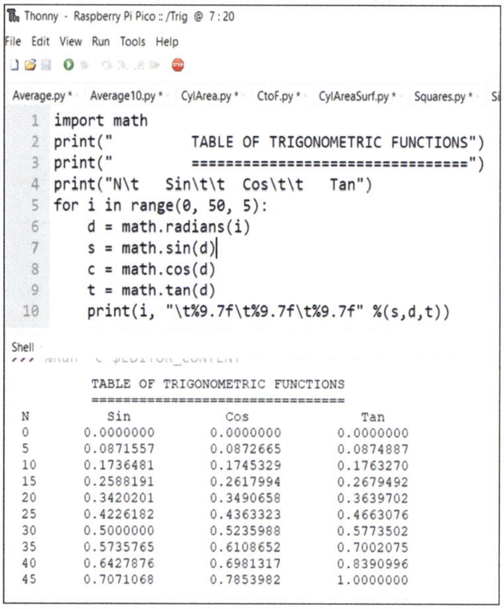

Figure 2.32 Program: Trig, and a sample output.

Example 9 — Trigonometric function of a required angle

In this example, an angle is read from the keyboard. Also, the user specifies whether the sine (s), cosine (c), or the tangent (t) of the angle is required.

Solution 9

The program is named **TrigUser**, and the program listing and an example run of the program are shown in Figure 2.33.

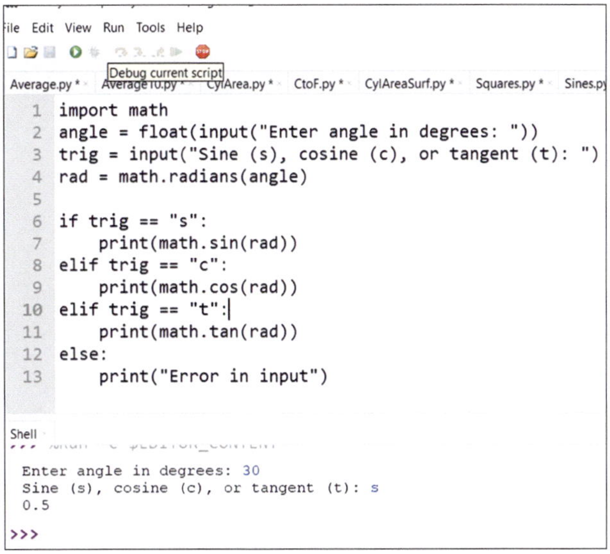

Figure 2.33: Program: TrigUser, and a sample output.

Example 10 — Series and parallel resistors

This program calculates the total resistance of a number of series- or parallel-connected resistors. The user specifies whether the connection is in series or in parallel. Additionally, the number of resistors used is also specified at the beginning of the program.

Solution 10

When a number of resistors are in series, then the resultant resistance is the sum of the resistance of each resistor. When the resistors are in parallel, then the reciprocal of the resultant resistance is equal to the sum of the reciprocal resistances of each resistor.
Figure 2.34 shows the program listing (program: **Serpal**). At the beginning of the program, a heading is displayed, and the program enters a **while** loop. Inside his loop, the user is prompted to enter the number of resistors in the circuit and whether they are connected in series or in parallel. Function **str** converts a number into its equivalent string. e.g. number 5 is converted into string "5". If the connection is serial (mode equals to **'s'**), then the value of each resistor is accepted from the keyboard and the resultant is calculated and displayed on the screen. If on the other hand the connection is parallel (mode is equals to **'p'**), then again the value of each resistor is accepted from the keyboard and the reciprocal of the number is added to the total. When all the resistor values are entered, the resultant resistance is displayed on the screen.

```
print("RESISTORS IN SERIES OR PARALLEL")
print("===============================")
yn = "y"

while yn == 'y':
  N = int(input("\nHow many resistors are there?: "))
  mode = input("Are the resistors series (s) or parallel (p)?: ")
```

```
  mode = mode.lower()
#
# Read the resistor values and calculate the total
#
  resistor = 0.0

  if mode == 's':
    for n in range(0,N):
       s = "Enter resistor " + str(n+1) + " value in Ohms: "
       r = int(input(s))
       resistor = resistor + r
    print("Total resistance = %d Ohms" %(resistor))

  elif mode == 'p':
    for n in range(0,N):
      s = "Enter resistor " + str(n+1) + " value in Ohms: "
      r = float(input(s))
      resistor = resistor + 1 / r
    print("Total resistance = %.2f Ohms" %(1 / resistor))
#
# Check if the user wants to exit
#
  yn = input("\nDo you want to continue?: ")
  yn = yn.lower()
```

Figure 2.34: Program: Serpal.

Figure 2.35 shows a typical run of the program.

```
RESISTORS IN SERIES OR PARALLEL
===============================

How many resistors are there?: 3
Are the resistors series (s) or parallel (p)?: s
Enter resistor 1 value in Ohms: 100
Enter resistor 2 value in Ohms: 150
Enter resistor 3 value in Ohms: 200
Total resistance = 450 Ohms

Do you want to continue?: y

How many resistors are there?: 2
Are the resistors series (s) or parallel (p)?: p
Enter resistor 1 value in Ohms: 100
Enter resistor 2 value in Ohms: 100
Total resistance = 50.00 Ohms

Do you want to continue?: n
```

Figure 2.35: Typical run of the Serpal program.

Example 11 — Words in reverse order

Write a program to read a word from the keyboard and then display the letters of this word in reverse order on the screen.

Solution 11

The required program listing is shown in Figure 2.36 (program: **Letters**). A word is read from the keyboard and stored in string variable **word**. Then the letters of this word are displayed in reverse order. An example run of the program is shown in Figure 2.36.

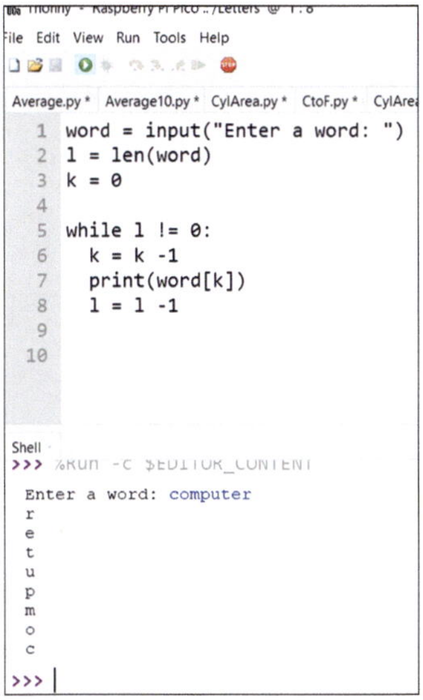

Figure 2.36: Program: Letters, and a sample output.

Example 12 — Calculator

Write a calculator program to carry out the four simple mathematical operations of addition, subtraction, multiplication, and division on two numbers received from the keyboard.

Solution 12

The required program listing is shown in Figure 2.37 (program: **Calc**). Two numbers are received from the keyboard and stored in variables **n1** and **n2**. Then, the required mathematical operation is received and it is performed. The result, stored in variable **result**, is displayed on the screen. The user is given the option of terminating the program.

```
any = 'y'
while any == 'y':
    print("\nCalculator Program")
    print("==================")

    n1 = float(input("Enter first number: "))
    n2 = float(input("Enter second number: "))
    op = input("Enter operation (+-*/): ")
```

```
if op =="+":
   result = n1 + n2
elif op == "-":
   result = n1 - n2
elif op == "*":
   result = n1 * n2
elif op == "/":
   result = n1 / n2
print("Result = %f" %(result))
any = input("\nAny more (yn): ")
```

Figure 2.37: Program: Calc.

An example run of the program is shown in Figure 2.38.

```
Calculator Program
==================
Enter first number: 25
Enter second number: 2
Enter operation (+-*/): *
Result = 50.000000

Any more (yn): y

Calculator Program
==================
Enter first number: 12
Enter second number: 2
Enter operation (+-*/): /
Result = 6.000000

Any more (yn): n
>>>
```

Figure 2.38: Example run of the program.

Example 13 — Dice

Write a program to simulate double dice, i.e. to display two random numbers between 1 and 6 every time it is run.

Solution 13

The required program listing is shown in Figure 2.39 (program: **Dice**). Here, the random-number generator **randint** is used to generate random numbers between 1 and 6 when the Enter key is pressed. The program is terminated when letter **x** (or **X)** is entered.

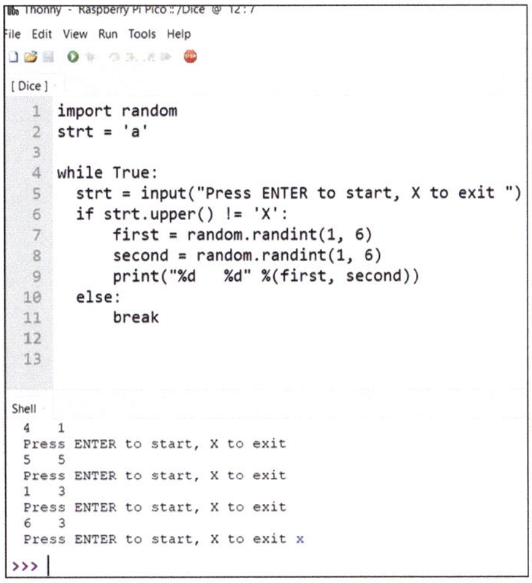

Figure 2.39: Program: Dice.

An example run of the program is shown in Figure 2.39.

Example 14 — Sorting lists

The names of 5 countries are stored in a list. Write a program to sort the names of these countries in alphabetical order and then display them.

Solution 14

The program is named **Sort**, and its listing and an example run are shown in Figure 2.40.

Figure 2.40: Program: Sort, and an example output.

Example 15 — File processing (writing)

In this example, a text file called **MyFile.txt** will be created and text **Hello from Raspberry Pi Pico!** will be written to this file.

Solution 15

The program is named **Filew** and its listing and an example run are shown in Figure 2.41.

The fie is opened in write (**w**) mode and the text is written in it using function **write**. Notice here that **fp** is the file handle.

```
print("Open the file and write the text")
fp = open("MyFile.txt", "w")
fp.write("Hello from Raspberry Pi Pico!\n")
fp.close()
print("End of file operation")
```

```
Shell
Open the file and write the text
End of file operation
```

Figure 2.41: Program: Filew.

Example 16 — File processing (reading)

In this example, the text file **MyFile.txt** created in the previous example is opened and its contents is displayed on the screen.

Solution 16

The program is named **Filer**, and its listing and an example run are shown in Figure 2.42. The fie is opened in read (**r**) mode and its contents is displayed.

```
print("Open the file and read its contents")
fp = open("MyFile.txt", "r")
str = fp.read(80)
fp.close()
print(str)
```

```
hell
Open the file and read its contents
Hello from Raspberry Pi Pico!
```

Figure 2.42: Program: Filer.

Example 17 — Squares and cubes of numbers

Write a program to tabulate the squares and cubes of numbers from 1 to 10.

Solution 17

The program is named **Cubes**, and its listing an example run are shown in Figure 2.43.

```
print("Squares and cubes of numbers")
print(' N  N*N  N*N*N')
for i in range(1,11):
    print('{0:2d} {1:3d} {2:4d}'.format(i, i*i, i*i*i))
```

```
Shell
Squares and cubes of numbers
 N  N*N  N*N*N
 1   1     1
 2   4     8
 3   9    27
 4  16    64
 5  25   125
 6  36   216
 7  49   343
 8  64   512
 9  81   729
10 100  1000
```

Figure 2.43: Program: Cubes, and an example output.

Example 18 — Multiplication timetable

Write a program to read a number from the keyboard and then display the timetable for this number from 1 to 12.

Solution 18

The program is named **Times**, and its listing and an example run are shown in Figure 2.44.

```
num = int(input("Enter a number: "))
print("Timetable of number ", num)
for i in range(1, 13):
    print(num, 'x', i, '=', num*i)
```

```
Shell
Enter a number: 5
Timetable of number  5
5 x 1 = 5
5 x 2 = 10
5 x 3 = 15
5 x 4 = 20
5 x 5 = 25
5 x 6 = 30
5 x 7 = 35
5 x 8 = 40
5 x 9 = 45
5 x 10 = 50
5 x 11 = 55
5 x 12 = 60
```

Figure 2.44: Program: Times, and an example output.

Example 19 — Odd or even

Write a program to read a number from the keyboard, then check and display if this number is odd or even.

Solution 19

The program is named **OddEven**, and its listing and an example run are shown in Figure 2.45.

```
num = int(input("Enter a number: "))
if (num % 2) == 0:
   print("Number {0} is Even".format(num))
else:
   print("Number {0} is Odd".format(num))
```

```
Enter a number: 15
Number 15 is Odd
```

Figure 2.45: Program: OddEven, and an example output.

Example 20 — Binary, octal, and hexadecimal

Write a program to read a decimal number from the keyboard. Convert this number into binary, octal, and hexadecimal and display on the screen.

Solution 20

The program is named **Conv**, and its listing and an example run are shown in Figure 2.46.

```
dec = int(input("Enter a number: "))
print("The decimal value of", dec, "is:")
print("in binary: ",bin(dec))
print("in octal: ",oct(dec))
print("in hexadecimal: ",hex(dec))
```

```
Enter a number: 254
The decimal value of 254 is:
in binary:  0b11111110
in octal:  0o376
in hexadecimal:  0xfe
```

Figure 2.46: Program: Conv, and an example output.

Example 21 — Add two matrices

Write a program to add two given matrices and display the elements of the new matrix.

Solution 21

The program is named **AddMatrix**, and its listing and an example run are shown in Figure 2.47.

```
A = [[5,4,2],
     [6 ,3,1],
     [2 ,8,3]]

B = [[2,4,2],
     [0,4,10],
     [8,2,8]]

res = [[0,0,0],
       [0,0,0],
       [0,0,0]]

for i in range(len(A)):
   for j in range(len(A[0])):
       res[i][j] = A[i][j] + B[i][j]

for i in res:
   print(i)
```

```
>>> %Run -c $EDITOR_CONTENT

[7, 8, 4]
[6, 7, 11]
[10, 10, 11]
```

Figure 2.47: Program: AddMatrix, and an example output.

Chapter 3 • Raspberry Pi Pico Simple Hardware Projects

3.1 Overview

In this Chapter we will be developing simple hardware projects with the Raspberry Pi Pico, using the Thonny text editor. The following sub-headings will be given for each project where applicable:

- Title
- Description
- Aim
- Block Diagram
- Circuit Diagram
- Program Listing
- Suggestions for future work

All the programs in this Chapter have been developed using the Thonny on a PC, with the Raspberry Pi Pico connected to the USB port of the PC.

3.2 Project 1: Flashing LED – Using the on-board LED

Description: In this project the on-board LED is flashed every second.

Aim: The aim of this project is to make the reader familiar with some basic GPIO control statements.

Program listing: Figure 3.1 shows the program listing (Program: **LEDINT**). At the beginning of the program modules **machine** and **utime** are imported to the program. LED is then assigned to port pin GP25 and it is configured as an output. The remainder of the program runs in a loop forever, until stopped by the user. Inside this loop the LED is turned ON by the statement **LED.value(1)**. After a delay of one second the LED is turned OFF by the statement **LED.value(0)**. Function **utime.sleep(n)** creates **n** seconds of delay in the program.

```
#----------------------------------------------------------
#            FLASHING THE ON-BOARD LED
#            =========================
#
# In this program the on-board LED (at GP25) is flashed
# every second
#
# Author: Dogan Ibrahim
# File  : LEDINT.py
# Date  : February, 2021
#-----------------------------------------------------------
import machine
import utime
```

```
LED = machine.Pin(25, machine.Pin.OUT)          # LED at GP25

while True:                                     # DO FOREVER
    LED.value(1)                                # LED ON
    utime.sleep(1)                              # Wait 1 second
    LED.value(0)                                # LED OFF
    utime.sleep(1)                              # Wait 1 second
```

Figure 3.1: Program: LEDINT.

In Figure 3.1, **import machine** module imports other functions in addition to **Pin**. We can simplify the program by importing only the **Pin** functions as shown in Figure 3.2 (Program: **LEDINT2**). You may have to stop the program by selecting **Run** followed by **Stop/Restart backend** before being able to save a new program while a program is already running on Pico.

```
#----------------------------------------------------------
#             FLASHING THE ON-BOARD LED
#             =========================
#
# In this program the on-board LED (at GP25) is flashed
# every second. In this version only module Pin is imported
#
# Author: Dogan Ibrahim
# File  : LEDINT2.py
# Date  : February, 2021
#-----------------------------------------------------------
from machine import Pin
import utime

LED = Pin(25, Pin.OUT)                      # LED at GP25

while True:                                 # DO FOREVER
    LED.value(1)                            # LED ON
    utime.sleep(1)                          # Wait 1 second
    LED.value(0)                            # LED OFF
    utime.sleep(1)                          # Wait 1 second
```

Figure 3.2: Program: LEDINT2.

The **machine** module supports the following functions (we will see in later Chapters how to use these functions):

- Pin
- Timer
- ADC

- I^2C and Soft I^2C
- SPI and SoftSPI
- WDT
- PWM
- UART

The general format of the machine.Pin function is:

```
machine.Pin(pin, mode, pull, value, alt)
```

for more information, go to
https://docs.micropython.org/en/latest/library/machine.Pin.html

The parameters of a pin can be re-initialized using the following function:

```
Pin.init(pin, mode, value, drive, at)
```

Where **pin** is the pin number.

Parameter **mode** can take the following values:

`Pin.IN`	- pin is configured as input
`Pin.OUT`	- pin is configured as output
`Pin.OPEN_DRAIN`	- pin is configured as open-drain output
`Pin.ALT`	- pin is configured as an alternative function

Parameter **pull** can take the following values:

`NONE`	- no internal pull-up or pull-down resistors
`Pin.PULL_UP`	- internal pull-up resistor enabled
`Pin.PULL_DOWN`	- internal pull-down resistor enabled

Parameter **value** is valid only for Pin.OUT and Pin.OPEN_DRAIN modes and it specifies the initial output pin value (if specified).
Parameter **alt** specifies an alternate function for the pin (port dependent). This parameter is valid only for PIN.ALT and Pin.ALT_OPEN_DRAIN modes.

A pin can be set/reset using one of the following functions:

`Pin.value(1)`	- set pin to logic 1
`Pin.value(0)`	- set pin to logic 0

Some other useful **machine** functions are:

`machine.reset()`	- reset the device (same as pressing the external RESET button)

`machine.reset_cause)`	- return the cause of the reset
`machine.disable_irq()`	- disable interrupt requests
`machine.enable_irq()`	- enable interrupt requests
`machine.freq()`	- returns the CPU frequency

3.3 Project 2: External flashing LED

Description: In this project an external LED is connected to the Pico. The LED is flashed every second as in the previous project.

Aim: The aim of this project is to show how an external LED can be connected to the Pico.

Block diagram: Figure 3.3 shows the block diagram of the project.

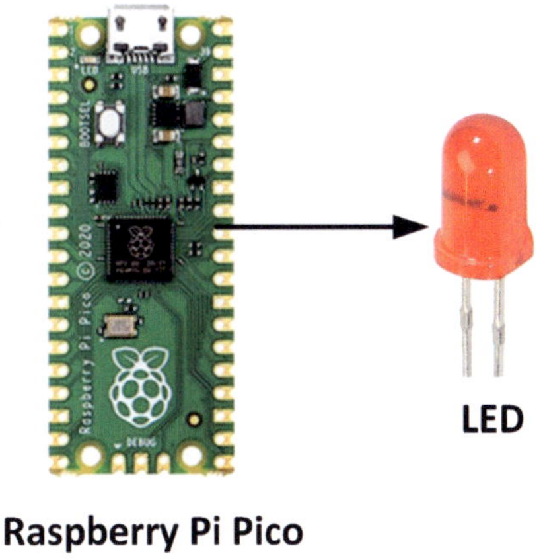

Figure 3.3: Block diagram of the project.

Circuit diagram: The circuit diagram of the project is shown in Figure 3.4. The LED is connected to port pin GP0 of Pico through a current-limiting resistor.

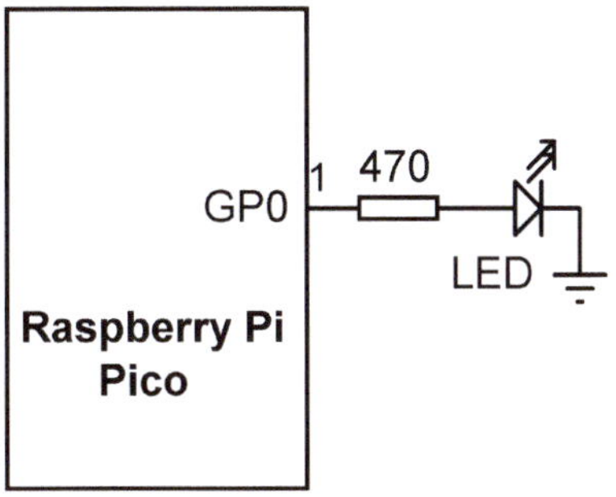

Figure 3.4: Circuit diagram of the project.

The LED can be connected either in current-sourcing or in current-sinking mode. In current-sourcing mode (Figure 3.5) the LED is turned ON when logic HIGH is applied to the port pin. In current-sinking mode (Figure 3.6) the LED is turned ON when logic LOW is applied to the port pin.

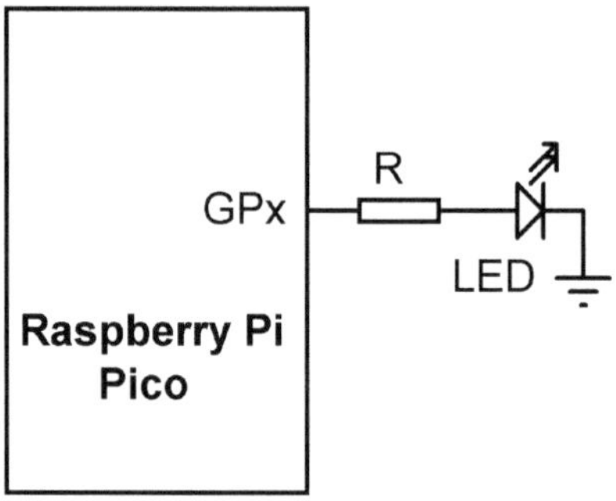

Figure 3.5: LED in current-sourcing mode.

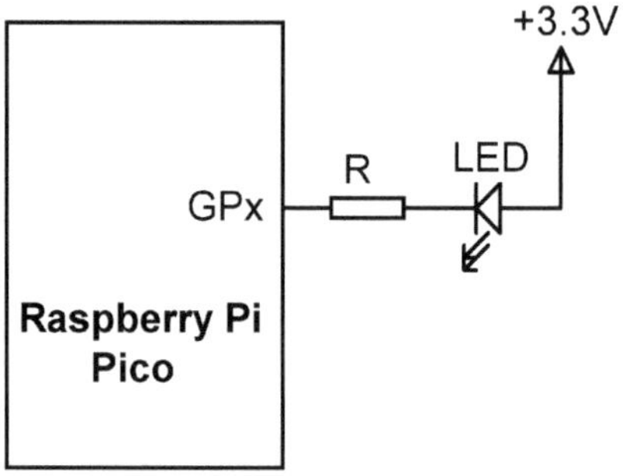

Figure 3.6: LED in current-sinking mode.

The required value of the current limiting resistor can be calculated as follows. In current-sourcing mode, assuming the output HIGH voltage is +3.3 V, the voltage drop across the LED is 2 V, and the current through the LED is 3 mA, the required value of the current limiting resistor is:

$$R = (3.3 - 2) / 3 = 433 \text{ ohms}$$

So we will choose 470 ohms as the nearest practical resistor value.

Program listing: Figure 3.7 shows the program listing (Program: **ExtFlash.py**).

```
#--------------------------------------------------------
#                FLASHING AN EXTERNAL LED
#                ========================
#
# In this program an external LED is connected to port pin
# GP0 (pin 1). The LED is flashed every second
```

```
#
# Author: Dogan Ibrahim
# File  : ExtFlash.py
# Date  : February, 2021
#-----------------------------------------------------------
from machine import Pin
import utime

LED = Pin(0, Pin.OUT)                   # LED at GP0

while True:                             # DO FOREVER
    LED.value(1)                        # LED ON
    utime.sleep(1)                      # Wait 1 second
    LED.value(0)                        # LED OFF
    utime.sleep(1)                      # Wait 1 second
```

Figure 3.7 Program: ExtFlash.py.

Figure 3.8 shows the Fritzing diagram of the project built on a breadboard.

Figure 3.8: Project built on a breadboard.

3.4 Project 3: Flashing SOS in Morse

Description: In this project an external LED flashes the SOS signal in Morse code (three dots, followed by three dashes, followed by three dots) continuously. In this project, a dot is represented with the LED being ON for 0.25 seconds (Dot time) and a dash is represented with the LED being ON for 1 second (Dash time). The delay between the dots and dashes is set to 0.2 second (GAP time). This process is repeated continuously after 2 seconds of delay.

The block diagram and circuit diagram of this project are the same as in Figure 3.3 and Figure 3.4, respectively.

Program listing. Figure 3.9 shows the program listing (Program: **SOS**). At the beginning of the program the dot, dash, and gap times are defined. Then a loop is formed using a **while** statement. Inside this loop two **for** loops are formed, each iterating 3 times. The first loop displays three dots, while the second loop displays three dashes. This process is repeated after 2 seconds of delay.

```
#---------------------------------------------------------
#                    LED FLASHING SOS
#                    ================
#
# In this program an external LED is connected to port pin
# GP0 (pin 1). The LED flashes the SOS signal
#
# Author: Dogan Ibrahim
# File  : SOS.py
# Date  : February, 2021
#---------------------------------------------------------
from machine import Pin
import utime

Dot = 0.25                       # Dot time
Dash = 1.0                       # Dash time
Gap = 0.2                        # Gap time
ON = 1                           # ON
OFF = 0                          # OFF

LED = Pin(0, Pin.OUT)            # LED at GP0

while True:                      # DO FOREVER
    for i in range(0, 3):
        LED.value(ON)            # LED ON
        utime.sleep(Dot)         # Wait Dot time
        LED.value(OFF)           # LED OFF
        utime.sleep(Gap)         # Wait Gap time

    utime.sleep(0.5)             # 0.5 second delay

    for i in range(0, 3):
        LED.value(ON)            # LED ON
        utime.sleep(Dash)        # Wait Dash time
        LED.value(OFF)           # LED OFF
        utime.sleep(Gap)         # Wait Gap time

    utime.sleep(2)               # Wait 2 seconds
```

Figure 3.9: Program: SOS.

Suggestions: You could easily replace the LED with a buzzer to make the SOS signal audible. There are two types of buzzers: active and passive. Passive buzzers require an audio signal to be sent to them and the frequency of the output signal depends on the frequency of the supplied signal. Active buzzers are ON/OFF type devices producing audible sound when activated. In his project we can use an active buzzer with a transistor switch (any NPN type transistor can be used) as shown in Figure 3.10.

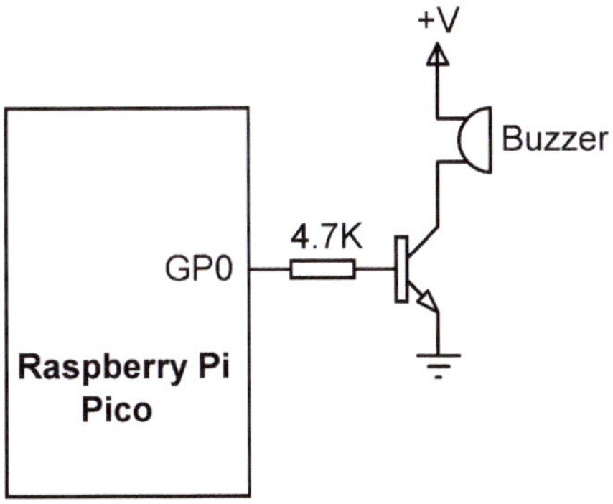

Figure 3.10: Using an active buzzer.

3.5 Project 4: Flashing LED – using a timer

Description: This project is very similar to Project 2 where an external LED is connected to port pin GP0 of the Pico. In this project a timer is used to flash the LED every 500 ms.

Aim: The aim of this project s to show how a timer can be used in a program.
The block diagram and circuit diagram of this project are the same as in Figure 3.3 and Figure 3.4, respectively.

Program listing. Figure 3.11 shows the program listing (Program: **LEDTimer**). Here, a timer is initialized which calls function **Flash_LED** twice (**freq = 2.0**) a second in a periodic manner. Notice that the LED is flashed using the **toggle** function.

```
#-----------------------------------------------------------
#                LED FLASHING USING A TIMER
#                ==========================
#
# In this program an external LED is connected to port pin
# GP0 (pin 1). The LED flashes every second using a timer
#
# Author: Dogan Ibrahim
# File  : LEDTimer.py
# Date  : February, 2021
#------------------------------------------------------------
from machine import Pin, Timer

LED = Pin(0, Pin.OUT)
```

```
tim = Timer()

def Flash_LED(timer):
    global LED
    LED.toggle()

tim.init(freq = 2.0, mode = Timer.PERIODIC, callback = Flash_LED)
```

Figure 3.11: Program: LEDTimer.

3.6 Project 5: Alternately flashing LEDs

Description: In this project two LEDs are connected to the Pico. The LEDs flash alternately every 500 ms.

Aim: The aim of this project is to show how multiple LEDs can be connected to the Pico.

Block diagram: Figure 3.12 shows the block diagram of the project.

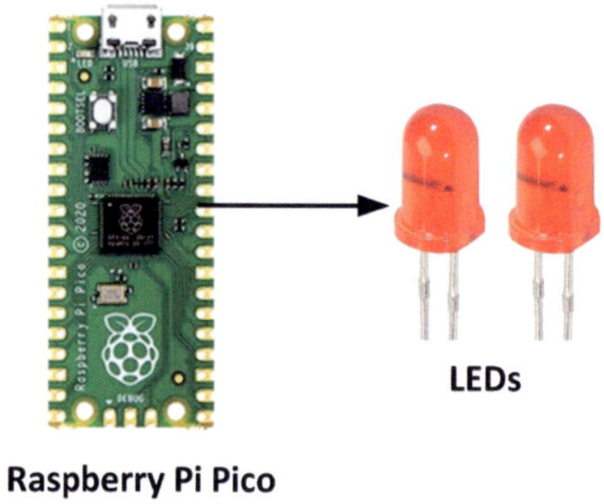

Figure 3.12: Block diagram of the project.

Circuit diagram: The circuit diagram of the project is shown in Figure 3.13. The LEDs are connected to port pins GP0 and GP1 through 470-ohm current limiting resistors.

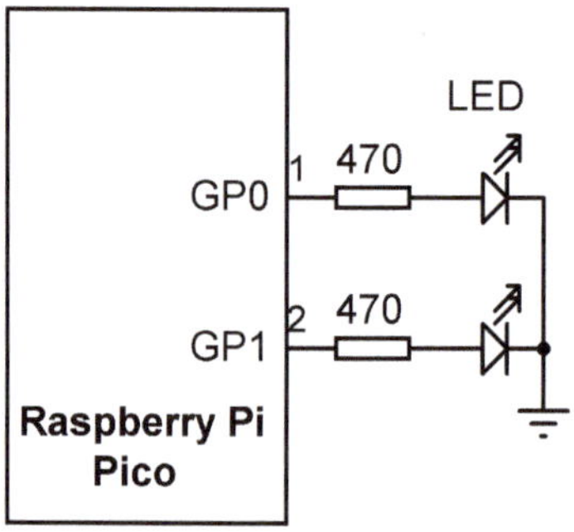

Figure 3.13: Circuit diagram of the project.

Program listing: Figure 3.14 shows the program listing (Program: **LED2**).

```
#----------------------------------------------------------
#                 ALTERNATELY FLASHING LEDs
#                 =========================
#
# In this program two external LEDs are connected to pins
# GP0 (pin 1) and GP1 (pin 2). The LEDs flash alternately
# every 500ms
#
# Author: Dogan Ibrahim
# File  : LED2.py
# Date  : February, 2021
#-----------------------------------------------------------
from machine import Pin
import utime

LED1 = Pin(0, Pin.OUT)
LED2 = Pin(1, Pin.OUT)

while True:
    LED1.value(1)
    LED2.value(0)
    utime.sleep(0.5)
    LED1.value(0)
    LED2.value(1)
    utime.sleep(0.5)
```

Figure 3.14: Program: LED2.

Figure 3.15 shows the Fritzing diagram of the project built on a breadboard.

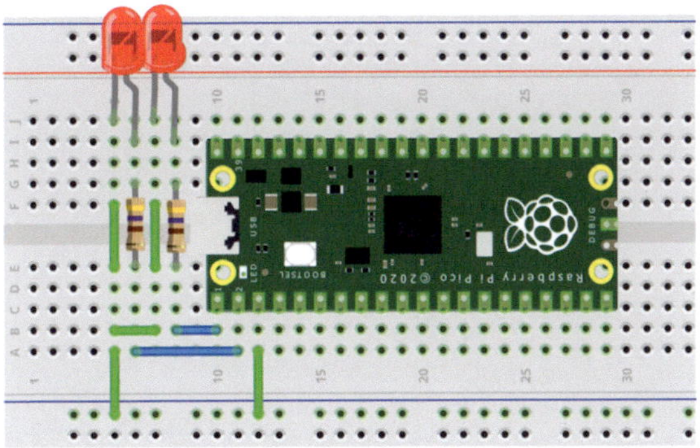

Figure 3.15: Project built on a breadboard.

3.7 Project 6: Changing the LED flashing rate – using pushbutton interrupts

Description: In this project an external LED is connected to port pin GP0 of the Pico. Additionally, two pushbuttons are connected to port pins GP1 and GP2. At the start of the program the LED flashes every second. Pushbutton at GP1 is named **Faster** and pressing this button flashes the LED faster. Similarly, pushbutton at GP2 is named **Slower**, and pressing this button flashes the LED slower.

Aim: The aim of this project is to show how pushbuttons can be connected to the Pico, and how the state of a button can be read.

Block diagram: Figure 3.16 shows the block diagram of the project.

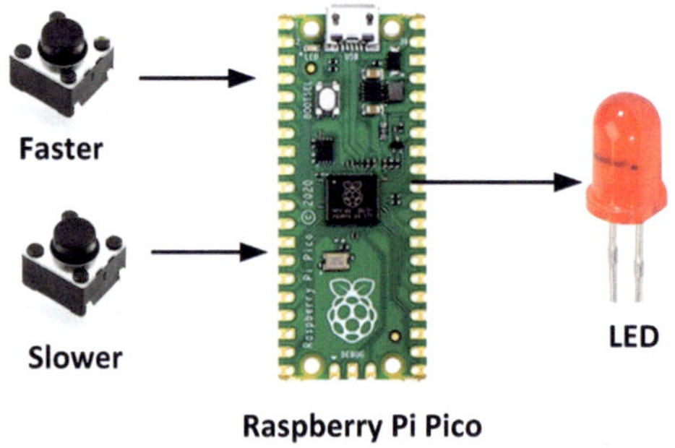

Figure 3.16: Block diagram of the project.

Circuit diagram: The circuit diagram of the project is shown in Figure 3.17. The LED is connected through a 470-ohm current limiting resistor. The two pushbuttons are connected through 10-kohm resistors. The default state of the pushbuttons is at logic 1, being pulled-up through the resistors. Pressing a pushbutton changes its output state to logic 0.

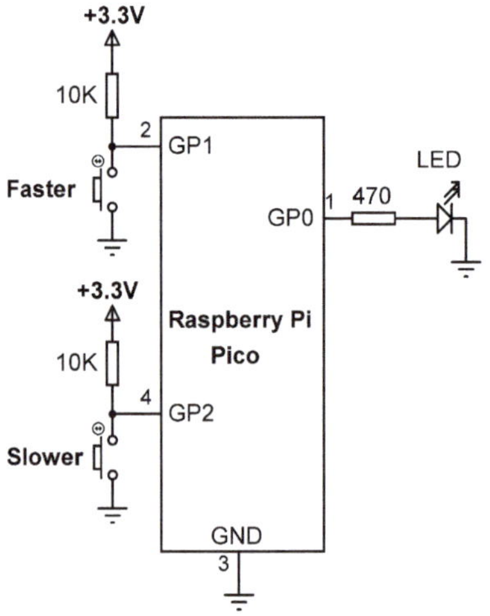

Figure 3.17: Circuit diagram of the project.

Program listing: Figure 3.18 shows the program listing (Program**: LEDrate**). At the beginning of the program LED is assigned to pin GP0, and pushbuttons **Faster** and **Slower** are assigned to ports GP1 and GP2 respectively. The default flashing rate is set to one second and is stored in variable **dly**. The program is external-interrupt-based. Pressing either of the pushbuttons creates an interrupt. For example, the interrupt for pushbutton **Faster** is configured using the following function call:

```
Faster.irq(handler=Flash_Faster, trigger=Faster.IRQ_FALLING)
```

Where **Flash_Faster** is the name of the interrupt service routine where **dly** is decremented. The interrupt is configured to happen on the falling edge of the pushbutton, i.e. when the pushbutton is pressed (the normal state of the pushbuttons is at logic 1, being pulled-up by resistors). Inside the interrupt service routine **Flash_Faster** variable **dly** is declared as **global** so that it can be accessed. Its value is then decremented by 100ms (0.1 second). The Interrupt service routine for pushbutton **Slower** is done similarly where the delay is incremented by 100 ms each time the button is pressed.

The other external interrupt modes are:

`Pin.IRQ_FALLING`	- interrupt on falling edge (high-to-low)
`Pin.IRQ_RISING`	- interrupt on rising edge (low-to-high)
`Pin.IRQ_LOW_LEVEL`	- interrupt on low level
`Pin.IRQ_HIGH_LEVEL`	- interrupt on high level

The above values can be OR'ed together to trigger on multiple events. We can also specify the interrupt priority with the keyword **priority**, where higher values represent higher priorities.
An interrupt **wake** parameter can be specified with the values **None**, **machine.IDLE**, **machine.SLEEP**, or **machine.DEEPSLEEP**.
Additionally, a parameter called **hard** with the values of **False** or **True** can be specified. If this parameter is set to **True**, then hardware interrupts are used which yields faster response.

```
#-----------------------------------------------------------
#                CHANGE THE LED FLASHING RATE
#                ============================
#
# In this program an external LED and two pushbuttons are
# connected to Pico. Pressing Faster flashes the LED faster,
# and pressing Slower flashes the LED slower
#
# Author: Dogan Ibrahim
# File  : LEDrate.py
# Date  : February, 2021
#------------------------------------------------------------
from machine import Pin
```

```
import utime

LED = Pin(0, Pin.OUT)                          # LED at pin GP0
Faster = Pin(1, Pin.IN)                        # Faster at pin GP1
Slower = Pin(2, Pin.IN)                        # Slower at pin GP2
dly = 1.0                                      # Default delay

#
# This is the interrupt service routine. Whenever pushbutton
# Faster is pressed, the program jumps here and decrements
# delay to make the flashing faster
#
def Flash_Faster(Faster):
   global dly
   dly = dly - 0.1

#
# This is the interrupt service routine. Whenever pushbutton
# Slower is pressed, the program jumps here and increments
# delay to make the flashing slower
#
def Flash_Slower(Slower):
    global dly
    dly = dly + 0.1

#
# Configure the external interrupts
#
Faster.irq(handler=Flash_Faster,trigger=Faster.IRQ_FALLING)
Slower.irq(handler=Flash_Slower,trigger=Slower.IRQ_FALLING)

#
# Main program loop
#
while True:
    LED.value(1)                              # LED ON
    utime.sleep(dly)                          # Delay dly
    LED.value(0)                              # LED OFF
    utime.sleep(dly)                          # Delay dly
```

Figure 3.18: Program LEDrate.

Figure 3.19 shows the project built on a breadboard.

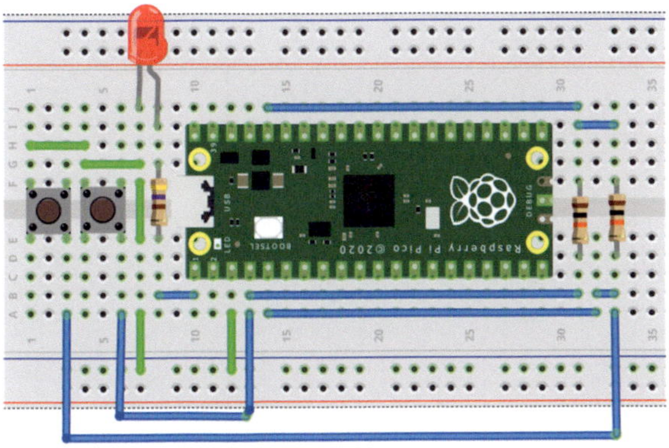

Figure 3.19: Project built on a breadboard.

Using the internal pull-up resistors

We can simplify the circuit diagram of Figure 3.17 by removing the external resistors and using the internal pull-up resistors. The simplified circuit diagram is shown in Figure 3.20. The modified program listing (Program: **LEDrate2**) is shown in Figure 3.21 where the option **pull = Pin.PULL__UP** is added to the input configuration statements.

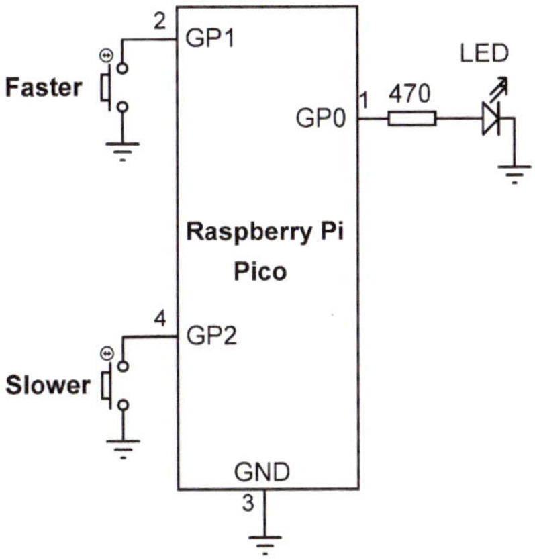

Figure 3.20: Modified circuit diagram.

```
#----------------------------------------------------------
#                CHANGE THE LED FLASHING RATE
#                ============================
#
# In this program an external LED and two pushbuttons are
# connected to Pico. Pressing Faster flashes the LED faster,
# and pressing Slower flashes the LED slower
# In this modified version, internal pull-ups are used
#
# Author: Dogan Ibrahim
# File  : LEDrate2.py
```

```
# Date   : February, 2021
#------------------------------------------------------------
from machine import Pin
import utime

LED = Pin(0, Pin.OUT)
Faster = Pin(1, Pin.IN, pull=Pin.PULL_UP)
Slower = Pin(2, Pin.IN, pull=Pin.PULL_UP)
dly = 1.0

#
# This is the interrupt service routine. Whenever pushbutton
# Faster is pressed, the program jumps here and decrements
# delay to make the flashing faster
#
def Flash_Faster(Faster):
   global dly
   dly = dly - 0.1

#
# This is the interrupt service routine. Whenever pushbutton
# Slower is pressed, the program jumps here and increments
# delay to make the flashing slower
#
def Flash_Slower(Slower):
    global dly
    dly = dly + 0.1

#
# Configure the external interrupts
#
Faster.irq(handler=Flash_Faster,trigger=Faster.IRQ_FALLING)
Slower.irq(handler=Flash_Slower,trigger=Slower.IRQ_FALLING)

#
# Main program loop
#
while True:
    LED.value(1)                        # LED ON
    utime.sleep(dly)                    # Delay dly
    LED.value(0)                        # LED OFF
    utime.sleep(dly)                    # Delay dly
```

Figure 3.21: Program LEDrate2.

3.8 Project 7: Alternately flashing red, green, and blue LEDs – RGB

Description: This is a very simple project where an RGB LED is connected to the Raspberry Pi Pico and the red, green, and blue colours are flashed alternately every 500 ms.

Aim: The aim of this project is to show how an RGB LED can be used in a Raspberry Pi Pico project.

Background Information: As shown in Figure 3.22, the RGB LED is a 4-pin device which incorporates Red, Green and Blue LEDs. Each colour LED is assigned a pin, where the fourth pin is the ground. By activating different LEDs at different brightness, we can generate many different colours. In this project a common cathode RGB LED is used. Notice that the cathode pin of the RGB LED is the longer pin.

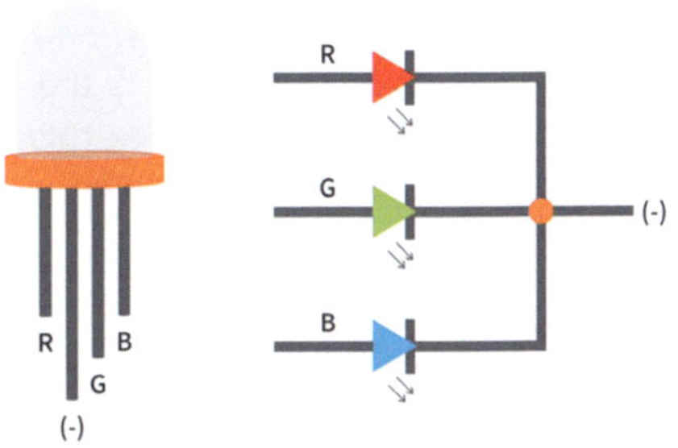

Figure 3.22: RGB LED (from CircuitBread).

Block Diagram: Figure 3.23 shows the block diagram of the project.

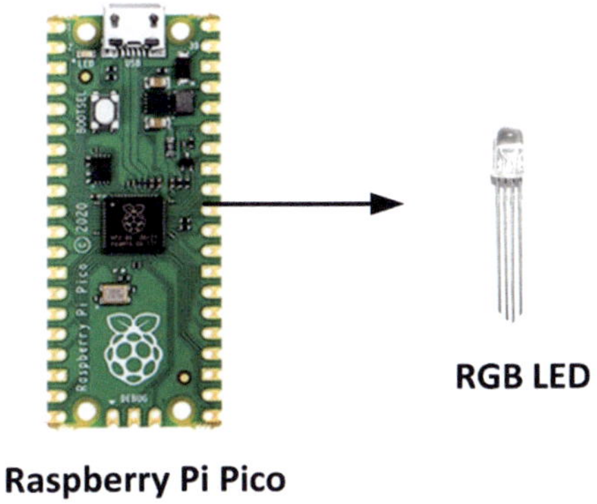

Figure 3.23: Block diagram of the project.

Circuit Diagram: The circuit diagram of the project is shown in Figure 3.24. The Red, Green, and Blue pins are connected to port pins GP0, GP1, and GP2 respectively through 470-ohm current limiting resistors.

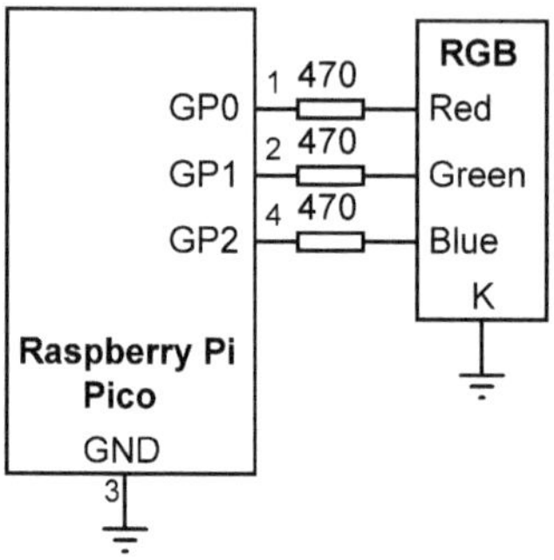

Figure 3.24: Circuit diagram of the project.

Program Listing: The program is very simple and is shown in Figure 3.25 (program: **RGB**). At the beginning of the program the RED, GREEN, and BLUE LEDs are assigned to the 0, 1, and 2 port pins respectively, and the LED ports are configured as outputs. The remainder of the program runs in an endless loop. Inside this loop the RED, GREEN, and BLUE LEDs are turned ON and OFF with 0.5-second delay between each output.

```
#----------------------------------------------------------
#                  ALTERNATELY FLASHING RGB LED
#                  ============================
#
# In this program an RGB LED is connected to Pico.The three
# colours of the LED are flashed alternately every 500ms
#
# Author: Dogan Ibrahim
# File  : RGB.py
# Date  : February, 2021
#-----------------------------------------------------------
from machine import Pin
import utime

Red = Pin(0, machine.Pin.OUT)
Green = Pin(1, Pin.OUT)
Blue = Pin(2, Pin.OUT)

Red.value(0)
Green.value(0)
Blue.value(0)

while True:
    Red.value(1)
    utime.sleep(0.5)
    Red.value(0)
    Green.value(1)
    utime.sleep(0.5)
```

```
Green.value(0)
Blue.value(1)
utime.sleep(0.5)
Blue.value(0)
```

Figure 3.25: The RGB program.

Figure 3.26 shows the project built on a breadboard.

Figure 3.26: Project built on a breadboard.

3.9 Project 8: Randomly flashing red, green, and blue LEDs — RGB

Description: In this project the RGB LEDs flash randomly, where the Red, Green, or the Blue LEDs are randomly ON or OFF.

The block diagram and the circuit diagram are the same as in Figure 3.23 and 3.24, respectively.

Program listing: Figure 3.27 shows the program listing (Program: **RGB2**). Random numbers are generated either as 0 or 1 for each colour, and these numbers are used either to turn ON or OFF a colour LED.

```
#----------------------------------------------------------
#                    RANDOMLY FLASHING RGB LED
#                    =========================
#
# In this program an RGB LED is connected to Pico.The three
# colours of the LED are flashed randomly every 500ms
#
# Author: Dogan Ibrahim
# File  : RGB2.py
# Date  : February, 2021
#-----------------------------------------------------------
from machine import Pin
import utime
```

```
import random

Red = Pin(0, Pin.OUT)
Green = Pin(1, Pin.OUT)
Blue = Pin(2, Pin.OUT)

while True:
    r = random.randint(0, 1)
    g = random.randint(0, 1)
    b = random.randint(0, 1)
    Red.value(r)
    utime.sleep(0.2)
    Green.value(g)
    utime.sleep(0.2)
    Blue.value(b)
    utime.sleep(0.2)
```

Figure 3.27: The RGB2 program.

3.10 Project 9: Rotating LEDs

Description: In this project, 4 LEDs are connected to the Pico. The LEDs display a pattern of rotating left as shown in Figure 3.28.

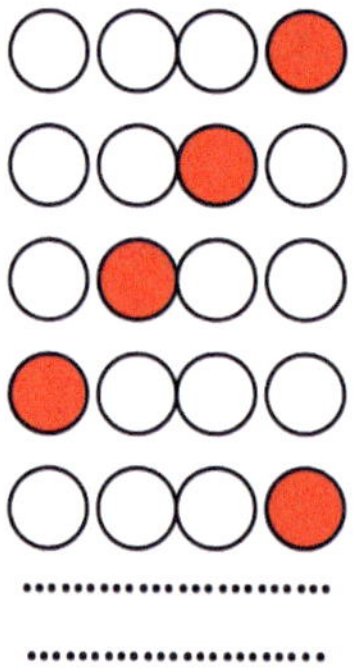

Figure 3.28: 'Rotating' LEDs.

Block diagram: Figure 3.29 shows the block diagram of the project.

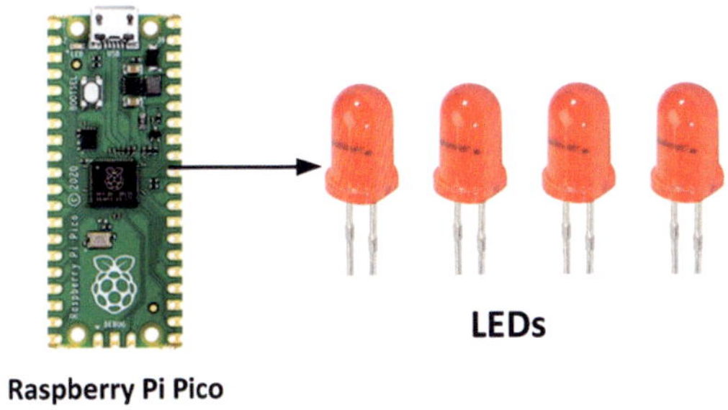

Figure 3.29: Block diagram of the project.

Circuit diagram: The circuit diagram of the project is shown in Figure 3.30. The LEDs are connected to the Pico through 470-ohm current limiting resistors.

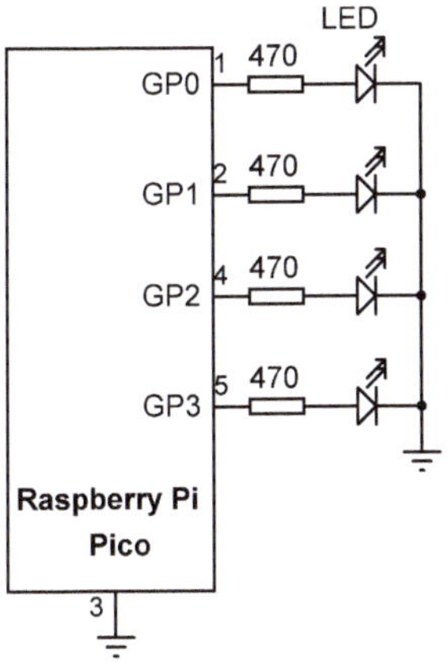

Figure 3.30: Circuit diagram of the project.

Program listing. Figure 3.31 shows the program listing (Program: ROTATE).

```
#----------------------------------------------------------
#                  ROTATING LEDs
#                  =============
#
# In this program 4 LEDs are connected to Pico. The LEDs
# display pattern of rotating to the left
#
# Author: Dogan Ibrahim
# File  : Rotate.py
# Date  : February, 2021
#-----------------------------------------------------------
from machine import Pin
import utime

LED1 = Pin(0, Pin.OUT)
```

```
LED2 = Pin(1, Pin.OUT)
LED3 = Pin(2, Pin.OUT)
LED4 = Pin(3, Pin.OUT)

while True:
    LED1.value(1)
    utime.sleep(0.5)
    LED1.value(0)
    LED2.value(1)
    utime.sleep(0.5)
    LED2.value(0)
    LED3.value(1)
    utime.sleep(0.5)
    LED3.value(0)
    LED4.value(1)
    utime.sleep(0.5)
    LED4.value(0)
```

Figure 3.31: Program: ROTATE.

More efficient program

The program given in Figure 3.31 can be made more efficient (Program: **ROTATE2**) and easier to understand by modifying it as shown in Figure 3.32. This is especially true if there are more than 4 LEDs.

```
#----------------------------------------------------------
#                  ROTATING LEDs
#                  =============
#
# In this program 4 LEDs are connected to Pico. The LEDs
# display pattern of rotating to the left
#
# Author: Dogan Ibrahim
# File  : Rotate2.py
# Date  : February, 2021
#-----------------------------------------------------------
from machine import Pin
import utime

LEDS = [0, 1, 2, 3]                     # LED ports
L = [0, 0, 0, 0]

for i in range(4):                      # Do for all LEDs
    L[i] = Pin(LEDS[i], Pin.OUT)        # All are outputs

while True:                             # Do forever
```

```
for i in range(4):
    L[i].value(1)                      # LED ON
    utime.sleep(0.5)                   # Wait 0.5 second
    L[i].value(0)                      # LED OFF
```

Figure 3.32: Modified program.

Figure 3.33 shows the project built on a breadboard.

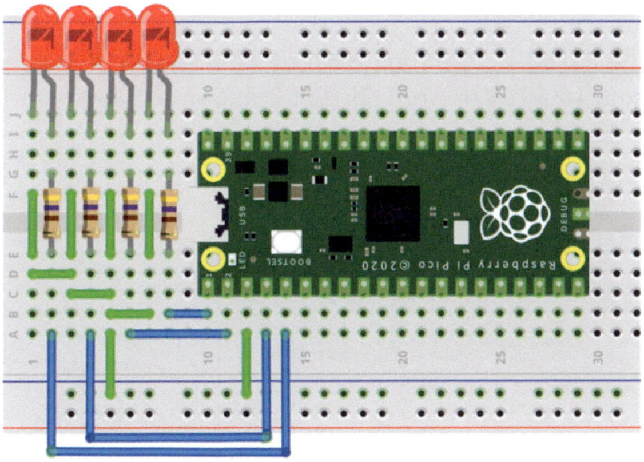

Figure 3.33: Project built on a breadboard.

3.11 Project 10: Binary-counting LEDs

Description: In this project, 8 LEDs are connected to the Pico. The LEDs count up in binary from 0 to 255 as shown in Figure 3.34, with a 1-second delay between each count.

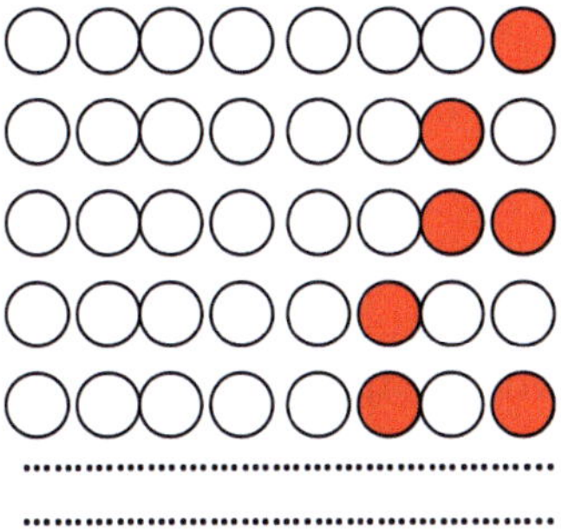

Figure 3.34: Binary counting LEDs.

Aim: The aim of this project is to show how a group of port pins can be combined and accessed as a parallel port.

Block diagram: Figure 3.35 shows the block diagram of the project.

Figure 3.35: Block diagram of the project.

Circuit diagram: The circuit diagram of the project is shown in Figure 3.36. The LEDs are connected to the Pico through 470-ohm current limiting resistors.

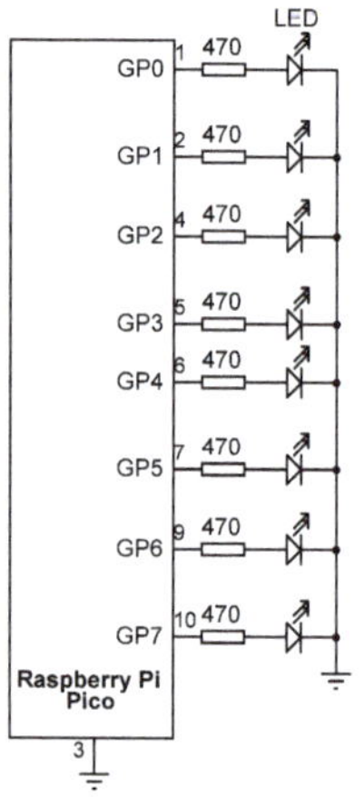

Figure 3.36: Circuit diagram of the project.

Program listing. Figure 3.37 shows the program listing (Program: **LEDCount**). All 8 GPIO ports used in the project are configured as outputs using the function **Configure_Port**. Notice that the **Configure_Port** function is general, and the list **DIR** sets the directions of the GPIO pins. An "O" sets as an output and an "I" sets as an input. Then, a loop is formed to execute forever and inside this loop the LEDs count up by one in binary. Variable **cnt** is used as the counter. Function **Port_Output** is used to control the LEDs. This function can take integer numbers from 0 to 255 and it converts the input number (x) into binary using the built-in function **bin**. Then the leading "0b" characters are removed from the output string **b** (**bin** function inserts characters "0b" to the beginning of the converted string). Then, the converted string **b** is made up of 8 characters by inserting leading 0s. The string is then sent to the PORT bit by bit, starting from the most-significant bit position.

```
#-----------------------------------------------------------
#                 BINARY COUNTING 8 LEDs
#                 ======================
#
# In this program 8 LEDs are connected to Pico. The LEDs
```

```
# count up in binary every second
#
# Author: Dogan Ibrahim
# File  : LEDCount.py
# Date  : February, 2021
#-----------------------------------------------------------
from machine import Pin
import utime

PORT = [7, 6, 5, 4, 3,  2,  1,  0]                # port connections
DIR = ["0","0","0","0","0","0","0","0"]          # port directons
L = [0]*8

#
# This function configures the port pins as outputs ("0") or
# as inputs ("I")
#
def Configure_Port():
   for i in range(0, 8):
      if DIR[i] == "0":
         L[i] = Pin(PORT[i], Pin.OUT)
      else:
         L[i] = Pin(PORT[i], Pin.IN)
   return

#
# This function sends 8-bit data (0 to 255) to the PORT
#
def Port_Output(x):
   b = bin(x)                               # convert into binary
   b = b.replace("0b", "")                  # remove leading "0b"
   diff = 8 - len(b)                        # find the length
   for i in range (0, diff):
      b = "0" + b                           # insert leading os

   for i in range (0, 8):
      if b[i] == "1":
         L[i].value(1)
      else:
         L[i].value(0)
   return

#
# Configure PORT to all outputs
#
Configure_Port()
```

```
#
# Main program loop. Count up in binary every second
#
cnt = 0
while True:
  Port_Output(cnt)                            # send cnt to port
  utime.sleep(1)                              # wait 1 second
  cnt = cnt + 1                               # increment cnt
  if cnt > 255:
     cnt = 0
```

Figure 3.37: Program LEDCount.

Figure 3.38 shows the project built on a breadboard.

Figure 3.38: Project built on a breadboard.

3.12 Project 11: Christmas lights (random flashing 8 LEDs)

Description: In this project, 8 LEDs are connected to the Pico as in the previous project. The LEDs flash randomly every 250 milliseconds just like fancy Christmas lights.

Aim: The aim of this project is to show how to generate random numbers between 1 and 255 and then shows how to use these numbers to turn the individual LEDs ON and OFF randomly.

The block diagram and circuit diagram of the project are given in Figure 3.35 and Figure 3.36 respectively.

Program listing: The program is called **XMAS** and the listing is shown in Figure 3.39. All the 8 GPIO ports used in the project are configured as outputs using the function **Configure_Port** as in the previous project. Then, a loop is formed to execute forever and inside this loop a random number is generated between 1 and 255, and this number is used as an argument to function **Port_Output.** The binary pattern corresponding to the generated number is sent to the port which turns the LEDs ON or OFF in a random manner.

```
#-----------------------------------------------------------
#                CHRISTMAS LIGHTS
#                ================
#
# In this program 8 LEDs are connected to Pico. The LEDs
# flash randomly
#
# Author: Dogan Ibrahim
# File  : XMAS.py
# Date  : February, 2021
#------------------------------------------------------------
from machine import Pin
import utime
import random

PORT = [7, 6, 5, 4, 3,  2,  1,  0]               # port connections
DIR = ["0","0","0","0","0","0","0","0"]          # port directons
L = [0]*8

#
# This function configures the port pins as outputs ("0") or
# as inputs ("I")
#
def Configure_Port():
   for i in range(0, 8):
      if DIR[i] == "0":
         L[i] = Pin(PORT[i], Pin.OUT)
      else:
         L[i] = Pin(PORT[i], Pin.IN)
   return

#
# This function sends 8-bit data (0 to 255) to the PORT
#
def Port_Output(x):
   b = bin(x)                                  # convert into binary
```

```
    b = b.replace("0b", "")                         # remove leading "0b"
    diff = 8 - len(b)                               # find the length
    for i in range (0, diff):
       b = "0" + b                                  # insert leading os

    for i in range (0, 8):
       if b[i] == "1":
          L[i].value(1)
       else:
          L[i].value(0)
    return

#
# Configure PORT to all outputs
#
Configure_Port()

#
# Main program loop. Count up in binary every second
#
while True:
  numbr = random.randint(1, 255)          # generate a random number
  Port_Output(numbr)                      # send cnt to port
  utime.sleep(0.25)                       # wait 250ms
```

Figure 3.39: Program: XMAS.

3.13 Project 12: Electronic dice

Description: In this project, 7 LEDs are arranged in the form of the faces of a dice and a pushbutton switch is used. When the button is pressed, the LEDs turn ON to display numbers 1 to 6 as if on a real dice. The display is turned OFF after 3 seconds, ready for the next game.

Aim: The aim of this project is to show how a dice can be constructed with 7 LEDs.

Block diagram: The block diagram of the project is shown in Figure 3.40.

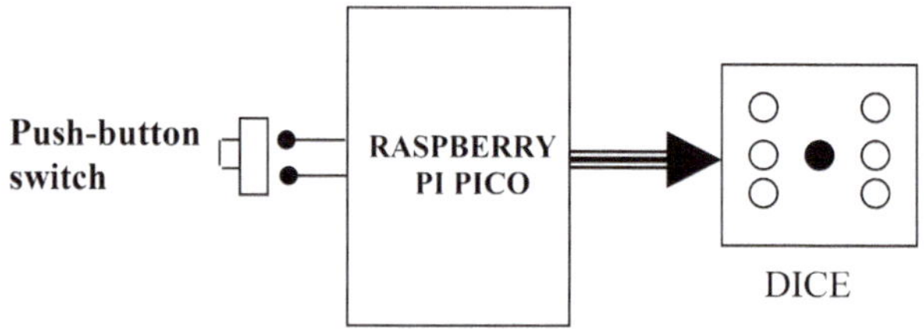

Figure 3.40: Block diagram of the project.

Figure 3.41 shows the LEDs that should be turned ON to display the 6 dice numbers.

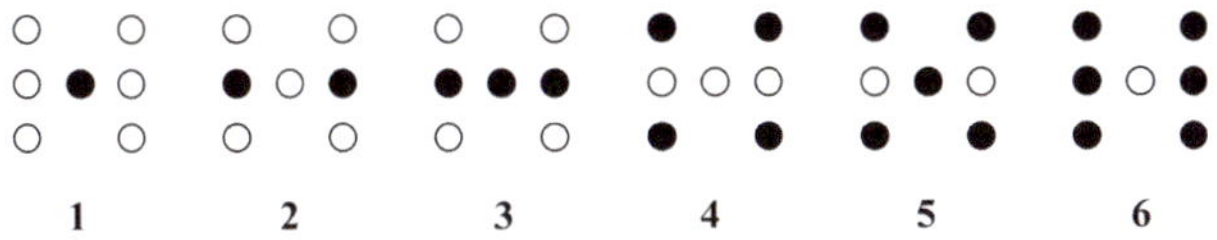

Figure 3.41: Numbers out of the program LED Dice.

Circuit diagram: The circuit diagram of the project is shown in Figure 3.42. Here, 8 GPIO pins are collected together to form a PORT. There are 7 LEDs, but 8 port pins are used in the form of a byte where the most-significant bit position is not used.

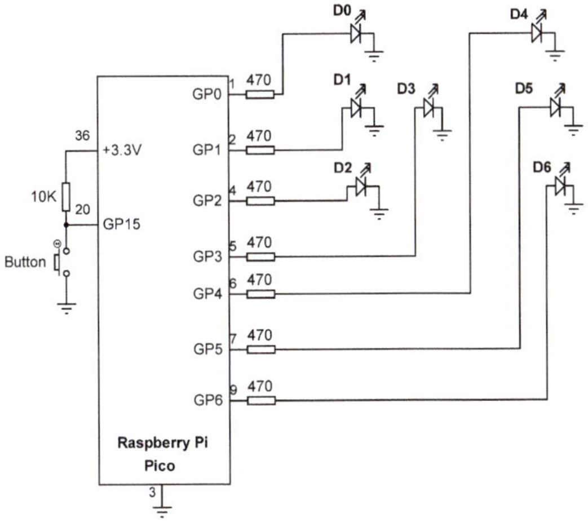

Figure 3.42: Circuit diagram of the project.

The pushbutton switch is connected to port pin GP15.

Table 3.1 gives the relationship between a dice number and the corresponding LEDs to be turned ON to imitate the faces of a real dice. For example, to display number 1 (i.e. only the middle LED is ON), we have to turn LED D3 ON. Similarly, to display number 4, we have to turn ON D0, D2, D4 and D6.

Required number	LEDs to be turned on
1	D3
2	D1, D5
3	D1, D3, D5
4	D0, D2, D4, D6
5	D0, D2, D3, D4, D6
6	D0, D1, D2, D4, D5, D6

Table 3.1: Dice number and LEDs to be turned ON.

The relationship between the required number and the data to be sent to the PORT to turn on the correct LEDs, is given in Table 3.2. For example, to display dice number 2, we have to send hexadecimal 0x22 to the PORT. Similarly, to display number 5, we have to send hexadecimal 0x5D to the PORT and so on.

Required number	PORT data (Hex)
1	0x08
2	0x22
3	0x2A
4	0x55
5	0x5D
6	0x77

Table 3.2: Required number and PORT data.

Program listing: The program is called **DICE** and the listing is shown in Figure 3.43. LED port pins are declared as a list in variable **PORT** and they are configured as outputs by using function **Configure_Port**. The bit pattern to be sent to the LEDs corresponding to each dice number is stored in hexadecimal format in a list called **DICE_NO** (see Table 3.2). GP15 is configured as an input pin and the pushbutton switch is connected to this pin to simulate the "throwing" of a dice. The state of the pushbutton is checked in the main program and when the button is pressed, function DICE is called to display a dice number between 1 and 6 for 3 seconds. After this time, all the LEDs are turned OFF to indicate that the program is ready to generate a new dice number. List **DICE_NO** is indexed to find the LEDs that should be turned ON, and the required bit pattern is sent to the PORT to display the dice number.

```
#----------------------------------------------------------
#                    DICE PROGRAM
#                    ============
#
# In this program 7 LEDs are connected to Pico to simlate
# a dice. When a pushbutton is pressed the LEDs display a
# dice number between 1 and 6
#
# Author: Dogan Ibrahim
# File  : DICE.py
# Date  : February, 2021
#-----------------------------------------------------------
from machine import Pin
import utime
import random

PORT = [7, 6, 5, 4, 3,  2,  1,  0]          # port connections
```

```
DICE_NO = [0, 0x08, 0x22, 0x2A, 0x55, 0x5D, 0x77]
L = [0]*8
Button = Pin(15, Pin.IN)

#
# This function configures the LED ports as outputs
#
def Configure_Port():
   for i in range(0, 8):
         L[i] = Pin(PORT[i], Pin.OUT)

#
# This function sends 8-bit data (0 to 255) to the PORT
#
def Port_Output(x):
   b = bin(x)                              # convert into binary
   b = b.replace("0b", "")                 # remove leading "0b"
   diff = 8 - len(b)                       # find the length
   for i in range (0, diff):
      b = "0" + b                          # insert leading os

   for i in range (0, 8):
      if b[i] == "1":
         L[i].value(1)
      else:
         L[i].value(0)
   return

#
# The program jumps here after the button is pressed
#
def DICE():
   n = random.randint(1, 6)               # generate a random number
   pattern = DICE_NO[n]                   # find the pattern
   Port_Output(pattern)                   # turn ON required LEDs
   utime.sleep(3)                         # wait for 3 seconds
   Port_Output(0)                         # turn OFF all LEDs
   return
#
# Configure PORT to all outputs
#
Configure_Port()

#
# Main program loop, check if Button is pressed
#
```

```
while True:
  if Button.value() == 0:                  # Button pressed?
     DICE()                                # Call DICE
  pass                                     # Do nothing
```

Figure 3.43: Program DICE.

3.14 Project 13: Lucky day of the week

Description: In this project, 7 LEDs are positioned in the form of a circle and are connected to the Raspberry Pi Pico. Each LED is assumed to represent a day of the week. Pressing a button generates a random number between 1 and 7 and lights up only one of the LEDs. The day name corresponding to this LED is assumed to be your lucky day of the week.

Block diagram: Figure 3.44 shows the block diagram of the project.

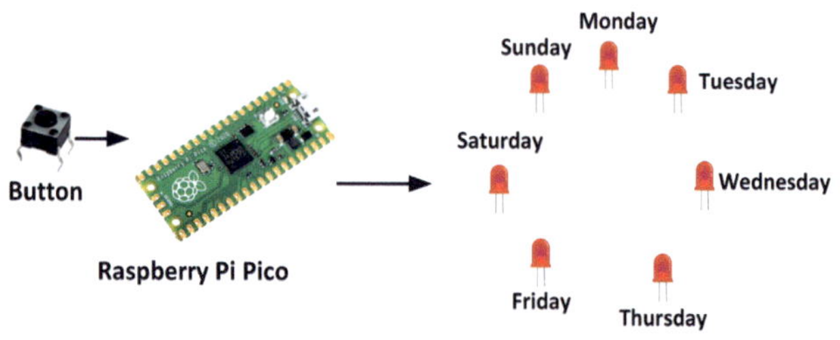

Figure 3.44: Block diagram of the project.

Circuit diagram: The circuit diagram of the project is shown in Figure 3.45, where 7 LEDs are connected to the Pico through current-limiting resistors. The button is connected to GP15. Normally the output of the button is at logic 1 and goes to logic 0 when the button is pressed.

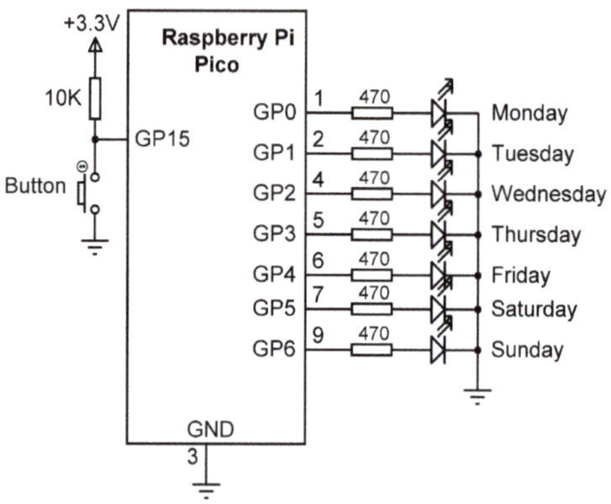

Figure 3.45: Circuit diagram of the project.

Program listing: Figure 3.46 shows the program listing (Program: **LuckyDay**). At the beginning of the program, all the 8 LED GPIO pins are combined into a single port and is addressed as a single 8-bit port using function **PORT_Output**. **utime.ticks_ms()** is used as the seed for the random number generator so that different sequence of numbers will be generated every time the program starts. This function returns an increasing millisecond counter with an arbitrary reference point, that wraps around after some value. An integer random number is generated between 1 and 7 and this number is used to turn ON one of the LEDs corresponding to a day of the week.

```
#-------------------------------------------------------
#                LUCKY DAY OF THE WEEK
#                =====================
#
# In this program 7 LEDs are connected to Pico where each
# LED represents a day of the week. Pressing a button
# turns ON one of the LEDs randomly and this corresponds to
# your lucky day of the week
#
# Author: Dogan Ibrahim
# File  : LuckyDay.py
# Date  : February, 2021
#--------------------------------------------------------
from machine import Pin
import utime
import random

PORT = [7, 6, 5, 4, 3,  2,  1,  0]        # port connections
L = [0]*8
Button = Pin(15, Pin.IN)

#
# This function configures the LED ports as outputs
#
def Configure_Port():
   for i in range(0, 8):
         L[i] = Pin(PORT[i], Pin.OUT)

#
# This function sends 8-bit data (0 to 255) to the PORT
#
def Port_Output(x):
   b = bin(x)                             # convert into binary
   b = b.replace("0b", "")                # remove leading "0b"
   diff = 8 - len(b)                      # find the length
   for i in range (0, diff):
      b = "0" + b                         # insert leading os

   for i in range (0, 8):
```

```
            if b[i] == "1":
               L[i].value(1)
            else:
               L[i].value(0)
      return
#
# Configure PORT to all outputs
#
Configure_Port()

#
# Main program loop, check if Button is pressed
#
print("Press the Button to display your lucky number...")

random.seed(utime.ticks_ms())

while Button.value() == 1:                  # If Button not pressed
   pass
r = random.randint(1, 7)                    # Generate random number
r = pow(2, r-1)                             # LED to be turned ON
Port_Output(r)                              # Send to LEDs
```

Figure 3.46: Program: LuckyDay.

3.15 Project 14: Door alarm with 7-colour flashing LED

Description: In this project, a miniature reed switch module is used together with a 7-colour flashing LED module. A small magnet is mounted on the door frame such that this magnet is very close to the reed switch and as a result the reed switch contacts are closed. When the door opens, the reed switch moves away from the magnet and as a result the reed switch contacts opens and this activates a 7-colour flashing LED module which flashes to indicate that the door is opened.

Aim: The aim of this project is to show how a mini reed switch module can be used together with a 7-colour flashing LED module to create a silent door alarm.

Sensors used: Two sensor modules are used in this project: The **KY-021** mini reed switch module, and the **KY-034** 7-colour flashing LED module. Figure 3.47 shows a picture of the **KY-021** module. This is a 3-pin module with the connections GND, +V, and Signal. The GND and +V pins are connected to the ground and power pins of the processor, respectively. The Signal pin can be connected to any general-purpose input/output pin. An on-board 10 kohm resistor is connected between the +V and the S pins as shown in Figure 3.47.

Figure 3.47: KY-021 mini reed switch module.

Figure 3.48 shows a picture of the **KY-034** 7-colour LED module. This is a 3-pin module where two GND pins are connected together. The other pin is the Signal pin. A 10 kohm resistor is connected to on-board pin V but is not used here. The module generates 7-colours when the Signal pin is connected.

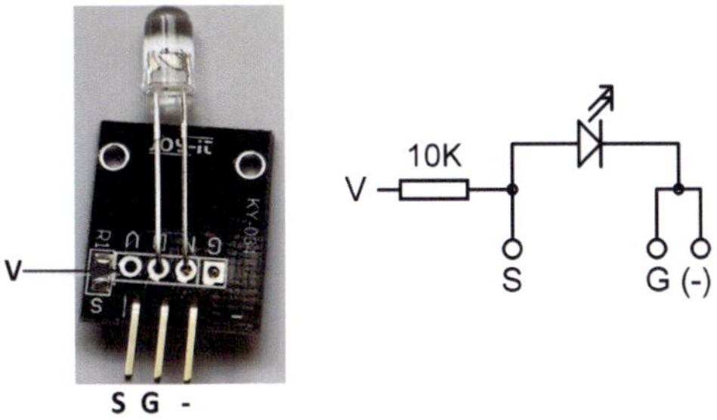

Figure 3.48: KY-034 7-colour LED module.

Background Information: Reed switches are electrical switches operated by applied magnetic field. These switches consist of a pair of ferromagnetic flexible metal contacts in a sealed glass envelope (see Figure 3.49). The contacts are normally open, closing when magnetic field (e.g. a magnet) is present near the contacts, and re-open i.e. return to their normal state when the magnetic field is removed. Reed switches are used in door and window mechanisms to detect when they are open or closed, and in many other security applications.

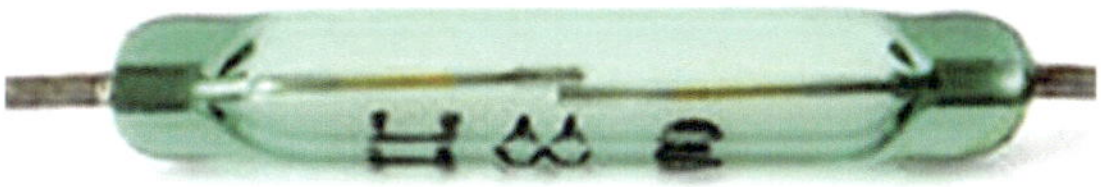

Figure 3.49: Typical reed switch in glass enclosure.

The 7-colour LED module has a built-in chip that controls the LED so that it flashes and cycles through 7 colours when power is applied to the LED. The operating voltage of the module is +3.3 V to +5 V. The module has pink, yellow, and green high brightness lights. The Flash module generates light of high brightness. By setting the LED ON and OFF with different durations we can get interesting flashing effects.

Block Diagram: The block diagram of the project is shown in Figure 3.50.

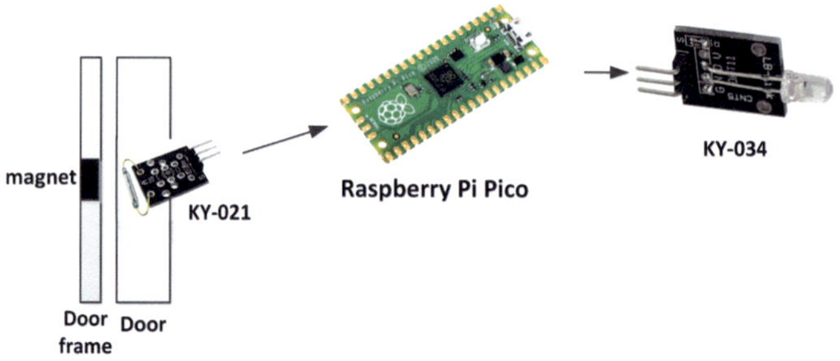

Figure 3.50: Block diagram of the project.

Circuit Diagram: The circuit diagram of the project is shown in Figure 3.51 for the case when the door is closed. Here, GP0 and GP1 of the Pico are connected to the **KY-021** reed switch and **KY-034** 7-colour LED, respectively. The reed switch output is pulled HIGH through a pull-up resistor and because the magnet is near the reed switch when the door is closed. As shown in Figure 3.52, this pin goes to logic HIGH when the door is opened (i.e. when the reed switch contacts open). The LED module is connected to the Pico through a 470-ohm current limiting resistor.

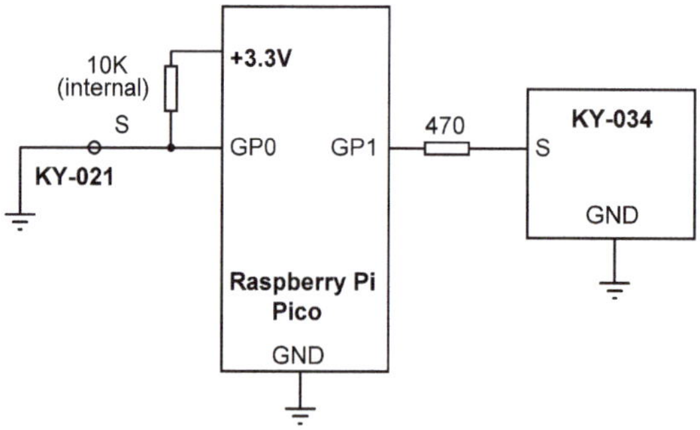

Figure 3.51: Door is closed.

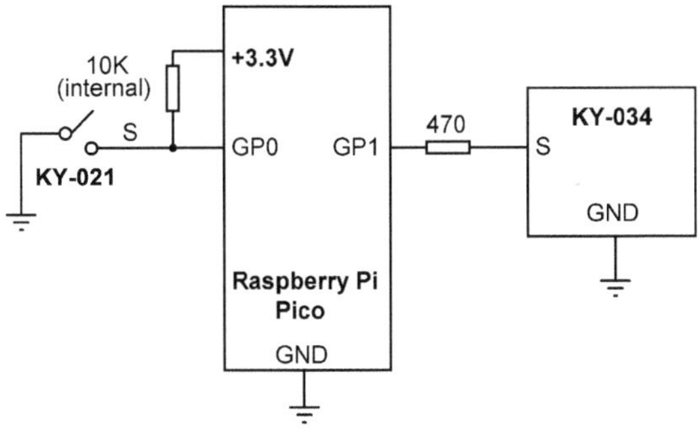

Figure 3.52: Door is open.

Program Listing: The program listing (**ReedDoor**) is shown in Figure 3.53. At the beginning of the program, the connections to **KY-021** and **KY-034** are defined, where GP0 and GP1 are configured as input and output respectively. The remainder of the program runs in an endless loop. Inside this loop, the state of the reed switch is checked and if it is at logic HIGH then it is assumed that the reed switch contacts are open i.e. the door is opened. As a result of this, the 7-color LED is activated to give visual indication that the door is opened.

```
#-----------------------------------------------------------
#                DOOR ALARM WITH 7-COLOUR FLASHING LED
#                =====================================
#
# In this program a reed switch is connected as an input and
# a 7-colour flashing LED is connected as an output. The LED
# flashes when the door is opened
#
# Author: Dogan Ibrahim
# File  : ReedDoor.py
# Date  : February, 2021
#------------------------------------------------------------
from machine import Pin

ReedSwitch = Pin(0, Pin.IN)
LED = Pin(1, Pin.OUT)

LED.value(0)

while True:
    door = ReedSwitch.value()
    if door == 1:
        LED.value(1)
    else:
        LED.value(0)
```

Figure 3.53: Raspberry Pi program listing.

Testing the program

When the program is run, you should see the LED flashing (door open condition). Place a magnet close to the reed switch (door closed condition) and the LED should stop flashing.

3.16 Project 15: 2-digit, 7-segment display

Description: In this project, a 7-segment LED display is used as a counter to count up every second from 0 to 99. Multi-digit 7-segment displays require continuous refreshing of their digits so that the human brain perceives the digits as lighting steady and non-flashing. The general technique used is to enable each digit for a short time (e.g., 10 ms) so that our eyes 'see' both digits as ON at any time. This process requires the digits to be enabled alternately and continuously. As a result of this, the processor cannot perform any other tasks and has to be busy all the time, refreshing the digits. One technique used in non-multitasking systems is to use timer interrupts and refresh the digits in the timer interrupt service routines. In this project, we will be employing a multitasking approach to refresh the display digits so that the processor can carry out other tasks. The aim of the project is to show how the digits of a multiplexed 2-digit 7-segment LED display can be refreshed, while the main program sends data to the display to count up in seconds from 00 to 99.

7-Segment LED Displays: Displaying data is one of the fundamental output activities of any microcontroller system. For example, displays are used to show the sensor data such as the temperature, humidity, pressure etc. There are several types of display devices that can be used in microcontroller-based systems. LCDs and 7-segment displays are probably two of the most used display devices. There are several types of LCDs, such as text-based LCD, graphics LCDs, colour LCDs, touch screen LCDs, etc. Most 7-segment displays are used to display numeric or alphanumeric values, and they can have one or more digits. One-digit displays can only display numbers from 0 to 9. Two-digit displays can display numbers from 0 to 99, three-digit displays numbers from 0 to 999, and so on. In this project a two-digit 7-segment display is used.

As shown in Figure 3.54, a 7-segment LED display basically consists of 7 LEDs connected such that numbers from 0 to 9 and some (basic) letters can be displayed. The display segments are identified by letters from **a** through **g**. Figure 3.55 shows the segment names of a typical 7-segment display.

Figure 3.54: Some 7-segment displays.

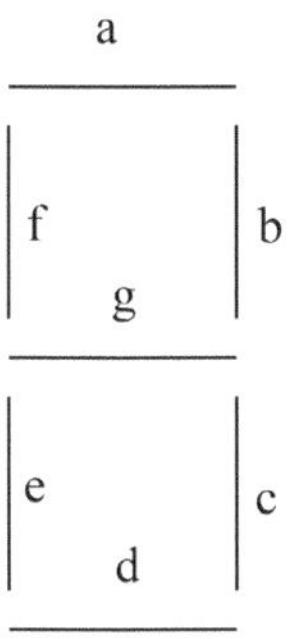

Figure 3.55: Segment names of a 7-segment display.

Figure 3.56 shows how numbers from 0 to 9 can be obtained by turning ON or OFF different segments of the display.

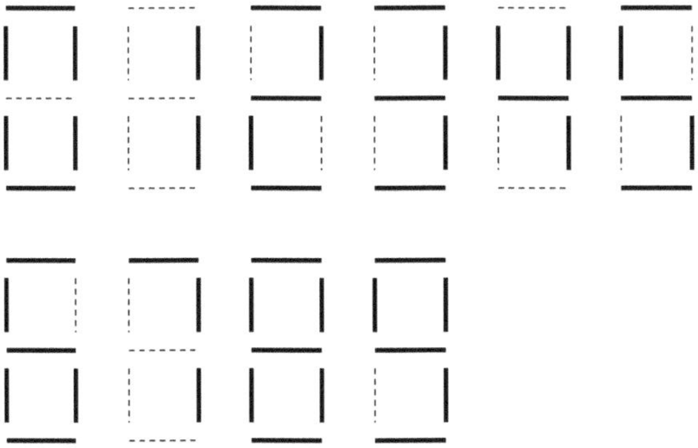

Figure 3.56: Displaying numbers 0 – 9.

7-segment LED displays are available in two different configurations: **common-cathode** and **common-anode**. As shown in Figure 3.57, in common-cathode configuration all the cathodes of all the segment LEDs are connected together to ground. The segments are then turned ON by applying a logic 1 to the required segment LED via current-limiting resistors. In common-cathode configuration, the 7-segment LED is connected to the microcontroller in current-sourcing mode.

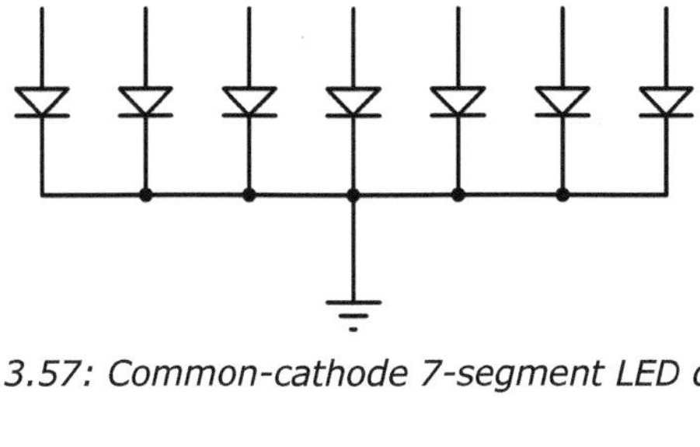

Figure 3.57: Common-cathode 7-segment LED display.

In a common-anode configuration, the anode terminals of all the LEDs are connected together as shown in Figure 3.58. This common point is then normally connected to the supply voltage. A segment is turned ON by connecting its cathode terminal to logic 0 via a current-limiting resistor. In common-anode configuration the 7-segment LED is connected to the microcontroller in current-sinking mode.

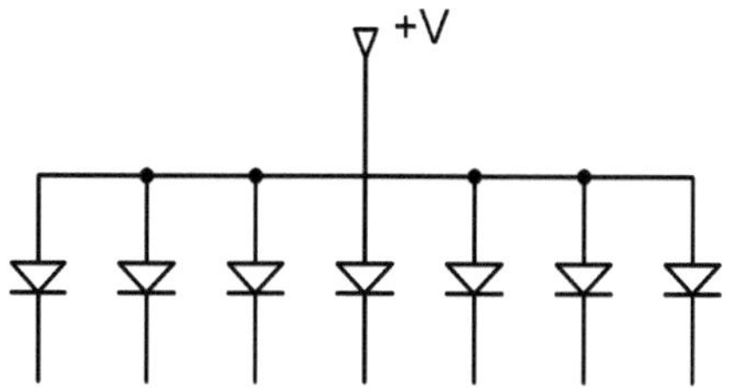

Figure 3.58: Common-anode, 7-segment LED display.

In multiplexed LED applications (for example, see Figure 3.59 for a 2-digit multiplexed LED display), the LED segments of all the digits are tied together and the common pins of each digit is turned ON separately by the microcontroller. By displaying each digit for several milliseconds, the brain cannot differentiate that the digits are not ON all the time. This way we can multiplex any number of 7-segment displays together. For example, to display number 57, we have to send 5 to the first digit and enable its common pin. After a few milliseconds, number 7 is sent to the second digit and the common point of the second digit is enabled. When this process is repeated continuously the user sees as if both displays are ON continuously.

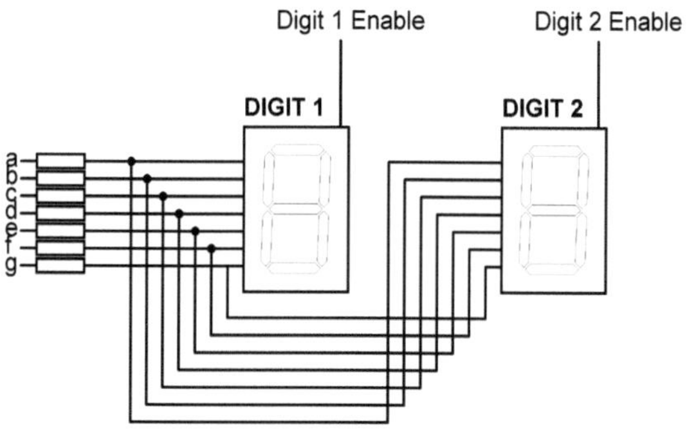

Figure 3.59: 2-digit, multiplexed, 7-segment LED display.

Some manufacturers provide multiplexed multi-digit displays in single packages. For example, we can purchase 2-, 4-, or 8-digit multiplexed displays in a single package. The display used in this project is the DC56-11EWA which is a red, 0.56-inch height, **common-cathode** two-digit multiplexed display with 18 pins, where the pin configuration is shown in Table 3.3. Basically, this display can be controlled from the microcontroller as follows:

- send the segment bit pattern for digit 1 to segments a to g;
- enable digit 1;
- wait for a few milliseconds;
- disable digit 1;

- send the segment bit patter for digit 2 to segments a to g;
- enable digit 2;
- wait for a few milliseconds;
- disable digit 2;
- repeat the above process continuously.

Pin no	Segment
1,5	e
2,6	d
3,8	c
14	digit 1 enable
17,7	g
15,10	b
16,11	a
18,12	f
13	digit 2 enable
4	decimal point1
9	decimal point 2

Table 3.3: Pin configuration of Type DC56-11EWA dual display.

The segment configuration of DC56-11EWA display is shown in Figure 3.60. In a multiplexed display application, the segment pins of corresponding segments are connected together. For example, pins 11 and 16 are connected as the common **a** segment. Similarly, pins 15 and 10 are connected as the common **b** segment and so on.

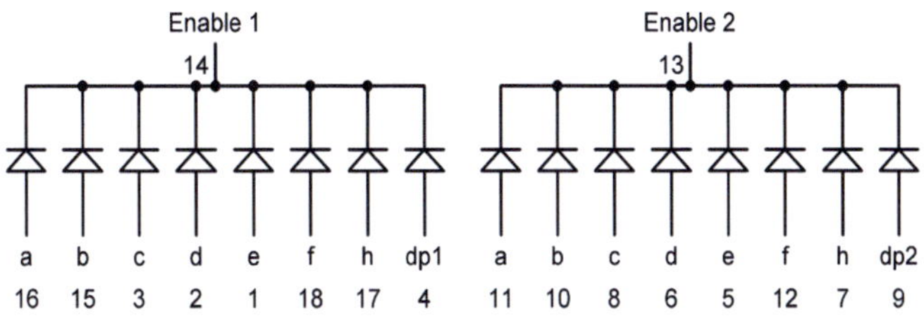

Figure 3.60: DC56-11EWA display segment configuration.

Block Diagram: Figure 3.61 shows the block diagram of the project.

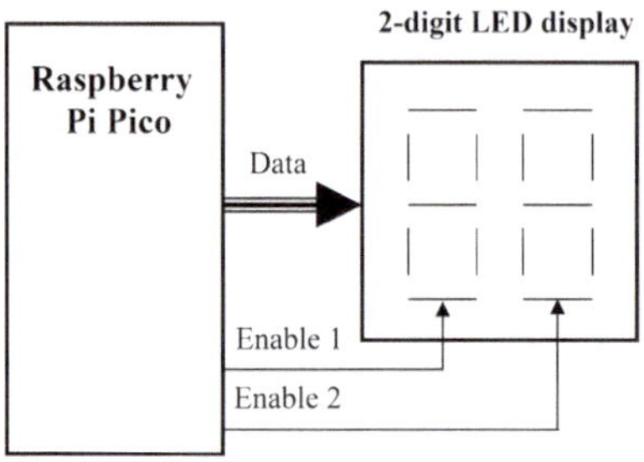

Figure 3.61: Block diagram of the project.

Circuit Diagram: The circuit diagram of the project is shown in Figure 3.62. In this project, the following pins of the Raspberry Pi Pico are used to interface with the 7-segment LED display:

7-Segment Display pin	Raspberry Pi Pico GPIO	Physical pin no.
a	0	1
b	1	2
c	2	4
d	3	5
e	4	6
f	5	7
g	6	9
E1	8 (via transistor)	11
E2	7 (via transistor)	10

7-segment display segments are driven from the port pins through 470-ohm current-limiting resistors. Digit-enable pins E1 and E2 are driven from port pins GP8 and GP7 respectively through two BC108 NPN transistors (any other NPN transistor can be used here), used as switches. The collectors of these transistors drive the segment digits. The segments are enabled when the base of the corresponding transistor is set to logic 1. Notice that the following pins of the display are connected together to form a multiplexed display:

16 and 11; 15 and 10; 3 and 8; 2 and 6; 1 and 5; 17 and 7; 18 and 12.

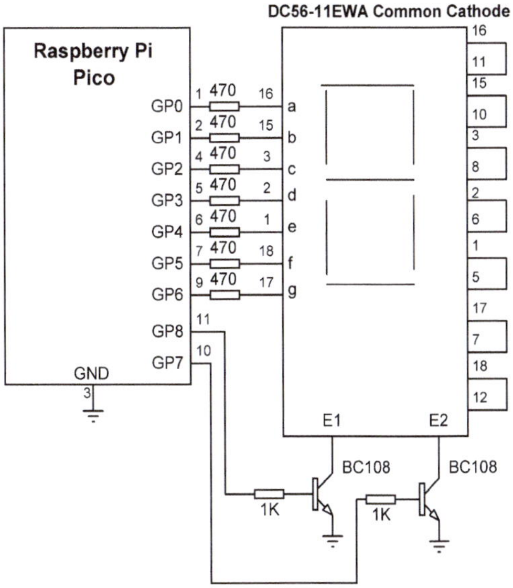

Figure 3.62: Circuit diagram of the project.

Program Listing: Before driving the display, we must know the relationship between the numbers to be displayed and the corresponding segments to be turned ON. This is shown below.

Number to be displayed	LED bit pattern (a,b,c,d,e,f,g)
0	1,1,1,1,1,1,0
1	0,1,1,0,0,0,0
2	1,1,0,1,1,0,1
3	1,1,1,1,0,0,1
4	0,1,1,0,0,1,1
5	1,0,1,1,0,1,1
6	1,0,1,1,1,1,1
7	1,1,1,0,0,0,0
8	1,1,1,1,1,1,1
9	1,1,1,1,0,1,1

Figure 3.63 shows the program listing (program: **SevenCount**). At the beginning of the program the connections between the LED segments and the GPIO pins are defined in list variable **LED_Segments**. Also the connections between the LED digits and the GPIO pins are defined in list variable **LED_Digits**. These GPIO pins are then configured as outputs and are all cleared to 0. Variable **count** is initialized to zero at the beginning of the program. Function **Refresh** is called periodically by the timer and this function refreshes the display to display the value of variable **count**. The display digits are refreshed every 10 ms.

If the number to be displayed is less than 10 then a 0 is inserted in front of the number so that the numbers 0 to 9 are displayed as 00 to 09. Variable **count** is incremented by one every second.

```
#-------------------------------------------------------------
#                 2-DIGIT 7-SEGMENT COUNTER
#                 ==========================
#
# In this program a 2-digit 7-segment display is connected
# to the Pico. The program counts up every second
#
# Author: Dogan Ibrahim
# File  : SevenCount.py
# Date  : February, 2021
#--------------------------------------------------------------
from machine import Pin, Timer
import utime

tim = Timer()
LED_Segments = [6, 5 ,4, 3, 2, 1, 0]
LED_Digits = [8, 7]
L = [0]*7
D = [0, 0]

#
# LED bit pattern for all numbers 0-9
#
LED_Bits ={
'0':(1,1,1,1,1,1,0),                        # 0
'1':(0,1,1,0,0,0,0),                        # 1
'2':(1,1,0,1,1,0,1),                        # 2
'3':(1,1,1,1,0,0,1),                        # 3
'4':(0,1,1,0,0,1,1),                        # 4
'5':(1,0,1,1,0,1,1),                        # 5
'6':(1,0,1,1,1,1,1),                        # 6
'7':(1,1,1,0,0,0,0),                        # 7
'8':(1,1,1,1,1,1,1),                        # 8
'9':(1,1,1,1,0,1,1)}                        # 9

count = 0                                   # Initialzie count
#
# This function configures the LED ports as outputs
#
def Configure_Port():
   for i in range(0, 7):
         L[i] = Pin(LED_Segments[i], Pin.OUT)
```

```
    for i in range(0, 2):
          D[i] = Pin(LED_Digits[i], Pin.OUT)


#
# Refresh the 7-segment display
#
def Refresh(timer):                                  # Thread Refresh
    global count
    cnt = str(count)                                 # into string
    if len(cnt) < 2:
       cnt = "0" + cnt                               # Make sure 2 digits
    for dig in range(2):                             # Do for 2 digits
       for loop in range(0,7):
           L[loop].value(LED_Bits[cnt[dig]][loop])
       D[dig].value(1)
       utime.sleep(0.01)
       D[dig].value(0)

#
# Configure PORT to all outputs
#
Configure_Port()

#
# Main program loop. Start the periodic timer and counting
#
tim.init(freq=50, mode=Timer.PERIODIC, callback=Refresh)

while True:                                # Do forever
    utime.sleep(1)                         # Wait a second
    count = count + 1                      # Increment count
    if count == 100:                       # If count = 100
        count = 0
```

Figure 3.63: Program: SevenCount.

Modified program

In the program shown in Figure 3.63, numbers under 10 are displayed with a leading 0 (e.g. 05). We can remove the leading zero by blanking all the segments of the left-hand digit if the number is less than 10. The number five, for example, is displayed as 5 and not as 05. The modified program listing (program: **SevenCount2**) is shown in Figure 3.64. Here, list **LED_Bits** is modified by adding a blank line where all the segment bits are set to 0. Additionally, a blank character is inserted to the front of string **cnt** if the number is less than 10 so that the leading digit is blanked.

```
#-----------------------------------------------------------
#                 2-DIGIT 7-SEGMENT COUNTER
#                 =========================
#
# In this program a 2-digit 7-segment display is connected
# to the Pico. The program counts up every second.
# In this version of the program leading zero is omitted
#
# Author: Dogan Ibrahim
# File  : SevenCount.py
# Date  : February, 2021
#------------------------------------------------------------
from machine import Pin, Timer
import utime

tim = Timer()
LED_Segments = [6, 5 ,4, 3, 2, 1, 0]
LED_Digits = [8, 7]
L = [0]*7
D = [0, 0]

#
# LED bit pattern for all numbers 0-9
#
LED_Bits ={
' ':(0,0,0,0,0,0,0),                # Blank
'0':(1,1,1,1,1,1,0),                # 0
'1':(0,1,1,0,0,0,0),                # 1
'2':(1,1,0,1,1,0,1),                # 2
'3':(1,1,1,1,0,0,1),                # 3
'4':(0,1,1,0,0,1,1),                # 4
'5':(1,0,1,1,0,1,1),                # 5
'6':(1,0,1,1,1,1,1),                # 6
'7':(1,1,1,0,0,0,0),                # 7
'8':(1,1,1,1,1,1,1),                # 8
'9':(1,1,1,1,0,1,1)}                # 9

count = 0                          # Initialzie count
#
# This function configures the LED ports as outputs
#
def Configure_Port():
   for i in range(0, 7):
         L[i] = Pin(LED_Segments[i], Pin.OUT)

   for i in range(0, 2):
```

```
        D[i] = Pin(LED_Digits[i], Pin.OUT)


#
# Refresh the 7-segment display
#
def Refresh(timer):                          # Thread Refresh
   global count
   cnt = str(count)                          # into string
   if len(cnt) < 2:
      cnt = " " + cnt                        # Make sure 2 digits
   for dig in range(2):                      # Do for 2 digits
      for loop in range(0,7):
          L[loop].value(LED_Bits[cnt[dig]][loop])
      D[dig].value(1)
      utime.sleep(0.01)
      D[dig].value(0)

#
# Configure PORT to all outputs
#
Configure_Port()

#
# Main program loop. Start the periodic timer and counting
#
tim.init(freq=50, mode=Timer.PERIODIC, callback=Refresh)

while True:                                 # Do forever
   utime.sleep(1)                           # Wait a second
   count = count + 1                        # Increment count
   if count == 100:                         # If count = 100
       count = 0
```

Figure 3.64: Program: SevenCount2.

3.17 Project 16: 4-digit, 7-segment display seconds counter

Description: In this project a 7-segment, 4-digit multiplexed LED display is used as a counter to count up every second from 0 to 9999. The project is very similar to the previous project, but here 4 digits are used instead of 2.

The operation of a 4-digit multiplexed display (Figure 3.65) is similar to the 2-digit display, where the LED segments of all the digits are tied together and the common pins of each digit are turned ON separately by the microcontroller. By displaying each digit for several milliseconds, the eye can not differentiate that the digits are not ON all the time. This way we can multiplex any number of 7-segment displays together. For example, to display number 5734, we must send '5' to the first digit and enable its common pin. After a few milliseconds, number '7' is sent to the second digit and the common point of the second digit is enabled, and so on. When this process is repeated continuously, the user perceives both displays as ON continuously.

Figure 3.65: 4-digit, multiplexed 7-segment LED display.

The display used in this project is the DC56-11EWA, which is a red 0.56-inch height common-cathode two-digit multiplexed display having 18 pins, where the pin configuration is shown in Table 3.3. Two such display modules are used to construct a 4-digit display. Each module has its own E1 and E2 enable pins.
In a multiplexed display application, the segment pins of corresponding segments are connected together. For example, pins 11 and 16 are connected as the common **a** segment. Similarly, pins 15 and 10 are connected as the common **b** segment and so on.

Block Diagram: Figure 3.66 shows the block diagram of the project.

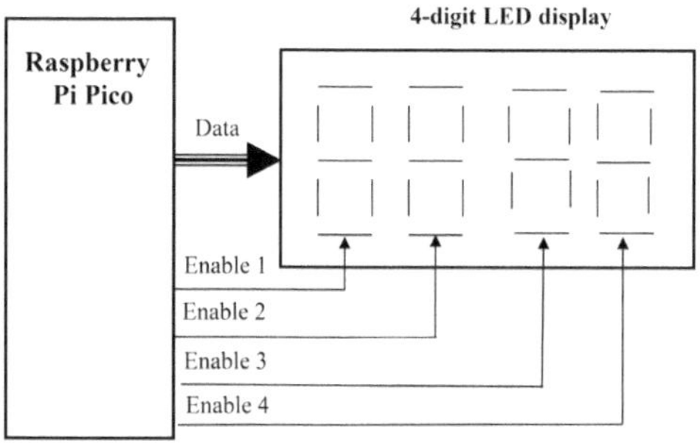

Figure 3.66: Block diagram of the project.

Circuit Diagram: The circuit diagram of the project is shown in Figure 3.67. In this project, the following pins of the Raspberry Pi Pico are used to interface with the 7-segment LED display:

7-Segment Display Pin	Raspberry Pi Pico GPIO	Physical Pin No.
a	0	1
b	1	2
c	2	4
d	3	5
e	4	6
f	5	7
g	6	9
E1	7 (via transistor)	10
E2	8 (via transistor)	1
E1	9 (via transistor)	12
E2	10 (via transistor)	14

The 7-segment display segments are driven from the port pins through 470-ohm current limiting resistors. Digit-enable pins E1, E2 of the first module and E1, E2 of the second module are driven from port pins GP7, GP8, GP9, and GP10 respectively through four BC108 NPN transistors used as switches (any other NPN, small-signal transistor can be used here). The collectors of these transistors drive the segment digits. The segments are enabled when the base of the corresponding transistor is set to logic 1. Notice that the following pins of the display are interconnected to form a multiplexed display:

16 and 11; 15 and 10; 3 and 8; 2 and 6; 1 and 5; 17 and 7; 18 and 12.

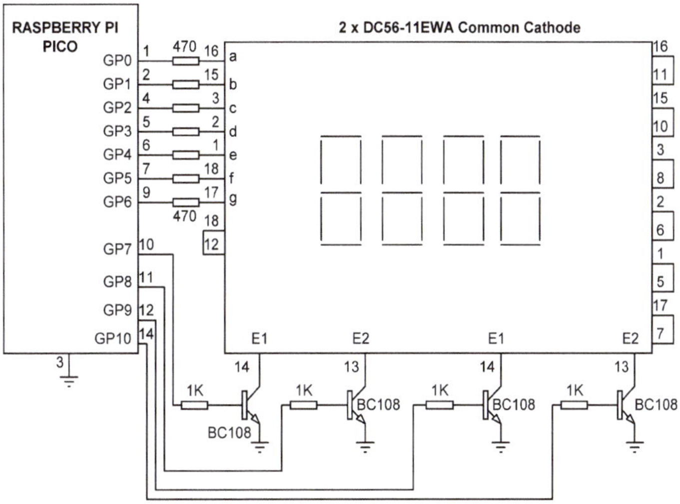

Figure 3.67: Circuit diagram of the project.

Program Listing: Figure 3.68 shows the program listing (Program: **SevenCount4**). At the beginning of the program, the modules used in the program are imported. The program is very similar to the one with 2 digits. Here, the list **LED_Digits** contains 4 numbers which are the digit-enable pins of the four 7-segment LED modules. Function **Refresh** is very similar to the function with 2 digits, except that here we had to make sure that the number to be displayed (**count**) consists of 4 digits. If the number is less than 4 digits, spaces are inserted in front of it to blank the display for these digit positions. Notice that 'digit count' runs from 0 to 4 and not from 0 to 2 which was the case with the 2-digit display. The delay between the digit-enables is reduced to 5 ms since we have 4 digits, and quicker refreshing is required. Variable **count** starts from 0 at the beginning of the program by default. It is incremented by 1 every second. When the count reaches 10000 it is reset back to 0.

```
#------------------------------------------------------------
#                4-DIGIT 7-SEGMENT SECONDS COUNTER
#                ==================================
#
# In this program a 4-digit 7-segment display is connected
# to the Pico. The program counts up every second.
# In this version of the program leading zero is omitted
#
# Author: Dogan Ibrahim
# File  : SevenCount4.py
# Date  : February, 2021
#-------------------------------------------------------------
from machine import Pin, Timer
import utime

tim = Timer()
LED_Segments = [6, 5 ,4, 3, 2, 1, 0]
LED_Digits = [7, 8, 9, 10]
L = [0]*7
D = [0, 0, 0, 0]


#
# LED bit pattern for all numbers 0-9
#
LED_Bits ={
' ':(0,0,0,0,0,0,0),                # Blank
'0':(1,1,1,1,1,1,0),                # 0
'1':(0,1,1,0,0,0,0),                # 1
'2':(1,1,0,1,1,0,1),                # 2
'3':(1,1,1,1,0,0,1),                # 3
'4':(0,1,1,0,0,1,1),                # 4
'5':(1,0,1,1,0,1,1),                # 5
'6':(1,0,1,1,1,1,1),                # 6
'7':(1,1,1,0,0,0,0),                # 7
```

```
'8':(1,1,1,1,1,1,1),              # 8
'9':(1,1,1,1,0,1,1)}              # 9

count = 0                         # Initialzie count

#
# This function configures the LED ports as outputs
#
def Configure_Port():
   for i in range(0, 7):
         L[i] = Pin(LED_Segments[i], Pin.OUT)

   for i in range(0, 4):
         D[i] = Pin(LED_Digits[i], Pin.OUT)


#
# Refresh the 7-segment display
#
def Refresh(timer):                               # Thread Refresh
   global count
   cnt = str(count)                               # into string
   if len(cnt) == 3:                              # 3 digits?
      cnt = " " + cnt                             # Make sure 4 digits
   elif len(cnt) == 2:                            # 2 digits?
       cnt = "  " + cnt                           # MAke sure 4 digits
   elif len(cnt) == 1:                            # 1 digit?
       cnt = "   " + cnt                          # MAke sure 4 digits
   for dig in range(4):                           # Do for 4 digits
      for loop in range(0,7):
          L[loop].value(LED_Bits[cnt[dig]][loop])
      D[dig].value(1)
      utime.sleep(0.005)
      D[dig].value(0)

#
# Configure PORT to all outputs
#
Configure_Port()

#
# Main program loop. Start the periodic timer and counting
#
tim.init(freq=50, mode=Timer.PERIODIC, callback=Refresh)

while True:                       # Do forever
```

```
utime.sleep(1)                    # Wait a second
count = count + 1                 # Increment count
if count == 10000:                # If count = 10000
    count = 0
```

Figure 3.68: Program: SevenCount4.

3.18 LCDs

In microcontroller-based systems we usually want to interact with the system — for example, to enter a parameter, to change the value of a parameter, or to display the output of a measured variable. Data is usually entered to a system using a switch, a small keypad, or a full-blown keyboard. Data is usually displayed using an indicator such as one or more LEDs, 7-segment displays, or LC (liquid-crystal) type displays. LCDs have the advantages that they can display alphanumeric as well as graphical data. Some LCDs have 40 or more character lengths with the capability to display data on several lines. Some other LCDs can be used to display graphical images (graphical LCDs, or simply GLCDs), such as animation. Some displays are available in single- or multi-colour, while others incorporate backlighting so that they can be viewed in dimly lit conditions.

LCDs can be connected to a microcontroller either in parallel form or through the I^2C interface. Parallel LCDs (e.g. the Hitachi HD44780) are connected using more than one data line and several control lines, and the data gets transferred in parallel form. It is common to use either 4 or 8 data lines and two or more control lines. Using a 4-wire connection saves I/O pins but it is slower since the data is transferred in two stages. I^2C based LCDs on the other hand are connected to a microcontroller using only 2 wires, carrying 'data' and 'clock'. I^2C-based LCDs are in general much easier to use and require less wiring, but they cost more than the parallel ones. In this Chapter we will be learning to use both parallel and I^2C based LCDs in projects.

The programming of LCDs is a complex task and requires a good understanding of the internal operations of the LCD controllers, including knowledge of their exact timing requirements. Fortunately, there are several libraries that can be used to simplify the use of both parallel and serial LCDs.

The HD44780 LCD module

Although there are several types of LCDs, the HD44780 is currently one of the most popular LCD modules used in industry as well as by hobbyists (Figure 3.69). This module is an alphanumeric monochrome display and comes in different sizes. Modules with 16 columns are popular in most small applications, but other modules with 8, 20, 24, 32, or 40 columns are also available. Although most LCDs have two lines (or rows) as the standard, it is possible to purchase models with 1 or 4 lines. LCD displays are available with standard 14-pin connectors, although 16-pin modules are also available, providing terminals for backlighting. Table 3.4 gives the pin configuration and pin functions of a 16-pin LCD module. A brief summary of the pin functions is given below.

Pin no	Name	Function
1	VSS	Ground
2	VDD	+ ve Supply
3	VEE	Contrast
4	RS	Register Select
5	R/W	Read/Write
6	E	Enable
7	D0	Data bit 0
8	D1	Data bit 1
9	D2	Data bit 2
10	D3	Data bit 3
11	D4	Data bit 4
12	D5	Data bit 5
13	D6	Data bit 6
14	D7	Data bit 7
15	A	Backlight anode (+)
16	K	Backlight cathode (GND)

Table 3.4: Pin configuration of HD44780 LCD module.

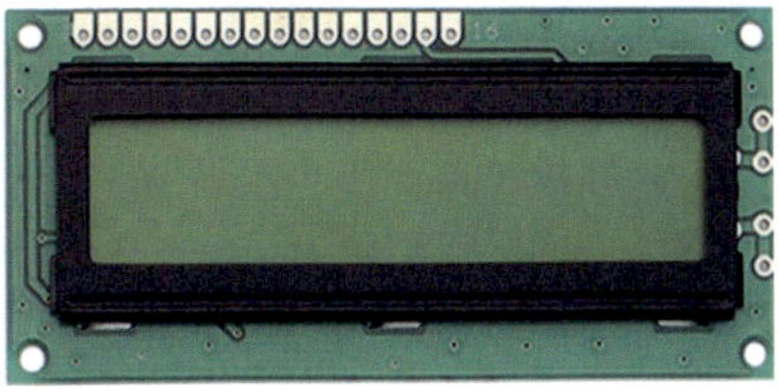

Figure 3.69: HD44780-compatible parallel LCD.

V_{SS} (pin 1) and V_{DD} (pin 2) are the Ground and Power Supply pins. The supply voltage should be +5 V.

V_{EE} is pin 3 and this is the contrast control pin used to adjust the contrast of the display. The arm of a 10-kohm potentiometer is normally connected to this pin and the other two terminals of the potentiometer are connected to the ground and power supply pins. The contrast of the display is adjusted by rotating the potentiometer arm.

Pin 4 is the Register Select (RS) and when this pin is LOW, data transferred to the display is treated as commands. When RS is HIGH, character data can be transferred to and from the display.

Pin 5 is the Read/Write (R/W) line. This pin is pulled LOW in order to write commands or character data to the LCD module. When this pin is HIGH, character data or status information can be read from the module. This pin is normally connected permanently LOW so that commands or character data can be sent to the LCD module.

Enable (E) is pin 6 which is used to initiate the transfer of commands or data between the LCD module and the microcontroller. When writing to the display, data is transferred only on the HIGH to LOW transition of this pin. When reading from the display, data becomes available after the LOW to HIGH transition of the enable pin and this data remains valid as long as the enable pin is at logic HIGH.
Pins 7 to 14 are the eight data bus lines (D0 to D7). Data can be transferred between the microcontroller and the LCD module using either a single 8-bit byte, or as two 4-bit nibbles. In the latter case only the upper four data lines (D4 to D7) are used. 4-bit mode has the advantage that four less I/O lines are required to communicate with the LCD. The 4-bit mode is slower, however, since the data is transferred in two stages. In this book we shall be using the 4-bit interface only.
Pins 15 and 16 are for background brightness control. To enable the background brightness, a 220-ohm resistor should be connected from pin 15 to +5 V supply, and pin 16 should be connected to ground.
In 4-bit mode the following pins of the LCD are used. The R/W line is permanently connected to ground. This mode uses 6 GPIO port pins of the microcontroller:

V_{SS}, V_{DD}, V_{EE}, E, R/S, D4, D5, D6, D7.

In the next section we will be creating an LCD library of functions that can be used to send data and text to standard HD44780 type character LCDs.

3.19 Project 17: LCD functions – displaying text

Description: In this project we will develop a number of functions that can be used to send data and text to 16×2 character type LC displays.

Aim: The aim of this project is to develop a library of functions that can be used to control LCDs. These functions can be used in projects to send text and numbers to LCDs.

Block diagram: Figure 3.70 shows the block diagram of the project.

Figure 3.70: Block diagram of the project.

Circuit diagram: The circuit diagram of the project is shown in Figure 3.71. The LCD is connected to the Pico using 4 data wires (D4 – D7) and 2 control wires (E and R/S). The connections between the LCD and Pico are as follows:

LCD pin	Pico pin
R/S	GP0
E	GP1
D4	GP2
D5	GP3
D6	GP4
D7	GP5

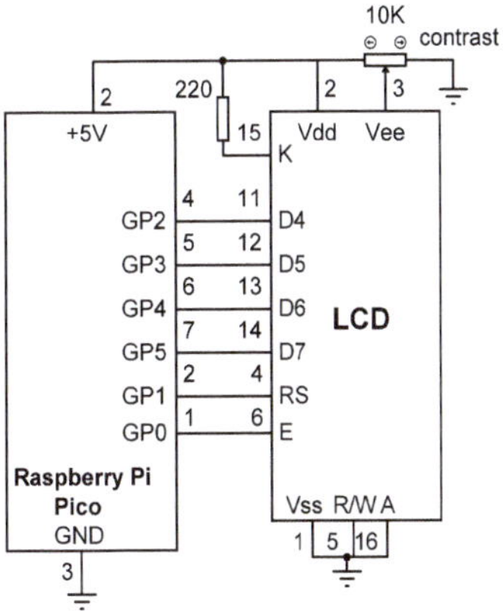

Figure 3.71: Circuit diagram of the project.

The contrast of the LCD is controlled using a 10-kohm potentiometer.

Program listing: Figure 3.72 shows the functions listing (Program: **LCD**). The connections between the LCD and the Pico are defined at the beginning and these can be changed if desired. The remainder of the functions should not be changed for proper control of the LCD. These functions implement the initialization and control of the LCD.

The following LCD control functions are available:

lcd_init: this is the LCD initialization function and must be called first before any other functions are called;
lcd_clear: clears the LCD;
lcd_home: homes the cursor (top left position);
lcd_cursor_blink: enables blinking cursor;
lcd_cursor_on: enables visible cursor;
lcd_cursor_off: disables visible cursor;
lcd_puts(s): displays string s;
lcd_putch(c): displays character c;
lcd_goto(col,row): positions thc cursor at the specified column and position. (0, 0) is the left corner of the LCD. First row is row 0, second row is row 1 and so on.

```
#-------------------------------------------------------
#                 PARALLEL LCD FUNCTIONS
#                 ======================
#
# These functions initialize and control the LCD
#
# Author: Dogan Ibrahim
# File  : LCD
# Date  : February 2021
#-------------------------------------------------------
from machine import Pin
import utime

EN = Pin(0, Pin.OUT)
RS = Pin(1, Pin.OUT)
D4 = Pin(2, Pin.OUT)
D5 = Pin(3, Pin.OUT)
D6 = Pin(4, Pin.OUT)
D7 = Pin(5, Pin.OUT)
PORT = [2, 3, 4, 5]
L = [0,0,0,0]

def Configure():
    for i in range(4):
       L[i] = Pin(PORT[i], Pin.OUT)

def lcd_strobe():
    EN.value(1)
    utime.sleep_ms(1)
    EN.value(0)
    utime.sleep_ms(1)

def lcd_write(c, mode):
    if mode == 0:
       d = c
    else:
       d = ord(c)
    d = d >> 4
    for i in range(4):
        b = d & 1
        L[i].value(b)
        d = d >> 1
    RS.value(mode)
    lcd_strobe()

    if mode == 0:
```

```
      d = c
   else:
      d = ord(c)
   for i in range(4):
       b = d & 1
       L[i].value(b)
       d = d >> 1
   RS.value(mode)
   lcd_strobe()
   utime.sleep_ms(1)
   RS.value(1)

def lcd_clear():
    lcd_write(0x01, 0)
    utime.sleep_ms(5)

def lcd_home():
    lcd_write(0x02, 0)
    utime.sleep_ms(5)

def lcd_cursor_blink():
    lcd_write(0x0D, 0)
    utime.sleep_ms(1)

def lcd_cursor_on():
    lcd_write(0x0E, 0)
    utime.sleep_ms(1)

def lcd_cursor_off():
    lcd_write(0x0C, 0)
    utime.sleep_ms(1)

def lcd_puts(s):
    l = len(s)
    for i in range(l):
       lcd_putch(s[i])

def lcd_putch(c):
    lcd_write(c, 1)

def lcd_goto(col, row):
    c = col + 1
    if row == 0:
        address = 0
    if row == 1:
        address = 0x40
```

```
        address = address + c - 1
        lcd_write(0x80 | address, 0)

    def lcd_init():
        Configure()
        utime.sleep_ms(120)
        for i in range(4):
            L[i].value(0)
        utime.sleep_ms(50)
        L[0].value(1)
        L[1].value(1)
        lcd_strobe()
        utime.sleep_ms(10)
        lcd_strobe()
        utime.sleep_ms(10)
        lcd_strobe()
        utime.sleep_ms(10)
        L[0].value(0)
        lcd_strobe()
        utime.sleep_ms(5)
        lcd_write(0x28, 0)
        utime.sleep_ms(1)
        lcd_write(0x08, 0)
        utime.sleep_ms(1)
        lcd_write(0x01, 0)
        utime.sleep_ms(10)
        lcd_write(0x06, 0)
        utime.sleep_ms(5)
        lcd_write(0x0C, 0)
        utime.sleep_ms(10)
    #================= END OF LCD FUNCTIONS ======================
```

Figure 3.72: Program LCD.

Displaying text

The following statement displays text **Hello from PICO** (these statements must follow the LCD functions given in Figure 3.72).

```
lcd_init()
lcd_puts('Hello from PICO')
```

3.20 Project 18: Seconds counter — LCD

Description: In this project we will count up every second and display the result on the LCD.

Aim: The aim of this project is to show how numeric data can be displayed on the LCD.

The block diagram and circuit diagram of the project are as in Figure 3.70 and Figure 3.71.

Program listing: The program is named **LCDCount**. The following statements must follow the LCD functions given in Figure 3.72.

```
lcd_init()
count = 0
while True:
        lcd_goto(0, 0)
        cntstr = str(count)
        lcd_puts(cntstr)
        count = count + 1
        utime.sleep(1)
```

Storing the LCD functions in a module library

We can easily combine all the LCD functions in a library and then import this library at the beginning of our program. The steps are given below.

- Open the program **LCD** (see Figure 3.72).
- Click at Thonny: **File** followed by **Save As.**
- Select **Raspberry Pi Pico** as the destination.
- Set the filename as **LCD.py** and click **OK.**

We can now import library LCD into our LCD based programs. For example, the program given in this project can be written as shown in Figure 3.73 (Program: LCDCount2). Notice that all the LCD functions must be preceded with word **LCD**.

```
#---------------------------------------------------------
#                LCD SECONDS COUNTER
#                ===================
#
# This program counts up every secon and displays on LCD
#
# Author: Dogan Ibrahim
# File  : LCDCount2.py
# Date  : February 2021
#-----------------------------------------------------------
import LCD
import utime

LCD.lcd_init()
count = 0

while True:
    LCD.lcd_goto(0, 0)
    cntstr = str(count)
```

```
LCD.lcd_puts(cntstr)
count = count + 1
utime.sleep(1)
```

Figure 3.73: Program LCDCount2.

3.21 Project 19: Reaction timer with LCD

Description: This is a reaction timer game. The idea of the game is to measure the reaction time of the user. The game consists of an LCD, an LED, and a pushbutton. The game starts with the user keeping one hand on the pushbutton. The LED turns ON at random times and as soon as it is ON, the user is expected to press the pushbutton. The elapsed time between seeing the LED lit and pressing the pushbutton is measured and displayed on the LCD as the reaction time of the user.

Block diagram: Figure 3.74 shows the block diagram of the project.

Figure 3.74: Block diagram of the project.

Circuit diagram: The circuit diagram of the project is shown in Figure 3.75. The LCD is connected as in the previous project. The LED and the pushbutton are connected to GP16 and GP17 respectively. An internal pull-up resistor is used at pin GP17, obviating the use of an external resistor.

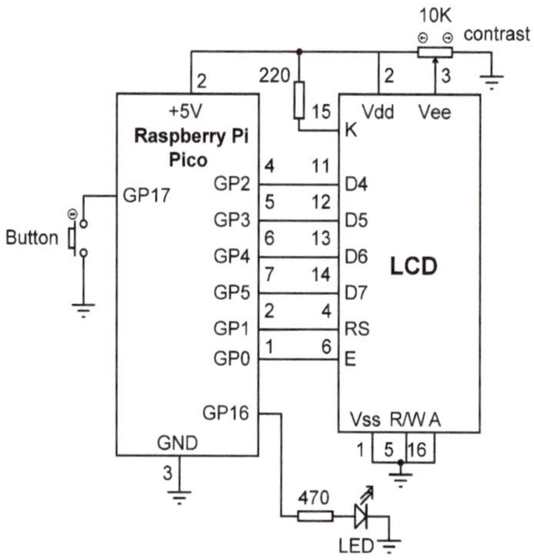

Figure 3.75: Circuit diagram of the project.

Program listing: Figure 3.76 shows the program listing (Program: **Reaction**). At the beginning of the program the LCD module, machine, **utime**, and the **random** module are all imported to the program. **Button** and **LED** are assigned to port pins GP17 and GP16 respectively. GP17 is pulled-up internally so that the state of this pin is logic 1 by default, and goes to logic 0 when the pushbutton is pressed. LCD library is then initialized by calling function **lcd_init**.

At the beginning of the main program the LED is turned OFF, and the program enters a **while** loop. Inside this loop the LCD is cleared, and a random number is generated between 3 and 10. This value is used to delay turning the LED ON so that the user does not know when the LED is going to be lit. At this point the LED is turned ON, a timer is started, and the button interrupt is enabled. The interrupt is configured to be activated on the falling edge of the pushbutton output (i.e. when the pushbutton is pressed). The main program then waits until the interrupt is serviced (i.e. while the **flag** is 0).

The program jumps to function **MyButton** as soon as the pushbutton is pressed. At the beginning of this program further interrupts are disabled by setting **handler = None**. Inside this function, the LED is turned OFF and the timer is stopped. The elapsed time is calculated by subtracting the current time from the time when the LED was turned ON. This time is converted into string and stored in variable **ReactionStr** and is displayed in the second row of the LCD in milliseconds. The text **Reaction Time:** is displayed at the first row of the LCD. As an example, if the reaction time is 500 ms, it is displayed in the following format:

Reaction Time:
500

Variable **flag** is then set to 1 so that the main program continues. At the same time the LCD is cleared. The game restarts as soon as the LCD is cleared.

```
#----------------------------------------------------------
#                  REACTION TIMER
#                  ==============
#
# This is a reaction timer program which measures the
# reaction of the user and displays on the LCD in ms.
# For a fast reaction time, the user should press the
# pushbutton as soon as the LED is lit
#
# Author: Dogan Ibrahim
# File  : Reaction.py
# Date  : February 2021
#------------------------------------------------------------
import LCD
from machine import Pin
import utime
import random

Button = Pin(17, Pin.IN, Pin.PULL_UP)
```

```
LED = Pin(16, Pin.OUT)
LCD.lcd_init()
flag = 0

#
# This is the interrupt service routine. The progra jumps
# here as soon as the pushbutton is pressed
#
def MyButton(pin):
    global flag
    Button.irq(handler = None)
    LED.value(0)
    TmrEnd = utime.ticks_ms()
    ReactionTime = utime.ticks_diff(TmrEnd, TmrStart)
    ReactionStr = str(ReactionTime)
    flag = 1
    LCD.lcd_puts("Reaction Time:")
    LCD.lcd_goto(0, 1)
    LCD.lcd_puts(ReactionStr)
    utime.sleep(3)

#
# Start of MAIN program
#
LED.value(0)
while True:
    flag = 0
    LCD.lcd_clear()
    rnd = random.randint(3, 10)
    utime.sleep(rnd)
    LED.value(1)
    TmrStart = utime.ticks_ms()
    Button.irq(handler=MyButton, trigger = Pin.IRQ_FALLING)
    while flag == 0:
       pass
```

Figure 3.76: Program Reaction.

3.22 Project 20: Ultrasonic distance measurement

Description: In this project an ultrasonic sensor module is used to measure the distance in front of a sensor. The distance is displayed on the LCD.

Aim: The aim of this project is to show how the ultrasonic sensor module can be used in a project to measure distance.

Ultrasonic sensors

In this project the popular HC-SR04 ultrasonic transmitter-receiver module is used (Figure 3.77). The basic features of this sensor module are:

- Operating voltage: 5 V
- Operating current: 2 mA
- Detection distance: 2 – 450 cm
- Input trigger signal: 10 µs TTL
- Sensor angle: 15 degrees or less

Figure 3.77: HC-SR04 ultrasonic sensor module.

The HC-SR04 has the following pin names and descriptions:

Vcc: Power input
Trig: Trigger input
Echo: Echo output
Gnd: Power ground

The basic principle of operation of the HC-SR04 ultrasonic sensor module is as follows (see Figure 3.78):

- a 10µs trigger pulse is sent to the module;
- the module then sends eight 40-kHz square wave signals to the target and sets the echo pin HIGH;
- the program starts a timer;
- the signal hits the target and echoes back to the module;
- when the signal is returned to the module the echo pin goes LOW;
- the timer is stopped;

the duration of the echo signal is calculated, and this is proportional to the distance to the target.
The distance to the object is calculated as follows.

Distance to object (in metres) = (duration of echo time in seconds * speed of sound) / 2

The speed of sound is 343 m/s, or 0.0343 cm/µs at 20 °C air temperature.
Therefore,

Distance to object (in cm) = (duration of echo time in µs) * 0.0343 / 2

or,

Distance to object (in cm) = (duration of echo time in µs) * 0.0171

For example, if the duration of the echo signal is 294 microseconds then the distance to the object is calculated as follows:

Distance to object (cm) = 294 * 0.0171 = 5.03 cm

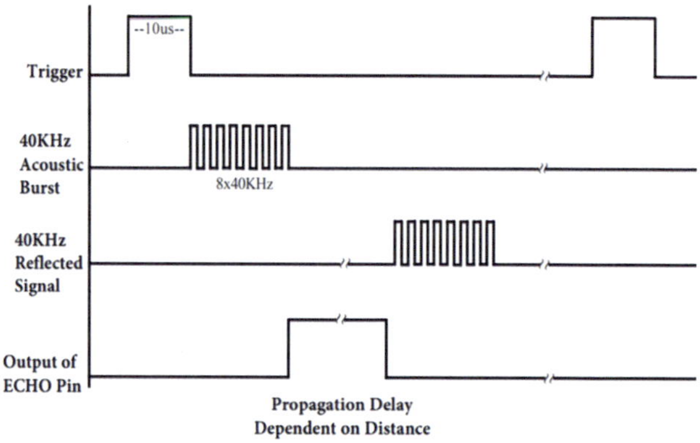

Figure 3.78: Operation of the ultrasonic sensor module.

Block Diagram: Figure 3.79 shows the block diagram of the project.

Figure 3.79: Block diagram of the project.

Circuit Diagram: Figure 3.80 shows the project circuit diagram. Notice that the sensor operates at +5 V and its output is not compatible with the Raspberry Pi Pico input. A resistive potential divider circuit is used to lower the sensor voltage to +3.3 V.

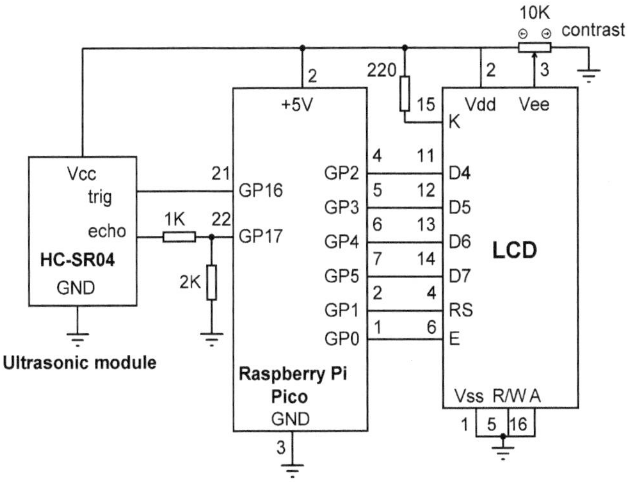

Figure 3.80: Circuit diagram of the project.

Program listing: Figure 3.81 shows the program listing (Program: **Ultrasonic**). At the beginning of the program, **trig** and the **echo** pins are configured. Inside the main program loop, a trigger pulse is sent for 10 microseconds and the program waits to receive the echo signal. After receiving the echo signal its duration is calculated and stored in the variable named Duration. Assuming that the speed of sound in air is 343 m/s (at air temperature 20 ºC), the distance to the object is calculated and stored in variable **distancecm**. This value is then displayed on the LCD as shown in Figure 3.81.

```
#------------------------------------------------------------
#            ULTRASONIC DISTANCE MESUREMENT
#            ==============================
#
# In this project a HC-SR04 type ultrasonic sensor module is
# connected to the Raspberry Pi Pico. The program displays
# distance to an object in-front of the sensor
#
# Author: Dogan Ibrahim
# File  : Ultrasonic.py
# Date  : February 2021
#--------------------------------------------------------------
from machine import Pin
import utime
import LCD

trig = Pin(16, Pin.OUT)                          # trig pin
echo = Pin(17, Pin.IN)                           # echo pin

LCD.lcd_init()                                   # Init LCD
```

```
while True:
    trig.value(0)
    utime.sleep_us(5)                         # Wait until settled

    trig.value(1)                             # Send trig pulse
    utime.sleep_us(10)                        # 10 microseconds
    trig.value(0)                             # Remove trig pulse

    while echo.value() == 0:                  # Wait for echo 1
        pass
    Tmrstrt = utime.ticks_us()

    while echo.value() == 1:                  # Wait for echo 0
        pass
    Tmrend = utime.ticks_us()

    Duration = utime.ticks_diff(Tmrend, Tmrstrt)
    distancecm = Duration * 0.0171
    LCD.lcd_clear()
    D = "Dist = " + str(distancecm)[:6] + " cm"
    LCD.lcd_puts(D)
    utime.sleep(1)
```

Figure 3.81: Program: Ultrasonic.

Figure 3.82: Example display on the LCD.

3.23 Project 21: Height of a person (stadiometer)

Description: Stadiometers are electronic devices used to measure the height of a person. In this project an ultrasonic sensor module is used to measure the height of a person. The height of the stadiometer is assumed to be 200 cm. The height of the person is displayed on the LCD.

Aim: The aim of this project is to show how the ultrasonic sensor module can be used to make a stadiometer

Block diagram: Figure 3.83 shows the block diagram of the project. The person whose height is to be measured stands below the stadiometer.

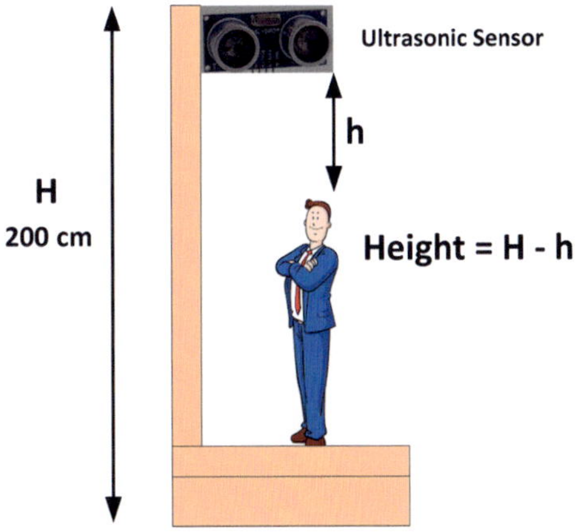

Figure 3.83: Block diagram of the project.

Circuit diagram: The circuit diagram of the project is identical to the one in Figure 3.80.

Program listing: Figure 3.84 shows the program listing (Program: **Stadiometer**). At the beginning of the program the height of the stadiometer is specified (**H = 200 cm**). The program then calculates the distance between the sensor and the top of the head of the person (**h**) The height of the person is given by **H – h**.

```
#-------------------------------------------------------------
#           PERSON HEIGHT MEASUREMENT (STADIOMETER)
#           =======================================
#
# In this project a HC-SR04 type ultrasonic sensor module is
# connected to the Raspberry Pi Pico. The program measures the
# height of a person
#
# Author: Dogan Ibrahim
# File  : Stadiometer.py
# Date  : February 2021
#---------------------------------------------------------------
from machine import Pin
import utime
import LCD

trig = Pin(16, Pin.OUT)                      # trig pin
echo = Pin(17, Pin.IN)                       # echo pin

LCD.lcd_init()                               # Init LCD
H = 200                                      # Height of stadiometer

while True:
    trig.value(0)
```

```
        utime.sleep_us(5)                          # Wait until settled

        trig.value(1)                              # Send trig pulse
        utime.sleep_us(10)                         # 10 microseconds
        trig.value(0)                              # Remove trig pulse

        while echo.value() == 0:                   # Wait for echo 1
            pass
        Tmrstrt = utime.ticks_us()

        while echo.value() == 1:                   # Wait for echo 0
            pass
        Tmrend = utime.ticks_us()

        Duration = utime.ticks_diff(Tmrend, Tmrstrt)
        h = Duration * 0.0171
        LCD.lcd_clear()
        Height = H - h
        D = "H = " + str(Height)[:5] + " cm"
        LCD.lcd_puts(D)
        utime.sleep(1)
```

Figure 3.84: Program: Stadiometer.

3.24 Project 22: Ultrasonic reverse parking aid with buzzer

Description: In this project the ultrasonic sensor module is used together with an active buzzer to help while reverse parking our car. As the distance to the objects get smaller, the buzzer sound faster to warn the driver that the objects at the rear of the vehicle are nearer.

Aim: The aim of this project is to show how the ultrasonic sensor module can be used to help reverse-park our car.

Block Diagram: Figure 3.85 shows the block diagram of the project.

Figure 3.85: Block diagram of the project.

Circuit diagram: The circuit diagram of the project is shown in Figure 3.86. The circuit is basically same as Figure 3.80, but there is no LCD. Also an active buzzer is added to port pin GP18 of the Raspberry Pi Pico.

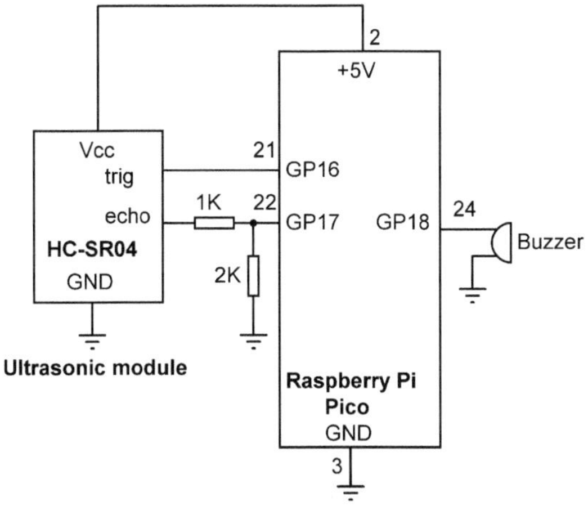

Figure 3.86: Circuit diagram of the project.

Program listing: Figure 3.87 shows the program listing (Program: **Parking**). After finding the distance to the obstacle, the program creates a delay value depending on the distance of the obstacle. As the car gets closer to the obstacle, this delay value is made smaller, causing the buzzer to sound faster (more frequently) to alert the driver that the car is getting close to the obstacle. If on the other hand the car gets further away from the obstacle, the delay is made larger so that the buzzer sounds slower (less frequently) to inform the driver that the obstacle is not very close.

```
#----------------------------------------------------------
#           ULTRASONIC REVERSE CAR PARKING AID
#           ==================================
#
# In this project a HC-SR04 type ultrasonic sensor module is
# connected to the Raspberry Pi Pico. Additionally, a buzzer
# is connected. The project sounds the buzzer as the car gets
# near an obstacle.The buzzer sounds faster as the car gets
# nearer an object
#
# Author: Dogan Ibrahim
# File  : Parking.py
# Date  : February 2021
#------------------------------------------------------------
from machine import Pin
import utime

trig = Pin(16, Pin.OUT)                   # trig pin
echo = Pin(17, Pin.IN)                    # echo pin

Buzzer = Pin(18, Pin.OUT)                 # Buzzer at pin 18
Buzzer.value(0)                           # Turn OFF buzzer
```

```
while True:
    trig.value(0)
    utime.sleep_us(5)                     # Wait until settled

    trig.value(1)                         # Send trig pulse
    utime.sleep_us(10)                    # 10 microseconds
    trig.value(0)                         # Remove trig pulse

    while echo.value() == 0:              # Wait for echo 1
        pass
    Tmrstrt = utime.ticks_us()

    while echo.value() == 1:              # Wait for echo 0
        pass
    Tmrend = utime.ticks_us()

    Duration = utime.ticks_diff(Tmrend, Tmrstrt)
    distance = Duration * 0.0171

#
# Now sound the buzzer accordingly.The sounding should be faster
# as the car gets neareer the object.This is done by changing the
# delay in the duration of the sound
#

    if distance > 100:
        dely = 0
    elif distance > 70 and distance < 90:
        dely = 600
    elif distance > 50 and distance < 70:
        dely = 400
    elif distance > 30 and distance < 50:
        dely = 300
    elif distance > 10 and distance < 30:
        dely = 200
    elif distance < 10:
        dely = 10

    if distance < 100:
        Buzzer.value(1)
        utime.sleep_ms(dely)
        Buzzer.value(0)
        utime.sleep_ms(dely)
```

Figure 3.87: Program: Parking.

Chapter 4 • Using Analogue-To-Digital Converters (ADCs)

4.1 Overview

Most sensors in real life are analogue, supplying analogue output voltages or currents which are proportional to the measured variable. Without using ADCs, such sensors cannot be directly connected to digital computers. In this Chapter we will learn how to use the ADC channels of the Raspberry Pi Pico.

Most ADCs for general purpose applications are 8-bits or 10-bits wide, although some higher-grade professional ones are 16 or even 32-bit wide. The conversion time of an ADC is one of its important specifications. This is the time taken for the ADC to convert an analogue input into digital. The smaller the conversion time, the better. Some cheaper ADCs give the converted digital data in serial format, while some more expensive, professional ones provide parallel digital outputs.

The Raspberry Pi Pico has 5 ADC channels. Four of them are at pins GP26, GP27, GP28, and GP29 — known as analogue channels 0, 1, 2, and 3. The first 3 channels are available at the GPIO pins, and the 4th one can be used to measure the VSYS voltage of the board. There is also a built-in ADC channel 4 which is connected internally to a temperature sensor.

The Pico's ADC has a resolution of 12 bits, thus converting an analogue input voltage into 4096 (0 to 4095) levels. MicroPython however transforms the output into a 16-bits number, ranging from 0 to 65535.

The reference voltage of the ADC used on the Pico is +3.3 V. Using such an ADC, the resolution is 3300 mV / 65535 = 0.050 mV per bit, or 50 µV/bit. Therefore, an analogue input voltage of 0.050 mV gives digital output of 00000000 0000001, 0.1mV gives 00000000 00000010, and so on.

In this Chapter we will develop several projects using the ADC offered by the Pico.

4.2 Project 1: Voltmeter

Description: This is a simple voltmeter project where the voltage of an external voltage source is measured and displayed on the screen in millivolts.

Aim: The aim of this project is to show how the Pico ADC channels can be used to read analogue input voltage.

Circuit diagram: Figure 4.1 shows the circuit diagram of the project. In this project, the voltage to be measured is applied to analogue input GP26 (pin 31, channel 0). You must make sure that the input voltage does not exceed +3.3 V. If it is required to measure higher voltages, then you can use resistive potential divider circuits at the input of the ADC.

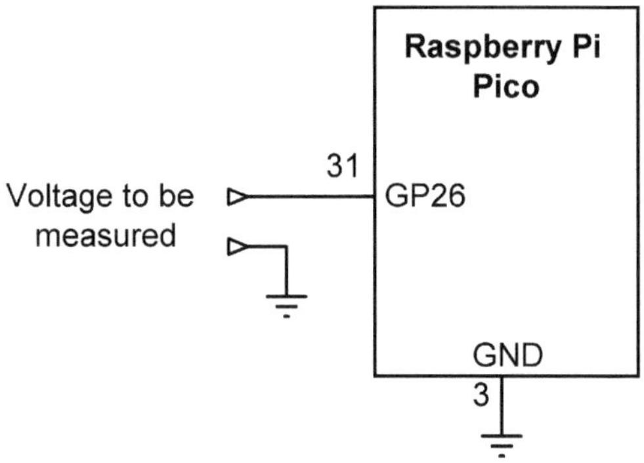

Figure 4.1: Circuit diagram of the project.

Program listing: Figure 4.2 shows the program listing and sample output from the program (Program: **Voltmeter**). At the beginning of the program module **ADC** of 'machine' is imported to the program and variable **AnalogIn** is assigned to analogue input channel 0. The conversion factor is then defined as 3300 / 65535. The value read from the analogue channel must be multiplied by this number in order to calculate the actual value of the measured voltage. The remainder of the program runs in a loop where the input voltage is read, converted to millivolts, and then displayed on the PC screen.

```
#---------------------------------------------------------
#                VOLTMETER
#                =========
#
# This is a voltmeter project. The voltage to me measured
# is applied to GP26 (pin 31) of the Pico
#
# Author: Dogan Ibrahim
# File  : Voltmeter.py
# Date  : February 2011
#-----------------------------------------------------------
from machine import ADC
import utime

AnalogIn = ADC(0)                               # ADC channel 0
Conv = 3300 / 65535                             # Conversion factor

while True:                                     # Do forever
    mV = AnalogIn.read_u16()                    # Read input
    mV = mV * Conv                              # Input in mV
    print("Voltage = %5.2f" %mV)                # Display
    utime.sleep(1)                              # Wait 1 second

Shell
Voltage = 53.98
Voltage = 53.98
Voltage = 53.17
Voltage = 53.17
```

Figure 4.2: Program: Voltmeter.

Displaying the voltage on the LCD

It is easy to modify the program to display the measured voltage on an LCD. First of all, build the circuit given in Figure 3.71 and apply the voltage to be measured to GP26 (pin 31) of the Pico, making sure that the voltage does not exceed +3.3 V. The program to display the measured voltage on the LCD (Program: **VoltLCD**) is shown in Figure 4.3.

```
#--------------------------------------------------------
#                        VOLTMETER
#                        =========
#
# This is a voltmeter project. The voltage to me measured
# is applied to GP26 (pin 31) of the Pico
# This version of the program displays the measured voltage
# on the LCD
#
# Author: Dogan Ibrahim
# File  : VoltLCD.py
# Date  : February 2021
#----------------------------------------------------------
from machine import ADC
import utime
import LCD

AnalogIn = ADC(0)                        # ADC channel 0
Conv = 3300 / 65535                      # Conversion factor
LCD.lcd_init()

while True:                              # Do forever
    mV = AnalogIn.read_u16()             # Read input
    mV = mV * Conv                       # Input in mV
    LCD.lcd_clear()                      # Clear screen
    mVstr = str(mV)                      # Convert to string
    LCD.lcd_puts(mVstr)                  # Display
    utime.sleep(1)                       # Wait 1 second
```

Figure 4.3: Program: VoltLCD.

4.3 Project 2: Temperature measurement – using the internal temperature sensor

Description: In this project, the internal temperature sensor of Pico is employed, and the measured temperature is displayed on the LCD.

Aim: The aim of this project is to show how the internal temperature sensor can be used to measure the temperature.

Circuit diagram: The circuit diagram of the project is same as in Figure 3.71.

Program listing: The internal temperature sensor is connected to ADC channel 4. The data read is converted into degrees Celsius using the following formula:

Temperature (in degrees Celsius) = 27 – (reading – 0.706) / 0.001721

The program listing is shown in Figure 4.4 (Program: **TempInt**). The program reads the data from ADC channel 4, converts it into volts, and then applies the above formula to convert into degrees Celsius. The calculated value is then displayed on the LCD. The program repeats every second. You can check that the temperature will increase if you touch the processor with the tip of your finger.

```
#--------------------------------------------------------
#                 TEMPERATURE MEASUREMENT
#                 =======================
#
# This program measures the temperature using the internal
# temperature sensor of the Pico and displyas on LCD
#
# Author: Dogan Ibrahim
# File  : TempInt.py
# Date  : February 2021
#----------------------------------------------------------
from machine import ADC
import utime
import LCD

AnalogIn = ADC(4)                         # ADC channel 4
Conv = 3.3 / 65535                        # Conversion factor
LCD.lcd_init()

while True:                               # Do forever
    V = AnalogIn.read_u16()               # Read temp
    V = V * Conv                          # Convert to Volts
    Temp = 27 - (V - 0.706) / 0.001721    # Convert to temp
    LCD.lcd_clear()                       # Clear screen
    Tempstr = str(Temp)                   # Convert to string
    LCD.lcd_puts(Tempstr)                 # Display
    utime.sleep(1)                        # Wait 1 second
```

Figure 4.4: Program: TempInt.

4.4 Project 3: Temperature measurement – using an external temperature sensor

Description: In this project, an external analogue temperature sensor is used to measure and display the ambient temperature on the LCD

Aim: The aim of this project is to show how an external analogue temperature can be used to measure the external temperature.

Block Diagram: Figure 4.5 shows the block diagram of the project.

Figure 4.5: Block diagram of the project.

Circuit diagram: The circuit diagram of the project is shown in Figure 4.6. In this project a TMP36 type temperature sensor chip is used (Figure 4.7) and it's connected to ADC channel 0. This chip provides analogue output voltage proportional to the measured temperature. The relationship between the measured temperature and the output voltage is given by:

$$T = (V_o - 500) / 10$$

Where T is the measured temperature in degrees Celsius, and V_o is the sensor output voltage in millivolts.

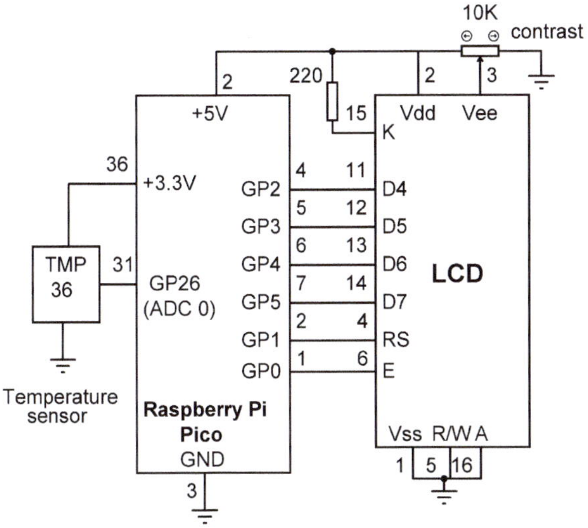

Figure 4.6: Circuit diagram of the project.

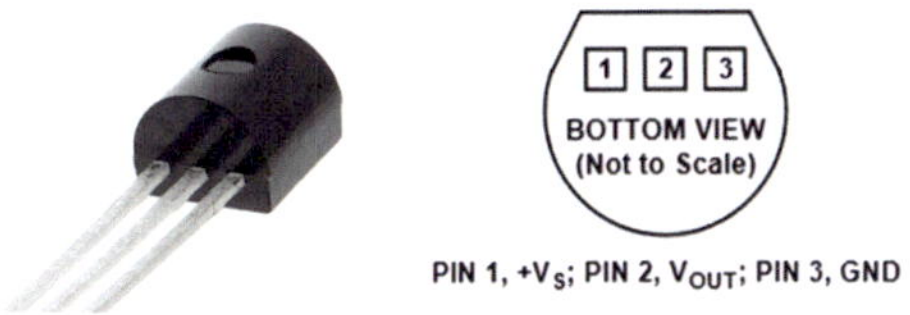

Figure 4.7: TMP36 sensor chip.

Program listing: Figure 4.8 shows the program listing (Program: TMP36). The sensor voltage is read in on ADC channel 0. This voltage is then converted into millivolts, the temperature is calculated in degrees Celsius, and gets displayed on the LCD every second. Notice that the output data is formatted so that only the first 5 digits of string **Temp** are displayed. As an example, the temperature is displayed in the following format:

nn.mm

```
#------------------------------------------------------------
#                  TEMPERATURE MEASUREMENT
#                  =======================
#
# This program measures the temperature using an external
# TMP36 type temperature sensor chip
#
# Author: Dogan Ibrahim
# File  : TMP36.py
# Date  : February 2021
#--------------------------------------------------------------
from machine import ADC
import utime
import LCD

AnalogIn = ADC(0)                         # ADC channel 0
Conv = 3300 / 65535                       # Conversion factor
LCD.lcd_init()

while True:                               # Do forever
    V = AnalogIn.read_u16()               # Read temp
    mV = V * Conv                         # Convert to Volts
    Temp = (mV - 500.0) / 10.0            # Convert to temp
    LCD.lcd_clear()                       # Clear screen
    Tempstr = str(Temp)[:5]               # Convert to string
    LCD.lcd_puts(Tempstr)                 # Display
    utime.sleep(1)                        # Wait 1 second
```

Figure 4.8: Program: TMP36.

4.5 Project 4: ON/OFF temperature controller

Description: Temperature control is important in many industrial, commercial, domestic, and chemical applications. A temperature control system basically consists of a temperature sensor, a heater, a fan (optional), an actuator to operate the heater, and a controller. A negative feedback is used to control the heater so that the temperature is at the desired set-point value. Accurate temperature control systems are based on the PID (Proportional + Integral + Derivative) algorithm.

In this project, an ON/OFF type simple control system is designed. ON/OFF temperature control systems commonly use relays to turn the heater ON or OFF depending on the set-point temperature and the measured temperature. If the measured temperature is below the set-point value, then the relay is activated which turns the heater ON. If on the other hand the measured temperature is above the set-point value, then the relay is de-activated to turn OFF the heater so that the temperature is lowered.
The project employs a type TMP36 sensor chip in conjunction with a heater and an LED, to control the temperature of a small room. The heater is turned **ON** by the relay if the measured room temperature (**RoomTemp**) is below the setpoint temperature (**SetTemp**), and it is turned **OFF** if it is above the setpoint value. The LED turns ON if the room temperature is below the set point value to indicate that the heater is ON. This process is repeated every 3 seconds.

The aim: The aim of this project is to show how an ON/OFF temperature controller system can be designed using a low-cost temperature sensor chip with the Raspberry Pi Pico.

Block diagram: Figure 4.9 shows the block diagram of the project.

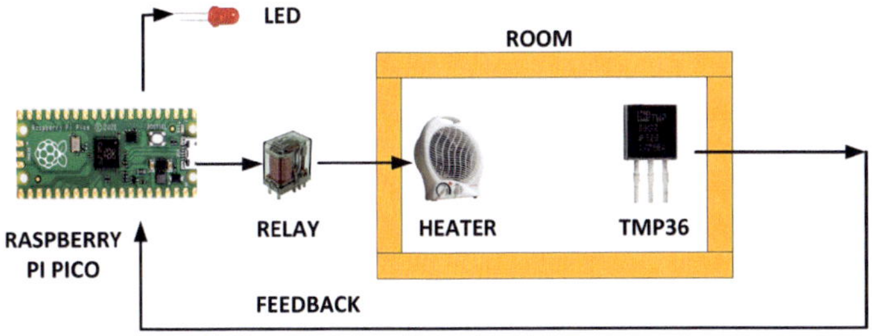

Figure 4.9: Block diagram of the project.

Circuit diagram: The circuit diagram of the project is shown in Figure 4.10. TMP36 sensor chip is connected to analogue channel 0 as in the previous project. The LED is connected to GP16 through a 470-ohm current-limiting resistor. The Relay is connected to GP17 and is activated when a logic 1 (+3.3V) is applied to it. The connections between the Raspberry Pi Pico ports and various components are as follows:

Raspberry Pi Pico	Component
GP26 (ADC0)	TMP36 out
GP16	LED
GP17	Relay

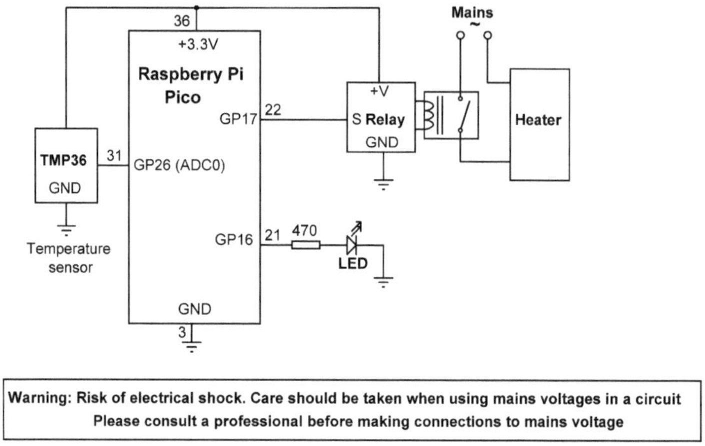

Figure 4.10: Circuit diagram of the project.

Operation of the project

The operation of the project is described in Figure 4.11 as a PDL (program description language).

```
BEGIN
    Read the set temperature (SetTemp)
    Read the maximum temperature (MaxTemp)
    DO FOREVER
        Read the room temperature (RoomTemp)
        IF SetTemp > RoomTemp THEN
            Activate relay
            LED ON
        ELSE
            Deactivate relay
            LED OFF
        ENDIF
        Wait 3 seconds
    ENDDO
END
```

Figure 4.11: PDL of the project.

Program listing: Figure 4.12 shows the program listing (Program: **ONOFF**). The desired temperature is set to 24 ºC and is stored in variable **SetTemp**. The **LED** and **Relay** are assigned to GP16 and GP17 respectively, which are configured as outputs and are turned OFF at the beginning of the program.

Inside the program loop, the room temperature (**RoomTemp**) is read and compared with the desired temperature (**SetTemp**). If the room temperature is below the desired value then both the heater and the LED are turned ON, otherwise they are both turned OFF. This process is repeated after 3 seconds of delay.

```
#-----------------------------------------------------------
#              ON-OFF TEMPERATURE CONTROLLER
#              =============================
#
# This is an ON-OFF temperature controller program. The
# project consists of a temperature sensor, an LED and a
# heater. The heater and the LED are turned ON if the room
# temperature (RoomTemp) is below the desired value (SetTemp)
#
# Author: Dogan Ibrahim
# File  : ONOFF.py
# Date  : February 2021
#-------------------------------------------------------------
from machine import ADC, Pin
import utime

AnalogIn = ADC(0)                       # ADC channel 0
Conv = 3300 / 65535                     # Conversion factor

SetTemp = 24.0                          # Desired temperature
LED = Pin(16, Pin.OUT)                  # LED at GP16
Relay = Pin(17, Pin.OUT)                # Relay at GP17
LED.value(0)                            # Turn OFF LED
Relay.value(0)                          # Turn OFF Relay

while True:                             # Do forever
    V = AnalogIn.read_u16()             # Read temp
    mV = V * Conv                       # Convert to Volts
    RoomTemp = (mV - 500.0) / 10.0      # Measured temperature
    if RoomTemp < SetTemp:              # If Room temp < desired
        Relay.value(1)                  # Turn Relay ON
        LED.value(1)                    # Turn LED ON
    else:
        Relay.value(0)                  # Turn Relay OFF
        LED.value(0)                    # Tuen LED OFF
    utime.sleep(3)                      # Wait 3 seconds
```

Figure 4.12: Program: ONOFF.

4.6 Project 5: ON/OFF temperature controller with LCD

Description: This project is similar to the previous project, but here additionally an LCD is connected to the project. The LCD shows both the desired temperature (**SetTemp**) and the measured room temperature (**RoomTemp**).

Block diagram: Figure 4.13 shows the block diagram of the project.

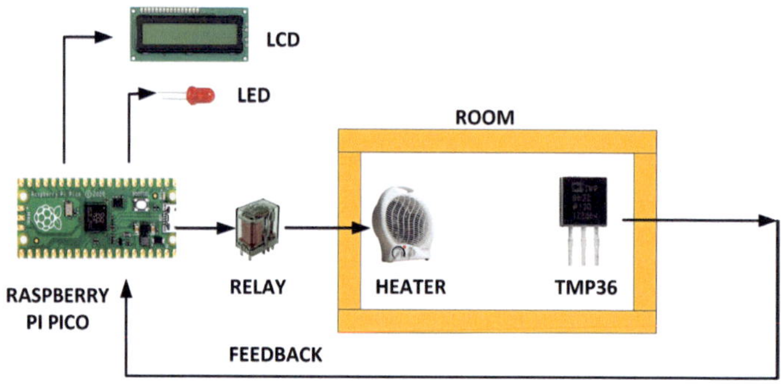

Figure 4.13: Block diagram of the project.

Circuit diagram: The circuit diagram of the project is shown in Figure 4.14. The LCD is connected to the Pico as in the previous LCD based projects. The TMP36, LED, and the Relay are connected as in the previous project.

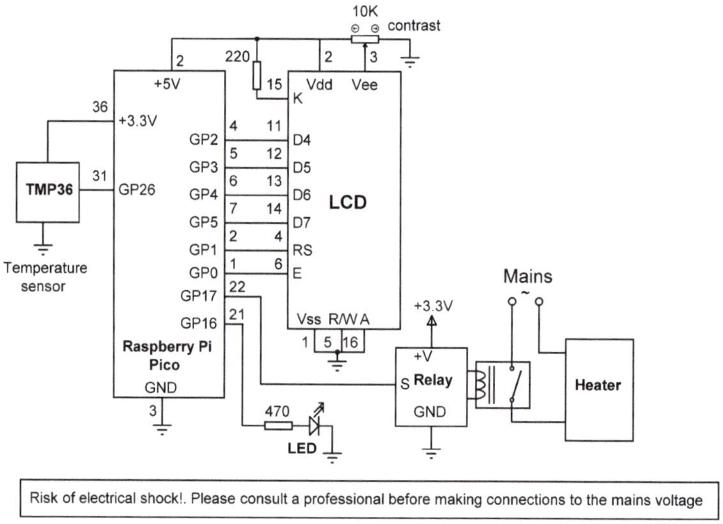

Figure 4.14: Circuit diagram of the project.

Program listing: Figure 4.15 shows the program listing (Program: **ONOFFLCD**). The program is very similar to the one given in Figure 4.12. Here, additionally the desired temperature and the room temperature are displayed in the following format, where the room temperature is updated continuously at every 3 seconds:

Row 0: **Set : 23.45**
Row 1: **Meas: 22.50**

```
#------------------------------------------------------------
#               ON-OFF TEMPERATURE CONTROLLER
#               =============================
#
# This is an ON-OFF temperature controller program. The
# project consists of a temperature sensor, an LED and a
# heater. The heater and the LED are turned ON if the room
# temp (RoomTemp) is below the desired value (SetTemp)
#
# An LCD is used to display the desired temperature at the
# top row, and room temperature at bottom row
#
# Author: Dogan Ibrahim
# File  : ONOFFLCD.py
# Date  : February 2021
#--------------------------------------------------------------
from machine import ADC, Pin
import utime
import LCD

LCD.lcd_init()                          # Initialize LCD
AnalogIn = ADC(0)                       # ADC channel 0
Conv = 3300 / 65535                     # Conversion factor

SetTemp = 24.0                          # Desired temperature
LED = Pin(16, Pin.OUT)                  # LED at GP16
Relay = Pin(17, Pin.OUT)                # Relay at GP17
LED.value(0)                            # Turn OFF LED
Relay.value(0)                          # Turn OFF Relay

LCD.lcd_clear()                         # Clear LCD
LCD.lcd_puts("Set : ")                  # Display Set :
LCD.lcd_puts(str(SetTemp)[:5])          # Display SetTemp

while True:                             # Do forever
    V = AnalogIn.read_u16()             # Read temp
    mV = V * Conv                       # Convert to Volts
    RoomTemp = (mV - 500.0) / 10.0      # Measured temperature
    LCD.lcd_goto(0, 1)                  # Cursor at 0,1
    LCD.lcd_puts("Meas: ")              # Display Meas:
    LCD.lcd_puts(str(RoomTemp)[:5])     # Display RoomTemp
    if RoomTemp < SetTemp:              # If Room temp < desired
        Relay.value(1)                  # Turn Relay ON
        LED.value(1)                    # Turn LED ON
    else:
        Relay.value(0)                  # Turn Relay OFF
```

```
        LED.value(0)                        # Turn LED OFF
    utime.sleep(3)                          # Wait 3 seconds
```

Figure 4.15: Program: ONOFFLCD.

4.7 Project 6: Measuring the ambient light intensity

Description: In this project, a light-dependent-resistor (LDR) is used to measure and display the ambient light intensity.

Block diagram: Figure 4.16 shows the block diagram of the project.

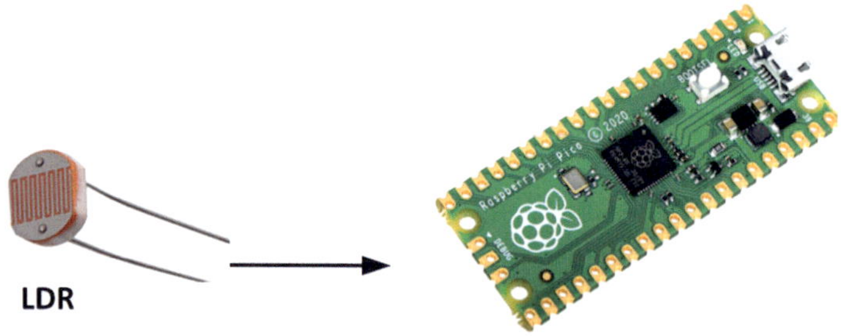

Figure 4.16: Block diagram of the project.

Background information: An LDR is an electronic component whose resistance changes with the light intensity that falls upon it. The resistance of the LDR drops with an increase in light intensity falling upon the device. Typically, the resistance at daylight is in the order of kilo-ohms (also: k-ohms or kΩ) and in dark it could be a few mega-ohms (also: megohms or MΩ). As a result, we can use such a device to measure the light intensity. Figure 4.17 shows the commonly used symbol of an LDR. A typical characteristic of an LDR is shown in Figure 4.18. LDRs are used in circuits in the form of resistive potential dividers. A fixed resistor is connected in series with the LDR, and the voltage across this resistor is measured. This voltage is proportional to the resistance of the LDR and consequently to the light intensity incident on the face of the LDR.

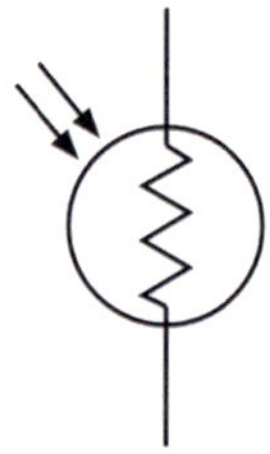

Figure 4.17: LDR circuit symbol.

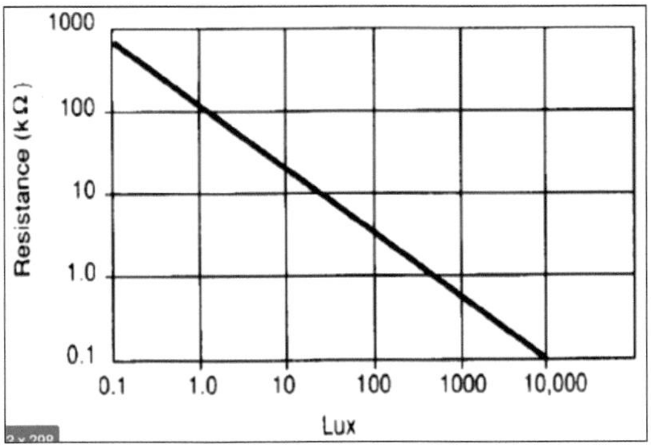

Figure 4.18: Typical LDR light/R characteristics.

Circuit diagram: The circuit diagram of the project is shown in Figure 4.19. A 10-kohm fixed resistor is used in the resistive potential divider circuit. The voltage across this resistor is measured using channel 0 of the ADC.

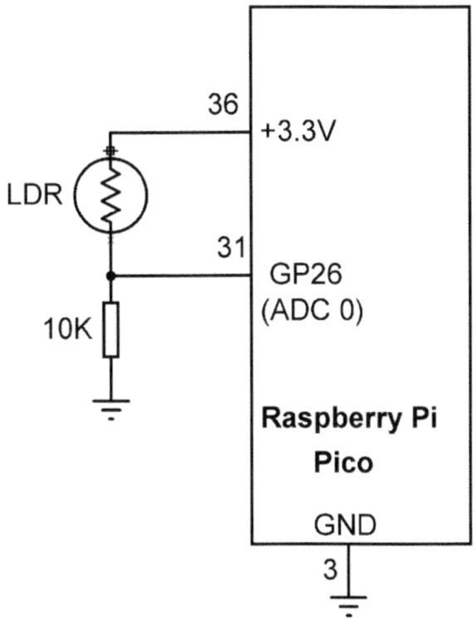

Figure 4.19: Circuit diagram of the project.

Program listing: Figure 4.20 shows the program listing (Program: **LDR**) together with output data. The program reads the analogue voltage across the fixed resistor. Notice that there is no need to know the absolute voltage. We can just use the digital value of the voltage (0 to 65535) read (**r** in this program). This value should be calibrated to give the intensity of the light in Lux.

```
#-------------------------------------------------------
#                   MEASURE THE LIGHT INTENSITY
#                   ===========================
#
# In this project an LCD is connected to the Pico in series
# with a fixed resistor. The program displays the volatge
# across the fixed resisor which is proportional to the
# light level falling on the LCD
#
# Author: Dogan Ibrahim
# File  : LDR.py
# Date  : February 2011
#---------------------------------------------------------
from machine import ADC
import utime

LDRin = ADC(0)                          # ADC channel 0

while True:                             # Do forever
    r = LDRin.read_u16()                # Read LDR
    print("ADC=",r)                     # Display ADC reading
    utime.sleep(1)                      # Wait 1 second

ADC= 38425
ADC= 38617
ADC= 38345
ADC= 38329
```

Figure 4.20: Program: LDR.

Calibration

A light-intensity meter is required to calibrate the readings. Measurements should be made at different light levels and a table should be created to list the lux readings of the meter and the corresponding output from the ADC. Then, a formula can be derived that describes the relationship between the light level and the ADC readings. Alternatively, this table can be indexed for a given ADC reading in order to find the corresponding light level. Interpolation can be applied for values between two readings.

4.8 Project 7: Ohmmeter

Description: This is an ohmmeter project. The project measures the value of an unknown resistor and displays it on the Thonny screen.

Circuit diagram: The circuit diagram of the project is shown in Figure 4.21. A fixed resistor (10 kohm) is used in series with the unknown resistor. The program measures the voltage across the fixed resistor and then calculates the value of the unknown resistor (R_x).

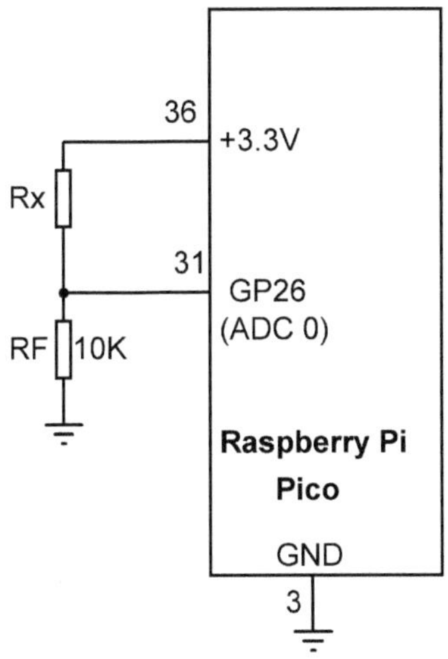

Figure 4.21: Circuit diagram of the project.

Program listing: Figure 4.22 shows the program listing (Program: **Ohmmeter**). If R_F is the fixed resistance and R_x is the unknown resistance, assuming the circuit is supplied from +3.3 V (3300 mV), the voltage at the output of the fixed resistor will be:

$$V = 3300 \times R_F / (R_F + R_x)$$

If we choose R_F to be 10 kΩ, then

$$V = 33000 / (10 + R_x)$$

Where V is in millivolts, and R_F and R_x are in kilo-ohms. As R_x changes from, say, 1 kΩ to 1 MΩ, the voltage across the fixed resistor will change from:

$$V = 33000 / 11 = 3000 \text{ mV}$$

into

$$V = 33000 / 1001 = 33 \text{ mV}$$

We can easily measure these voltages with the ADC. Therefore, the resistance measurement range of our ohmmeter is well below 1 kΩ and above 1 MΩ.

What we really want is to measure resistance R_x. We can write:

$$R_x = 3300 \times R_F / V - R_F$$

Remembering that the ADC resolution is 65535 steps and R_F = 10 kΩ, we can write:

$$R_x = 655350 / V_m - R_F$$

Where V_m is the digital value directly read from the ADC.

The voltage across the fixed resistor is read 5 times, and the value is averaged for higher accuracy.

```
#---------------------------------------------------------------
#                       OHMMETER
#                       ========
#
# In this project the value of an unknown resistor is measured
#
# Author: Dogan Ibrahim
# File  : Ohmmeter.py
# Date  : February 2021
#---------------------------------------------------------------
from machine import ADC
import utime

RF = 10                                         # RF = 10K
LDRin = ADC(0)                                  # ADC channel 0

while True:                                     # Do forever
    sum = 0
    for i in range(5):                          # Get 5 readings
        sum = sum + LDRin.read_u16()            # Read voltage
    Vm = sum / 5                                # Average
    Rx = 65535*RF / Vm - RF                     # Calculate Rx
    RxOhms = 1000 * Rx                          # Rx in Ohms
    print("Rx (Ohms)=%8.1f" %RxOhms)            # Display Rx
    utime.sleep(1)                              # Wait 1 second
```

Figure 4.22: Program: Ohmmeter.

An example output from the program is shown in Figure 4.23.

```
Shell
 Rx (Ohms)=    216.0
 Rx (Ohms)=    214.0
 Rx (Ohms)=    203.8
 Rx (Ohms)=    192.1
 Rx (Ohms)=    176.4
 Rx (Ohms)=    195.7
 Rx (Ohms)=    176.9
 Rx (Ohms)=    200.2
```

Figure 4.23: Example output.

4.9 Project 8: Internal and external temperature

Description: In this project, two temperature sensor chips are used: one to measure the external ambient temperature, and the other to measure the internal ambient temperature. Both readings are displayed on the LCD every 2 seconds.

Block diagram: Figure 4.24 shows the block diagram of the project.

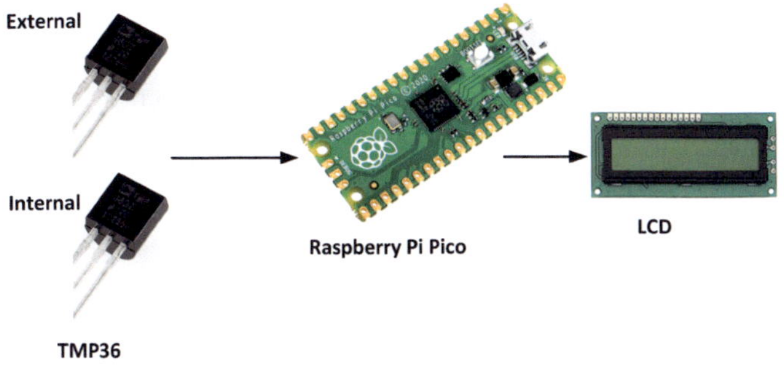

Figure 4.24: Block diagram of the project.

Circuit diagram: The circuit diagram of the project is shown in Figure 4.25. Two TMP36 type temperature sensor chips are used, one connected to channel 0 (external sensor) and the other one connected to channel 1 (internal sensor) of the ADC. The LCD is connected to the Pico as in the previous LCD-based projects.

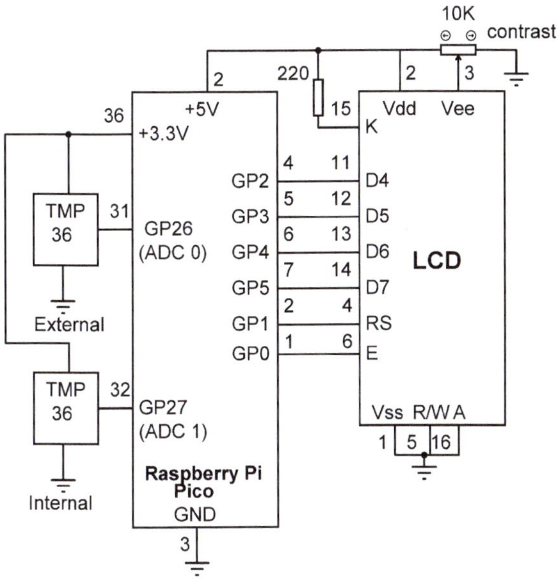

Figure 4.25: Circuit diagram of the project.

Program listing: Figure 4.26 shows the program listing (Program: **MultiTmp**). The external temperature sensor is named **ExtTemp** and gets assigned to channel 0. The internal temperature is named **IntTemp** and assigned to channel 1 of the ADC. Inside the program loop, the temperature of each channel is read, converted into degrees Celsius, and displayed on the LCD in the following format (top row displays the external temperature, bottom row displays the internal temperature):

Row 0: **Ext: nn.mm**
Row 1: **Int: pp.qq**

```
#----------------------------------------------------------------
#          EXTERNAL AND INTERNAL TEMPERATURE MEASUREMENT
#          =============================================
#
# This program measures the external and internal temperatures
# using two TMP36 type temperature sensor chips. Both external
# and internal temperatures are displayed on the LCD
#
# Author: Dogan Ibrahim
# File  : MultiTmp.py
# Date  : February 2011
#-----------------------------------------------------------------
from machine import ADC
import utime
import LCD

ExtTemp = ADC(0)                            # ADC channel 0
IntTemp = ADC(1)                            # ADC channel 1
Conv = 3300 / 65535                         # Conversion factor
LCD.lcd_init()

while True:                                 # Do forever
    Vext = ExtTemp.read_u16()               # Read channel 0
    mV = Vext * Conv                        # Convert to mV
    Tempext = (mV - 500.0) / 10.0           # External temp
    Vint = IntTemp.read_u16()               # Read channel 1
    mV = Vint * Conv                        # Convert to mV
    Tempint = (mV - 500.0) / 10.0           # Internal temp
    LCD.lcd_clear()                         # Clear screen
    Tempextstr = str(Tempext)[:5]           # Convert to string
    Tempintstr = str(Tempint)[:5]           # Convert to string
    LCD.lcd_puts("Ext: ")                   # Heading
    LCD.lcd_puts(Tempextstr)                # Display external
    LCD.lcd_goto(0, 1)                      # Cursor at row 1
    LCD.lcd_puts("Int: ")                   # Heading
    LCD.lcd_puts(Tempintstr)                # Display internal
    utime.sleep(2)                          # Wait 2 seconds
```

Figure 4.26: Program: MultiTmp.

4.10 Project 9: Using a thermistor to measure temperature

Description: In this project we will be reading the ambient temperature every second using the KY-013 temperature sensor (NTC thermistor) module, and then display it on the LCD.

Aim: The aim of this project is to show how the temperature of an NTC thermistor temperature sensor can be read, as well as learn to use an LCD in a project.

Background information: In this project, the type KY-013 analogue output NTC thermistor temperature sensor module is used. NTC thermistors are semiconductor devices whose resistances are inversely proportional to the temperature. Thus, as the temperature rises, their resistance falls and *vice versa*. As shown in Figure 4.27, this is a 3-pin module with the following pin assignment:

GND
+V
S (analogue output)

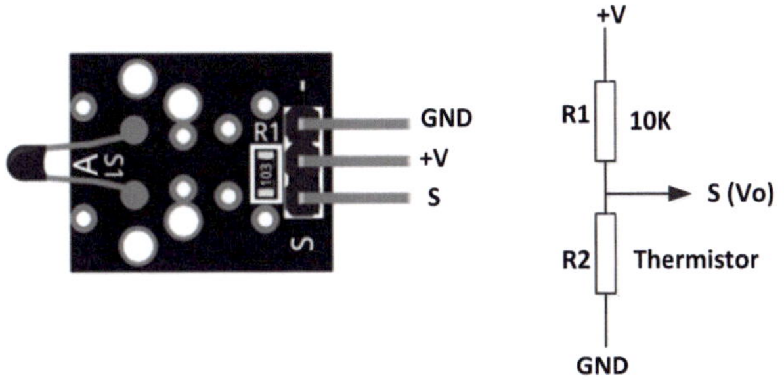

Figure 4.27: KY-013 module.

The sensor module is internally connected to a 10-kohm resistor as shown in the Figure to form a potential divider circuit. The voltage across the thermistor is read using an analogue port of the processor. This voltage is proportional to the temperature where the temperature is calculated using the well-known **Steinhart-Hart** equation. Different thermistors have different **Steinhart-Hart** coefficients, and it is required to know these coefficients in order to calculate the temperature of the thermistor used. For the KY-013, these coefficients are specified by the manufacturer as follows (your coefficients may be slightly different!):

$c1 = 0.001129148$
$c2 = 0.000234125$
$c3 = 0.\ 0000000876741$

Assuming the resistor is series with the thermistor, R1 = 10 kΩ (i.e. R1 = 10000 ohms), and a 16-bit ADC is used (0 to 65535 quantization levels) to read the thermistor voltage, the temperature is calculated as follows (see Figure 4.27).
First, calculate the resistance of the thermistor. From the potential divider circuit, the output voltage V_0 is given by:

$$V_o = V \times R2 / (R1 + R2) \quad (1)$$

Where V is the applied voltage. From this equation we find R2 as:

$$R2 = V_o \times R1 / (V - V_o) \quad (2)$$

With a 16-bit ADC, if Raw is the raw value read by the ADC then the actual physical voltage read, V_o, is given by:

$$V_o = Raw \times V / 65535 \quad (3)$$

From (3) and (2) we get:

$$R2 = [R1 \times Raw \times V / 65535] / (V - Raw \times V / 65535] \quad (4)$$

Equation (4) is simplified to give:

$$R2 = R1 / (65535 / Raw - 1) \quad (5)$$

or,

$$R2 = 10000 / (65535 / Raw - 1) \quad (6)$$

Knowing R2, the temperature is then given by the **Steinhart-Hart** equation:

$$T = \log(R2) \quad (7)$$

$$Tmp = 1 / (c1 + (c2 + (c3 \times T \times T)) \times T) \quad (8)$$

Now, we convert the temperature from Kelvin into Celsius:

$$Temp = Tmp - 273.15 \quad (9)$$

We will be using the above equations to calculate the temperature. Notice that the above calculations are only for a 10-kΩ resistor. You should check to make sure that you have the correct resistor installed on the KY-013 sensor module. **Notice that the reading is very sensitive to the resistor as well as to the thermistor parameters *c*1, *c*2, *c*3.**

Block diagram: Figure 4.28 shows the block diagram of the project.

Figure 4.28: Block diagram of the project.

Circuit diagram: The circuit diagram of the project is shown in Figure 4.29. The sensor is connected to channel 0 of the ADC (GP26, pin 31). The LCD is connected as in the previous projects using LCD.

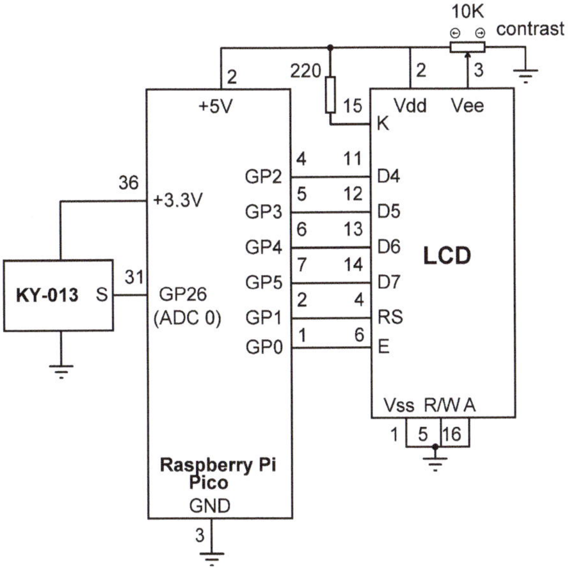

Figure 4.29: Circuit diagram of the project.

Program listing: Figure 4.30 shows the program listing (Program: **Thermistor**). At the beginning of the program variable Thermistor is assigned to channel 0 of the ADC and the LCD is initialized. Main program runs in a loop every 2 seconds. The thermistor data is read into variable Raw and then function Temperature is called to calculate the temperature. The LCD is cleared, heading Temperature (C) is displayed at the top row, and the temperature reading is formatted and displayed at the bottom row of the LCD in degrees Celsius in the following format:

Row 0: Temperature (C)
Row 1: nn.mm

```
#--------------------------------------------------------------
#               THERMISTOR TEMPERATURE MEASUREMENT
#               ==================================
#
# This program measures the ambient temperature using a
# low-cost NTC thermistor module (KY-013). The readings are
# displayed on the LCD
#
# Author: Dogan Ibrahim
# File  : Thermistor.py
# Date  : February 2021
#---------------------------------------------------------------
from machine import ADC
import utime
import math
import LCD

Thermistor = ADC(0)                         # ADC channel 0
LCD.lcd_init()                              # Initialize LCD

#
# Calculate the temperature using Steinhart-Hart equation
#
def Temperature(RawValue):
    c1 = 0.001129148
    c2 = 0.000234125
    c3 = 0.0000000876741
    R1 = 10000.0
    ADC_Res = 65535.0

    R2 = R1 / ((ADC_Res/RawValue - 1))
    T = math.log(R2)
    Tmp = 1.0 / (c1 + (c2 + (c3 * T * T)) * T)
    Temp = Tmp - 273.15
    return Temp

while True:                                  # Do forever
    Raw = Thermistor.read_u16()              # Read channel 0
    temp = Temperature(Raw)                  # Calculate temp
    LCD.lcd_clear()                          # Clear LCD
    LCD.lcd_puts("Temperature (C)")          # Display heading
    LCD.lcd_goto(0, 1)                       # Move cursor
    tempstr = str(temp)[:5]                  # Convert to string
    LCD.lcd_puts(tempstr)                    # Display temperature
    utime.sleep(2)                           # Wait 2 seconds
```

Figure 4.30: Program: Thermistor.

Note: We could also use the modified form of the Steinhart-Hart equation (known as the **B** parameter equation) if the parameters *c*1, *c*2, *c*3 are not known. The modified equation is:

$$1 / T = 1 / T_0 + 1 / B (\log(R / R_0))$$

where

T = the measured absolute temperature (take away 273.15 to find temperature in °C);

$\boldsymbol{T_0}$ = the absolute room temperature (equal to 298.15 K) at 25 °C;

B = the thermistor coefficient (usually quoted by the manufacturers, in the region of 3960);

R = the measured resistance of the thermistor;

$\boldsymbol{R_0}$ = the resistance of the thermistor at room temperature (usually quoted by the manufacturers, in the region of 10 kΩ).

Chapter 5 • Data Logging

5.1 Overview

The filing system of the Raspberry Pi Pico enables us to manipulate files in memory, which includes creating new files, reading from files, and writing to files. In this Chapter we will learn how to log the temperature data to files.

5.2 Project 1: Logging the temperature data

Description: In this project, we will create a file called **Temp.txt** and save the ambient temperature data every second, time-stamped with relative seconds. The data will be saved for 30 seconds, i.e. 30 records will be saved.

Aim: The aim of this project is to show how the temperature data (or any other data) can be saved in a file.

Block diagram: Figure 5.1 shows the block diagram of the project.

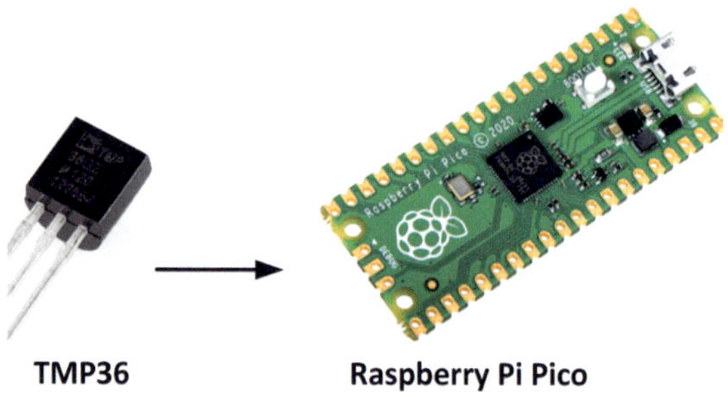

Figure 5.1: Block diagram of the project.

Circuit diagram: The circuit diagram is shown in Figure 5.2. TMP36 temperature sensor chip is connected to analogue channel 0 (GP26, pin 31).

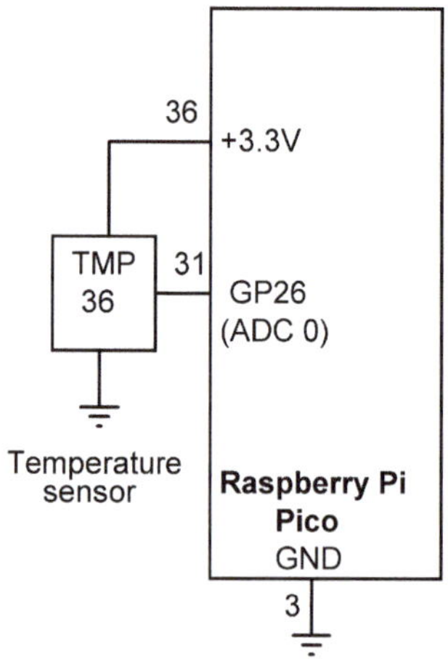

Figure 5.2: Circuit diagram of the project.

Program listing: Figure 5.3 shows the program listing (Program: **LogTemp**). At the beginning of the program, modules **ADC** of machine and **utime** are imported to the program. A new file is created (i.e. opened in write **w** mode) with the name **Temp.txt** and the heading **Ambient Temperature**, followed by a 'newline' character is written to the file. The remainder of the program runs in a **for** loop which is iterated 30 times. Inside this loop the temperature is read from TMP36, converted into degrees Celsius, and then saved in the file with the relative seconds. At the end of the loop, the file is closed, and the message **Data has been written to file...** is displayed on the screen.

```
#----------------------------------------------------------
#               LOGGING THE TEMPERATURE DATA
#               ============================
#
# This program measures the temperature using an external
# temperature sensor chip and logs the data every second
# for 30 seconds (i.e. 30 records)
#
# Author: Dogan Ibrahim
# File  : LogTemp.py
# Date  : February 2021
#------------------------------------------------------------
from machine import ADC
import utime

AnalogIn = ADC(0)                              # ADC channel 0
Conv = 3300 / 65535                            # Conversion factor

file = open("Temp.txt", "w")                   # Create a new file
file.write("Ambient Temperature\n")            # Write heading

for secs in range(30):                         # Do forever
    V = AnalogIn.read_u16()                    # Read temp
    mV = V * Conv                              # Convert to Volts
    Temp = (mV - 500.0) / 10.0                 # Convert to temp
    Tempstr = str(Temp)[:5]                    # Convert to string
    data = str(secs+1) + "    " + Tempstr + "\n"
    file.write(data)                           # Write to file
    utime.sleep(1)                             # Wait 1 second

file.close()                                   # Close file
print("Data has been written to file...")
```

Figure 5.3: Program: LogTemp.

The contents of the file can be displayed by on the Thonny screen by clicking **File**, followed by **Open**. Select **Raspberry Pi Pico**, and then click on file **Temp.txt** to display it as shown in Figure 5.4. Notice that it is important that you close a file after you finished writing to it, otherwise the data may not be saved securely. Also, by default a file is always opened in read mode as a text file. Files can also be opened in binary mode using the options **rb** and **wb** for read and write operations, respectively.

```
mp ] ×  [ Temp.txt ]
Ambient Temperature
1   25.18
2   25.18
3   23.65
4   25.42
5   25.02
6   25.10
7   25.18
8   25.58
9   23.33
10   25.26
11   25.10
12   25.18
13   25.42
```

Figure 5.4: Contents of file Temp.txt (only part of the file is shown).

5.3 Project 2: Reading the logged data

Description: In this project, the temperature data **Temp.txt** created in the previous project is open and its contents is displayed on the Thonny screen.

Aim: The aim of this project is to show how a file can be opened and its contents read and displayed on the PC screen.

Program listing: Figure 5.5 shows the program listing (Program: **ReadTemp**). At the beginning of the program, file **Temp.txt** is opened in read **r** mode. Function **file.read** is then used to read the data from the file and display (print) it in the Thonny screen.

Figure 5.5 shows the program and the data displayed on the Thonny screen.

```
#-----------------------------------------------------------
#                READ AND DISPLAY THE LOGGED DATA
#                ================================
#
# This program opens the file where the temperature data
# was saved and displays its contents on PC screen
#
# Author: Dogan Ibrahim
# File  : ReadTemp.py
# Date  : February 2011
#------------------------------------------------------------
file = open("Temp.txt", "r")                    # Open the file
print(file.read())                              # Read the data
file.close()
```

Shell

```
Ambient Temperature
1   25.18
2   25.18
3   23.65
4   25.42
5   25.02
6   25.10
7   25.18
8   25.58
9   23.33
10   25.26
11   25.10
12   25.18
13   25.42
```

Figure 5.5: Program: ReadTemp and the data displayed.

Function **read()** reads the entire contents of a file. If we want to read a line, we use the function **readline()**. An example is given below which reads and displays the first 3 lines of file **Temp.txt** (notice that an additional newline character is added to the end of each line):

```
file = open("Temp.txt", "r")            # Open the file
for i in range(3):                      # Read 3 lines
            print(file.readline())      # Display the data

file.close()                            # Close the file
```

Ambient Temperature

1 25.18
2 25.18

Chapter 6 • Pulse Width Modulation (PWM)

6.1 Overview

A digital form of Pulse Width Modulation (PWM; also written as *pulsewidth modulation*) is commonly used to drive heavy loads such as motors, actuators, heaters, and so on. As we shall see in this Chapter, PWM is basically a positive-going squarewave whose pulsewidth can be changed. By changing the pulsewidth, we can effectively change the average value of the voltage supplied to the load.

6.2 Basic theory of pulsewidth modulation

PWM is a commonly used technique for controlling the power delivered to analogue loads using digital waveforms. Although analogue voltages (and currents) can be used to control the delivered power, they have several drawbacks. Controlling large analogue loads require large voltages and currents that cannot easily be obtained using standard analogue circuits and DACs. Precision analogue circuits can be heavy, large, and expensive, and they are also sensitive to noise. By using the PWM technique, the average value of voltage (and current) fed to a load is controlled by switching the supply voltage ON and OFF at a fast rate. The longer the power on time, the higher the effective voltage supplied to the load.

Figure 6.1 shows a typical PWM waveform where the signal is basically a repetitive positive pulse, having the period T, ON time T_{ON} and OFF time of $T-T_{ON}$ seconds. The minimum and maximum values of the voltage supplied to the load are 0 and V_P respectively. The PWM switching frequency is usually set to be very high (usually in the order of several kHz) so that it does not affect the load that uses the power. The main advantage of PWM is that the load is operated efficiently since the power loss in the switching device is very low. When the switch is ON there is practically no voltage drop across the switch, and when the switch is OFF there is no current supplied to the load.

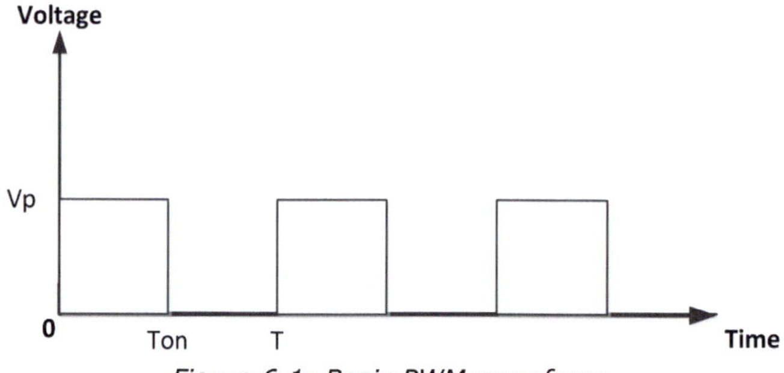

Figure 6.1: Basic PWM waveform.

The duty cycle D of a PWM waveform is defined as the ratio of the ON time to its period. Expressed mathematically,

$$D = T_{ON} / T$$

The duty cycle is usually expressed as a percentage and therefore,

$$D = (T_{ON} / T_{OFF}) \times 100\%$$

By varying the duty cycle between 0% and 100% we can effectively control the average voltage supplied to the load between 0 and V_p.

The average value of the voltage applied to the load can be calculated by considering a general PWM waveform shown in Figure 1. The average value *A* of waveform f(t) with period *T* and peak value y_{max} and minimum value y_{min} is calculated as:

$$A=\frac{1}{T}\int_{0}^{T} f(t)dt$$

or,

$$A=\frac{1}{T}\left(\int_{0}^{T_{ON}} y_{max}\, dt+\int_{T_{ON}}^{T} y_{min}\, dt\right)$$

In a PWM waveform, y_{min} = 0 and the above equation becomes

$$A=\frac{1}{T}\left(T_{ON}\, y_{max}\right)$$

or, $$A=D\, y_{max}$$

As it can be seen from the above equation, the average value of the voltage supplied to the load is directly proportional to the duty cycle of the PWM waveform and by varying the duty cycle we control the average load voltage. Figure 6.2 shows the average voltage for different values of the duty cycle.

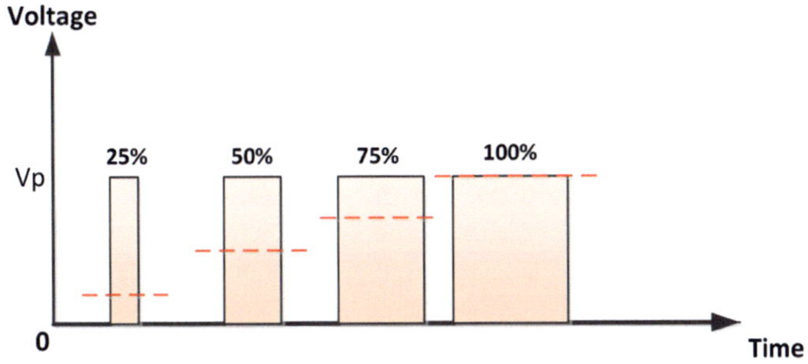

Figure 6.2: Average voltage (shown as dashed line) supplied to a load.

It is interesting to notice that with correct lowpass filtering, the PWM can be used as a DAC if the MCU does not have a DAC channel. By varying the duty cycle we can effectively vary the average analogue voltage supplied to the load.

6.3 PWM channels of the Raspberry Pi Pico

The Raspberry Pi Pico microcontroller has 16 programmable PWM channels. Figure 6.3 shows the pin configurations of these channels. Each channel is identified with a letter and a number, such as **PWM_A[0]**. Some of the 16 PWM channels located at left hand side of the microcontroller pins are duplicated at the right-hand side and only one of the duplicated channels can be used in an application.

Figure 6.3: PWM channels of the Pico.

The PWM channels can be accessed by one of two methods. For example, channel PW-M_A[0] connected to port pin GP0 can be accessed as:

```
import machine
ch = machine.PWM(machine.Pin(0))
```

or as

```
from machine import PWM, Pin
ch = PWM(Pin(0))
```

The frequency of the PWM waveform can be set using the following statement. For example, to set the frequency to 1000 Hz:

```
ch.freq(1000)
```

The duty cycle can be set between 0% and 100% by setting it from 0 to 65535. The duty cycle can be set using the following statement. For example, to set the duty cycle to 50%:

```
ch.duty_u16(32767)
```

Example projects are given in this Chapter using the PWM.

6.4 Project 1: Generate a 1000 Hz PWM waveform with 50% duty cycle

Description: In this project, we create a PWM waveform with a frequency of 1000 Hz and a duty cycle of 50%.

Aim: The aim of this project is to show how we can use the PWM functions.

Circuit diagram: In this project, port pin GP0 is used and an oscilloscope is connected to this pin to observe the waveform.

Program listing: The program listing is very simple. and it is given below.

```
from machine import Pin, PWM
ch = PWM(Pin(0))                    # PWM at GP0
ch.freq(1000)                       # Frequency = 1000Hz
ch.duty_u16(32767)                  # 50% duty cycle
while True:
            pass
```

Figure 6.4 shows the generated waveform on the oscilloscope. Here, the horizontal axis was 0.5ms/division and the vertical axis was 1 V/division. Clearly the period of the generated waveform is 1 ms (freq = 1000 Hz), duty cycle 50%, and the amplitude is about 3 V.

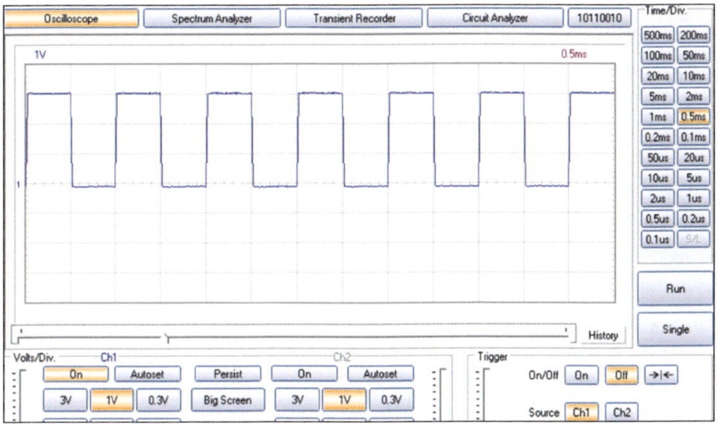

Figure 6.4: Generated PWM waveform.

Note: The author has generated clean and correct PWM waveforms to up to several MHz without any appreciable noise.

6.5 Project 2: Changing the brightness of an LED

Description: In this project, an external LED is connected to port pin GP0 through a 470-ohm current limiting resistor. The program changes the brightness of the LED by changing the duty cycle of the PWM voltage sent to the LED.

Aim: The aim of this project is to show how the PWM can be used in a project.
The block diagram and the circuit diagram of this project are as in Figure 3.3 and Figure 3.4 respectively.

Program listing: Figure 6.5 shows the program listing (Program: **LEDfade**). The frequency is set to 1000 Hz so that the LED light is steady (i.e. not flashing). As the duty cycle is increased from 0% to 100%, the LED brightness increases gradually.

```
#-----------------------------------------------------------
#              CHANGING THE BRIGHTNESS OF AN LED
#              =================================
#
# In this program and LED is connected to port pin GP0. The
# brightness of the LED is changed continuously by changing
# duty cycle of the voltage waveform from 0% to 100%
#
# Author: Dogan Ibrahim
# File  : LEDfade.py
# Date  : February 2011
#-------------------------------------------------------------
from machine import Pin, PWM
import utime

ch = PWM(Pin(0))                     # PWM at GP0
ch.freq(1000)                        # Frequency = 1000Hz

i = 0
while True:                          # Do forever
    ch.duty_u16(i)                   # Change duty cycle
    utime.sleep_ms(300)              # Delay 300ms
    i = i + 5000                     # Increment i
    if i > 65535:
        i = 0
```

Figure 6.5: Program: LEDfade.

6.6 Project 3: Varying the speed of a brushed DC motor

Description: This is a simple project where a small, brushed DC motor is connected to the PICO microcontroller through a power MOSFET. In addition, a potentiometer is connected to one of the analogue inputs of the microcontroller. In this project, the speed of the motor is varied by moving the potentiometer arm.

Block Diagram: Figure 6.6 shows the block diagram of the project. A motor driver (MOSFET) and a potentiometer are connected to the microcontroller.

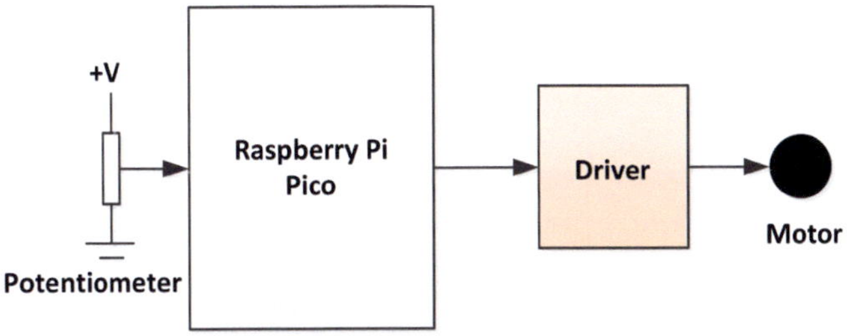

Figure 6.6: Block diagram of the project.

The DC motor In this project, is controlled using PWM waveforms as in the previous project. By varying the potentiometer arm, the analogue voltage read by the microcontroller is varied and this in turn changes the PWM duty cycle of the voltage applied to the motor, thus causing the motor speed to change.

Circuit diagram: The circuit diagram of the project is shown in Figure 6.7. The potentiometer is connected to channel 0 of the ADC (GP26, pin 31). The motor is connected to GP17 (pin 22) through an IRL540 type MOSFET switch. It is recommended to use an external power supply for the motor.

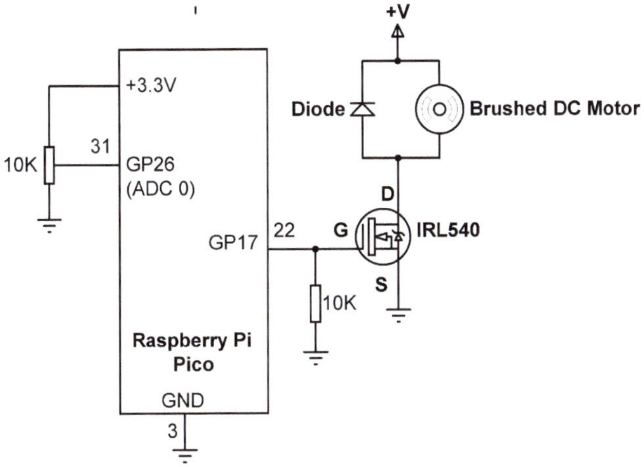

Figure 6.7: Circuit diagram of the project.

Program listing: Figure 6.8 shows the program listing (Program: **Motor**). The data read from the ADC varies between 0 and 65535 as the potentiometer arm is fully moved from one side to the other side. This data is used to change the duty cycle from 0% to 100%.

```
#------------------------------------------------------------
#              CHANGING THE MOTOR SPEED
#              ========================
#
# In this project a brushed DC motor is connected to the
# Pico.Additionally, a potentiometer is conencted to channel
# 0 of the ADC.Varying the potentiometer changes the motor speed
#
# Author: Dogan Ibrahim
# File  : Motor.py
# Date  : February 2021
#--------------------------------------------------------------
from machine import Pin, PWM, ADC

Pot = ADC(0)                           # Pot at channel 0
Motor = Pin(17, Pin.OUT)               # Motor at GP17

ch = PWM(Pin(17))                      # PWM at GP17
ch.freq(1000)                          # Frequency = 1000Hz

while True:                            # Do forever
    duty = Pot.read_u16()              # Read pot data
    ch.duty_u16(duty)                  # Change duty cycle
```

Figure 6.8: Program: Motor.

6.7 Project 4: Frequency generator with LCD

Description: This is a frequency generator project. A potentiometer and an LCD are connected to the Raspberry Pi Pico. By varying the potentiometer arm we change the frequency of the generated PWM waveform. The frequency of the generated waveform is displayed on the LCD. The duty cycle of the generated waveform is set at 50%. Frequencies up to about 65535 Hz can be generated by moving the potentiometer arm fully to one side.

Block diagram: Figure 6.9 shows the block diagram of the project.

Figure 6.9: Block diagram of the project.

Circuit diagram: The circuit diagram of the project is given in Figure 6.10. The potentiometer arm is connected to channel 0 of the ADC (GP0). The LCD is connected as in the previous LCD projects. Output PWM waveform is available at port pin GP16, pin 21).

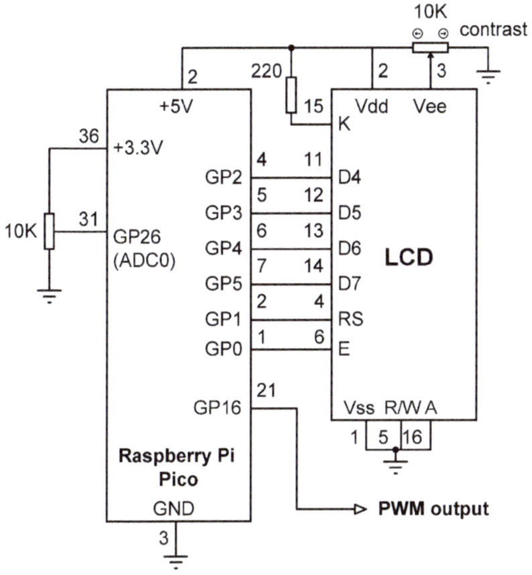

Figure 6.10: Circuit diagram of the project.

Program listing: Figure 6.11 shows the program listing (Program: **FreqGen**). At the beginning of the program, **Pot** is assigned to ADC channel 0; LCD is initialized and a message 'Frequency(Hz)' is displayed at the top row of the LCD. Inside the program loop the value of **Pot** is read and this is used to set the frequency of the PWM waveform. The duty cycle is set to 50%.

```
#-----------------------------------------------------------
#              FREQUENCY GENERATOR
#              ===================
#
# In this project a potentiometer is connected to channel 0
# of the Pico. Also, an LCD is connected. The program generates
# PWM waveforms of different frequencies as the potentiometer
```

```
# arm is moved
#
# Author: Dogan Ibrahim
# File  : FreqGen.py
# Date  : February 2011
#--------------------------------------------------------------
from machine import Pin, PWM, ADC
import LCD
import utime

Pot = ADC(0)                          # Pot at channel 0
LCD.lcd_init()

ch = PWM(Pin(16))                     # PWM at GP16
ch.freq(100)                          # Default freq
LCD.lcd_clear()
LCD.lcd_puts("Frequency(Hz)")

while True:                           # Do forever
    frequency = Pot.read_u16(         # Read pot data
    LCD.lcd_goto(0, 1)
    LCD.lcd_puts("                ")
    LCD.lcd_goto(0, 1)
    LCD.lcd_puts(str(frequency))
    ch.duty_u16(32767)
    ch.freq(frequency)                # Change the freuency
    utime.sleep(1)
```

Figure 6.11: Program FreqGen.

The frequency is displayed on the LCD in the following format:

Row 1: Frequency(Hz)
Row 2: nnnnnnn

6.8 PROJECT 5: Measuring the frequency and duty cycle of a PWM waveform

Description: In this project, the frequency and duty cycle of a PWM waveform is read and displayed on the Thonny screen.

Circuit diagram: The PWM waveform whose frequency and duty cycle is to be asserted is applied to port GP17 (pin 22). Make sure that the voltage is not greater than +3.3 V, otherwise you may damage the input circuitry of your Pico.

Program listing: Figure 6.12 shows the program listing (Program: **MeasPWM**). The program measures the Mark (i.e. logic 1) and Space (i.e. logic 0) timings of the PWM input waveform in microseconds. The duty cycle and the frequency are then calculated as follows:

Duty cycle (%) = 100 × Mark / (Mark + Space)
Frequency (kHz) = 1000 / (Mark + Space)

```
#-------------------------------------------------------------
#              MEASURE THE FREQUENCY AND DUTY CYCLE
#              ====================================
#
# In this project a PWM wave is applied to the PIco. The
# frequency and duty cycle of this wave are measured and
# displayed on the Thonny screen.
#
# Author: Dogan Ibrahim
# File  : MeasFreq.py
# Date  : February 2021
#---------------------------------------------------------------
from machine import Pin
import utime

PWMin = Pin(17, Pin.IN)                     # PWM wave input

while True:                                 # Do forever
    while True:
        if PWMin.value() == 1:              # Wait while 0
            break
    Tmr1Strt = utime.ticks_cpu()            # Start timer 1

    while True:
        if PWMin.value() == 0:              # Wait while 1
            break
    Tmr1End = utime.ticks_cpu()             # End

    while True:
        if PWMin.value() == 1:              # Wait while 0
            break

    Tmr2End = utime.ticks_cpu()             # End

    Mark = utime.ticks_diff(Tmr1End, Tmr1Strt)
    Space = utime.ticks_diff(Tmr2End, Tmr1End)
    duty = 100.0 * Mark / (Mark + Space)
    freqkHz = 1000.0 / (Mark + Space)
    print("Duty Cycle = %5.2f" % duty)
```

```
    print("Frequency (kHz) = ", freqkHz, "\n")
    utime.sleep(2)
```

Figure 6.12: Program: MeasPWM.

Example output from the program is shown in Figure 6.13.

```
Duty Cycle = 39.74
Frequency (kHz) =  1.20048

Duty Cycle = 35.05
Frequency (kHz) =  1.317523

Duty Cycle = 39.59
Frequency (kHz) =  1.203369
```

Figure 6.13: Example output.

6.9 PROJECT 6: Melody maker

Description: This project shows how PWM-type tones of different frequencies can be generated and sent to a passive buzzer device. The project shows how the simple melody *Happy Birthday* can be played on the buzzer.

Aim: The aim of this project is to show how various tones can be generated to create a simple melody.

Block diagram: The block diagram of the project is shown in Figure 6.14.

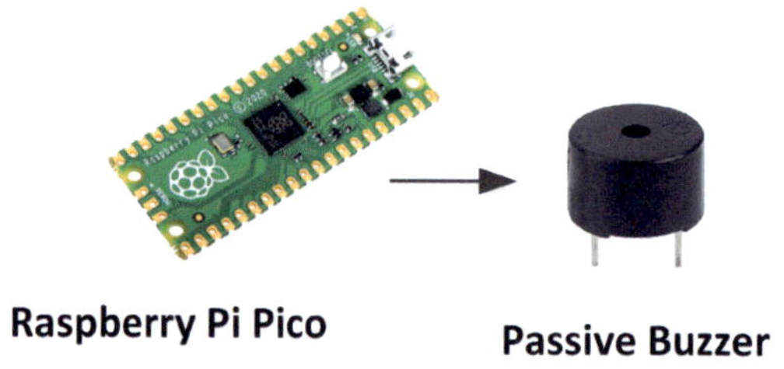

Figure 6.14: Block diagram of the Melody Maker project.

Circuit diagram: Figure 6.15 shows the circuit diagram of the project. A passive buzzer is connected to port GP0 (pin 1) of the Raspberry Pi Pico. A transistor switch is used to increase the voltage level of the buzzer (this can be omitted, and the buzzer can be directly connected to GP0 if desired. This however will give low output from the buzzer). Almost any old NPN, small-signal, bipolar transistor can be used in this project. The + terminal of the buzzer can be connected to either +3.3 V or to +5 V for higher output from the buzzer.

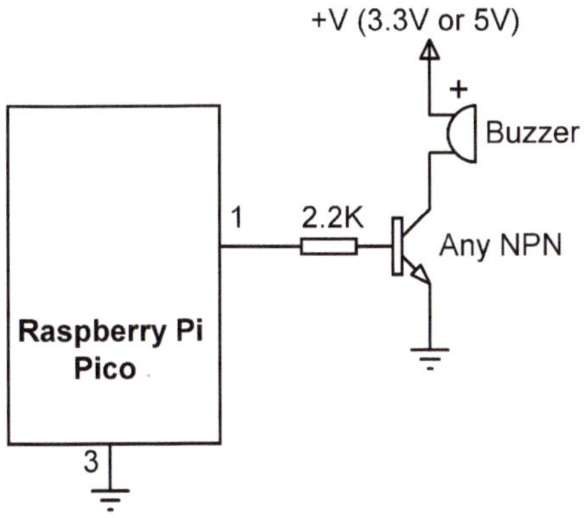

Figure 6.15: Circuit diagram of the project.

Melodies

When playing a melody each note is played for a certain duration and with a certain frequency. In addition, a certain gap is necessary between two successive notes. The frequencies of the musical notes starting from middle *C* (i.e. C_4) are given below. The harmonic of a note is obtained by doubling the frequency. For example, the frequency of C_5 is 2 × 262 = 524 Hz.

Notes	C_4	C_4#	D_4	D_4#	E_4	F_4	F_4#	G_4	G_4#	A_4	A_4#	B_4
Hz	261.63	277.18	293.66	311.13	329.63	349.23	370	392	415.3	440	466.16	493.88

To play the tune of a melody, we need to know its musical notes. Each note is played for certain duration and there is a certain time gap between two successive notes. The next thing we want is to know how to generate a sound with a required frequency and duration. In this project, we will be generating the classic Happy Birthday melody and thus we need to know the notes and their durations. These are given in the table below where the durations are in units of 400 milliseconds (i.e. the values given in the table should be multiplied by 400 to give the actual durations in milliseconds).

Note	C_4	C_4	D_4	C_4	F_4	E_4	C_4	C_4	D_4	C_4	G_4	F_4	C_4
Duration	1	1	2	2	2	3	1	1	2	2	2	3	1

Note	C_4	C_5	A_4	F_4	E_4	D_4	A_4#	A_4#	A_4	F_4	G_4	F_4
Duration	1	2	2	2	2	2	1	1	2	2	2	4

Program Listing: The program listing (program: **Melody**) is shown in Figure 6.16. The frequencies and durations of the melody are stored in two arrays called **frequency** and **duration** respectively. Before the main program loop the durations of each tone are calculated and stored in array **Durations** so that the main program loop does not have to spend time to do these calculations. Inside the program loop, the melody frequencies are generated with the required durations. Notice that the tone output is stopped by setting the duty cycle to 0. A small delay (100 ms) is introduced between each tone. The melody is repeated after 3 seconds of delay. You can try higher harmonics of the notes for clearer sound. For example, in Figure 6.16 the frequencies are multiplied by 2 to play the second harmonics.

```
#-----------------------------------------------------------------
#              MELODY MAKER - PLAY HAPPY BIRTHDAY
#              ==================================
#
# In this project a buzzer is connected to port pin GP0
# which is configured as a PWM output. The program plays the
# melody Happy Birthday
#
# Author: Dogan Ibrahim
# File  : Melody.py
# Date  : February 2021
#-----------------------------------------------------------
from machine import Pin, PWM
import utime

ch = PWM(Pin(0))                       # PWM output at GP0
MaxNotes = 25
Durations = [0]*MaxNotes
#
# Melody frequencis
#
frequency = [262,262,294,262,349,330,262,262,294,262,
                        392,349,262,262,524,440,349,330,294,466,
                        466,440,349,392,349]
#
# Frequency durations
#
duration = [1,1,2,2,2,3,1,1,2,2,2,3,1,1,2,2,2,2,
                       2,1,1,2,2,2,3]

for k in range(MaxNotes):
    Durations[k] = 400 * duration[k]

while True:                                     # Do forever
    for k in range(MaxNotes):                   # Do for all notes
        ch.duty_u16(32767)                      # Duty cycle
        ch.freq(2*frequency[k])                 # Play 2nd harmonics
        utime.sleep_ms(Durations[k])            # Durations
        utime.sleep_ms(100)                     # Wait
    ch.duty_u16(0)                              # Stop playing
    utime.sleep(3)                              # Stop 3 seconds
```

Figure 6.16: Program: Melody.

Suggestions for additional work

Modify the program given in Figure 6.16 by changing the durations between the notes and see its effects. How can you make the melody run quicker? Also, replace the buzzer with an audio amplifier and a speaker for higher quality and at the same time louder output.

Chapter 7 • Serial Communication (UART)

7.1 Overview

Serial communication is a simple means of sending data across long distances quickly and reliably. The most seen serial communication method is based on the RS-232 standard. In this standard data is sent over a single line from a transmitting device to a receiving device in bit-serial format at a pre-specified speed, also known as the Baud rate, or the number of bits sent each second. Typical Baud rates are 4800, 9600, 19200, 38400, etc.

RS-232 serial communication is a form of asynchronous data transmission where data is sent character-by-character. Each character is preceded with a start bit, seven or eight data bits, an optional parity bit, and one or more stop bits. The most commonly used format is eight data bits, no parity bit and one stop bit (8N1). Therefore, a data frame consists of 10 bits. With a Baud rate of 9600, we can transmit and receive 960 characters every second. The least significant data bit is transmitted first, and the most significant bit is transmitted last.

In standard RS-232 communication, logic high is defined to be at −12 V, and a logic 0 is at +12 V. Figure 7.1 shows how character "A" (ASCII binary pattern 0010 0001) is transmitted over a serial line. The signal line is normally idle at −12 V. The start bit is first sent by the line going from high to low. Then eight data bits are sent starting from the least significant bit. Finally, the stop bit is sent by raising the line from Low to High.

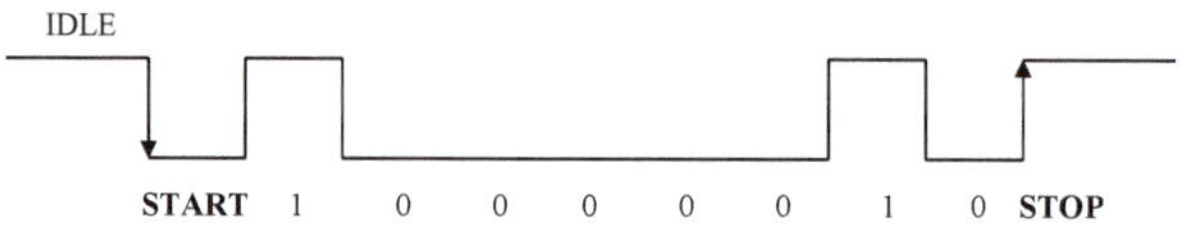

Figure 7.1: Sending character "A" across, in serial format.

In serial communication a minimum of three lines are used for communication: transmit (TX), receive (RX), and ground (GND). Some high-speed serial communication systems use additional control signals for synchronization, such as CTS, DTR, and so on. Some systems use software synchronization techniques where a special character (XOFF) is used to tell the sender to stop sending, and another character (XON) is used to tell the sender to recommence transmission. RS-232 devices are connected to each other using two types of connectors: 9-way connector, and 25-way connector. Table 7.1 shows the TX, RX, and GND pins of each types of connectors. The connectors used in RS232 serial communication are shown in Figure 7.2.

9-pin connector

Pin	Function
2	Transmit (TX)
3	Receive (RX)
5	Ground (GND)

25-pin connector

Pin	Function
2	Transmit (TX)
3	Receive (RX)
7	Ground (GND)

Table 7.1: Minimum pins required for RS232 serial communication.

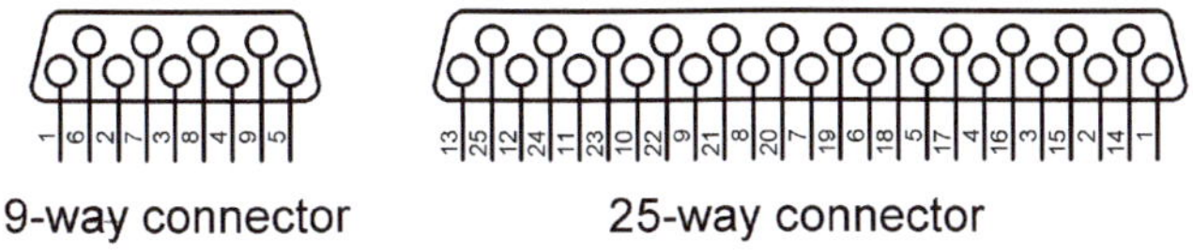

Figure 7.2: RS-232 connectors.

As described above, RS-232 voltage levels are at ±12 V. On the other hand, microcontroller input/output ports typically operate at 0 to +5 V voltage levels. It is therefore necessary to translate the voltage levels before a microcontroller can be connected to an RS-232 compatible device. Thus, the output signal from the microcontroller has to be converted into ±12 V, and the input from an RS-232 device must be converted into 0 to +5 V before it can be connected to a microcontroller. This voltage translation is normally done using special RS232 voltage converter chips. One such popular chip is the MAX232. This is a dual converter chip having the pin configuration as shown in Figure 7.3. This particular device requires four external 1-μF capacitors for its operation.

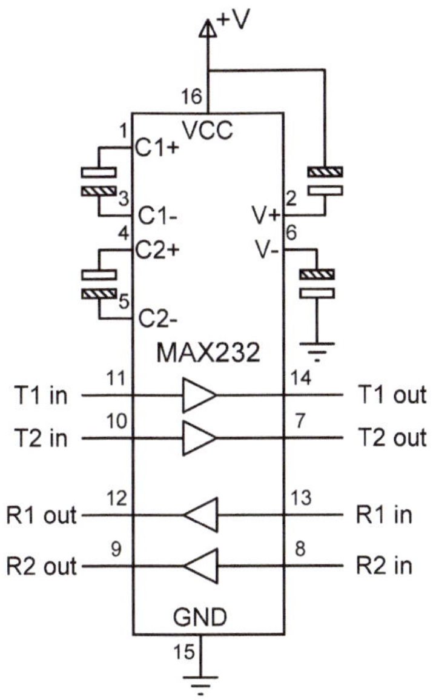

Figure 7.3: MAX232 pin configuration.

Nowadays, serial communication is done using standard TTL logic levels instead of ±12 V, where logic 1 is +5 V (or greater than +3 V) and logic 0 is 0 V. A serial line is idle when the voltage is at +5 V. The start bit is identified on the High-to-Low transition of the line, i.e. the transition from +5 V to 0 V.
In this Chapter we will develop a program to communicate between the Raspberry Pi Pico and an Arduino Uno microcontroller. Also, a program to communicate with a Raspberry Pi 4.

7.2 Raspberry Pi Pico UART serial ports

The Raspberry Pi Pico has two serial ports as shown in Figure 7.4. These are named as UART0 and UART1 where both have TX and RX pins as shown in the figure. Notice that a few ports share UART0 and UART1 and only one of each shared port can be used at any time.

Figure 7.4: Raspberry Pi Pico UART serial ports.

7.3 Project 1: Sending the Raspberry Pi Pico internal temperature to an Arduino Uno

Description: In this project we will be using a Raspberry Pi Pico and an Arduino Uno microcontroller jointly. The Pico will read the temperature from its internal sensor and send it to the Arduino over a serial link every 10 seconds. The Arduino will then display the received temperature on its monitor.

Aim: The aim of this project is to show how serial data can be sent to another device.

Block diagram: Figure 7.5 shows the block diagram of the project.

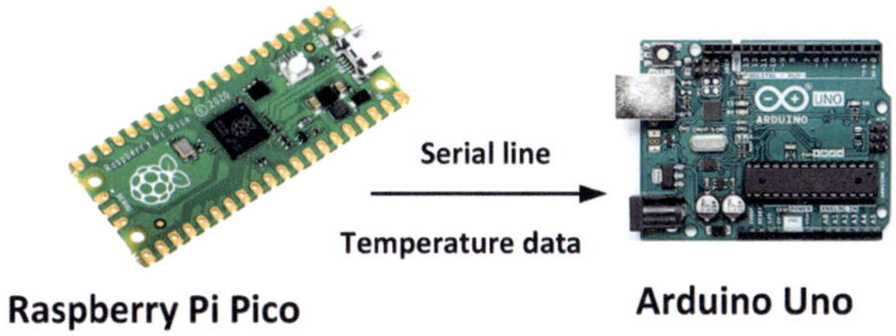

Figure 7.5: Block diagram of the Pico-temperature-to-Arduino project.

Circuit diagram: The circuit diagram of the project is shown in Figure 7.6. TX0 pin (at GP0) of the Raspberry Pi Pico is connected to pin 2 of the Arduino (this pin will be configured as a soft serial input in the Arduino program).

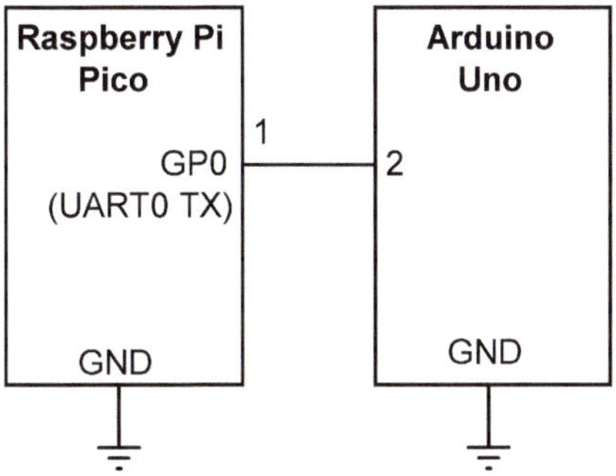

Figure 7.6: Circuit diagram of the project.

Raspberry Pi Pico program listing: Figure 7.7 shows the program listing (Program: **SerTemp**). At the beginning of the program variable AnalogIn is assigned to ADC channel 4 which is where the internal temperature sensor is connected to. UART 0 is then initialized at port GP0 with the speed of 9600 Baud. Inside the program loop the internal temperature is read, converted into degrees Celsius and finally sent to UART using function **write**. The data is sent with 2 digits before, and 2 digits after the decimal point. Also, the text **Degrees C**, followed by a 'newline' character ('\n') is sent.

Function UART can be used in one of two ways:

```
from machine import UART
uart = UART(id=0,baudrate=9600,bits=8,parity=None,stop=1)
```

Where **id** is the UART port number (e.g. 0 for TX0, RX0). By default, the number of bits is 8, parity is None, and stop bits is 1. If we are using GP0 with 9600 Baud, we can write the second statement as:

```
uart = UART(0, 9600)
```

We can alternatively use the UART as follows:

```
import machine
uart=machine.UART(id=0,baudrate=9600,bits=8,parity=None,stop=1 )
```

We can then use the following functions to send and receive data:

`uart.read(n)`	read n characters
`uart.read()`	read all available characters
`uart.readline()`	read a line
`uart.readinto(buf)`	read and store into the given buffer
`uart.write('xyz')`	write the characters

```
#------------------------------------------------------------
#        SERIAL LINK - SEND TEMPERATURE READING TO ARDUINO
#        ==================================================
#
# This project reads the internal temperature and sends it
# to Arduino Uno over a serial link at 9600 Baud
#
# Author: Dogan Ibrahim
# File  : SerTemp.py
# Date  : February 2021
#--------------------------------------------------------------
from machine import ADC, UART
import utime

AnalogIn = ADC(4)                        # ADC channel 4
Conv = 3.3 / 65535                       # Conversion factor

uart = UART(0, 9600)

while True:                              # Do forever
    V = AnalogIn.read_u16()              # Read temp
    V = V * Conv                         # Convert to Volts
    Temp = 27 - (V - 0.706) / 0.001721   # Convert to temp
    Tempstr = str(Temp)                  # Convert to string
    uart.write(Tempstr[:5])              # Send to UART
    uart.write(" Degrees C\n")
    utime.sleep(10)                      # Wait 10 seconds
```

Figure 7.7: Raspberry Pi Pico program: SerTemp.

Figure 7.8 shows the program listing (Program: **SerTemp2**) where library machine is imported to the program.

```
#------------------------------------------------------------
#              SERIAL LINK - SEND TEMPERATURE READING TO ARDUINO
#              =================================================
#
# This project reads the internal temperature and sends it
# to Arduino Uno over a serial link at 9600 Baud.
# This version of the program imports machine
#
# Author: Dogan Ibrahim
# File  : SerTemp2.py
# Date  : February 2021
#--------------------------------------------------------------
import machine
import utime

AnalogIn = machine.ADC(4)                 # ADC channel 4
Conv = 3.3 / 65535                        # Conversion factor

uart=machine.UART(id=0,baudrate=9600,bits=8,parity=None,stop=1 )

while True:                               # Do forever
    V = AnalogIn.read_u16()               # Read temp
    V = V * Conv                          # Convert to Volts
    Temp = 27 - (V - 0.706) / 0.001721    # Convert to temp
    Tempstr = str(Temp)                   # Convert to string
    uart.write(Tempstr[:5])               # Send to UART
    uart.write(" Degrees C\n")
    utime.sleep(10)                       # Wait 10 seconds
```

Figure 7.8: Raspberry Pi Pico program: SerTemp2.

Arduino Uno program listing: Figure 7.9 shows the Arduino Uno program listing (Program: **Temp.c**). The soft serial library is included at the beginning of the program and pins 2 and 3 are assigned to soft UART RX and TX, respectively. Inside the setup routine the baud rate of the monitor and the soft serial port are configured to 9600. Inside the main program loop the program waits until data arrives from the Raspberry Pi Pico. The data is received until and including a 'newline' character. The temperature data is then displayed on the Arduino IDE monitor as shown in Figure 7.10. Make sure that the Arduino IDE monitor Baud rate is set to 9600.

```
/************************************************************
 *                    TEMPERATURE DISPLAY
 *                    ===================
 * This program reads the analog temperature data from the
 * Raspberry Pi Pico over teh serial link and then displays
 * this data on the Arduino IDE monitor
```

```
 *
 * Author: Dogan Ibrahim
 * Date   : February, 2020
 * File   : Temp.c
 *****************************************************************/
#include <SoftwareSerial.h>
SoftwareSerial MySerial(2, 3);           // RX, TX

String Temp;
char ch;

void setup()
{
  Serial.begin(9600);                    // Monitor speed 9600
  MySerial.begin(9600);                  // Soft serial speed 9600
}

void loop()
{
  if(MySerial.available() > 0)           // Data available?
  {
    ch = MySerial.read();
    Temp.concat(ch);
    if(ch == ‘\n’)
    {
        Serial.print("Temperature = ");
        Serial.print(Temp);              // Display data
        Temp="";
    }
  }
}
```

Figure 7.9: Arduino Uno program: Temp.

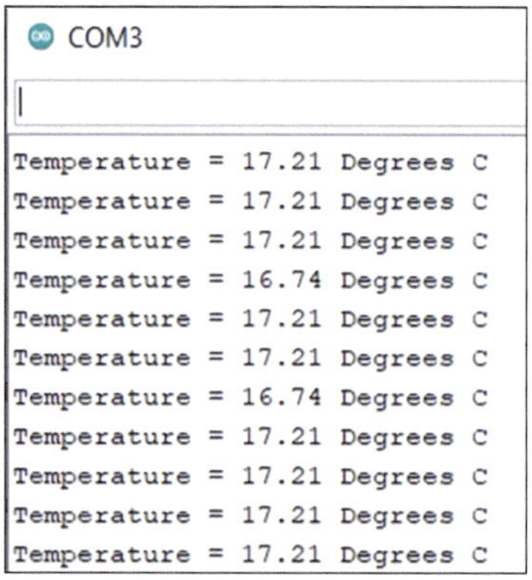

Figure 7.10: Data displayed by Arduino Uno.

7.4 Project 2: Receiving and displaying numbers from the Arduino Uno

Description: In this project we will be using a Raspberry Pi Pico and an Arduino Uno microcontroller as in the previous project. The program receives numbers counting up every second from the Arduino and displays them on the Thonny screen.

Aim: The aim of this project is to show how serial data can be received from another device.

Circuit diagram: Figure 7.11 shows the circuit diagram of the project. RX0 pin (at GP1) of the Raspberry Pi Pico is connected to pin 3 of the Arduino (this pin will be configured as a soft serial output in the Arduino program).

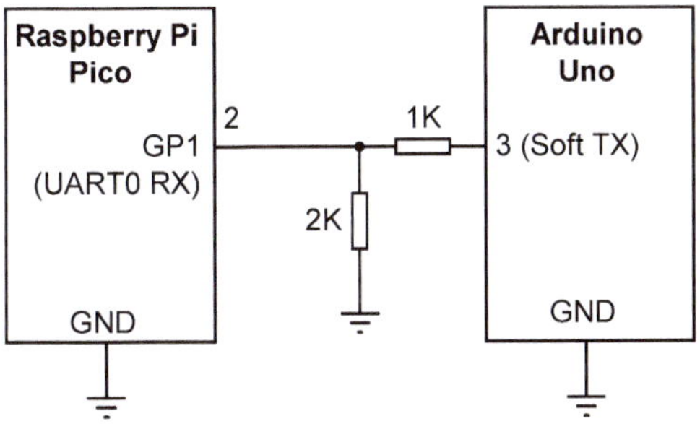

Figure 7.11: Circuit diagram of the project.

Raspberry Pi Pico program listing: Figure 7.12 shows the program listing (Program: **SerRecv**) together with the received data. At the beginning of the program UART 0 is initialized to 9600 Baud. The program loop receives data from the UART using function **readline**. The received data is decoded and displayed on the Thonny string.

```
#--------------------------------------------------------------
#       SERIAL LINK - READ DATA FROM ARDUINO
#       ====================================
#
# This project reads data from the Arduino Uno and displays
# on the Thonny screen
#
# Author: Dogan Ibrahim
# File  : SerRecv.py
# Date  : February 2011
#---------------------------------------------------------------
from machine import UART

uart = UART(0, 9600)

while True:                             # Do forever
    line = uart.readline()
    enc = line.decode('utf-8')
    print(enc)

Shell
2

3

4

5
```

Figure 7.12: Raspberry Pi Pico program: SerRecv and sample received data.

Arduino Uno program listing: Figure 7.13 shows the Arduino Uno program listing (Program: **Numbers.c**). The soft serial library is included at the beginning of the program and pins 2 and 3 are assigned to soft UART RX and TX respectively. Inside the setup routine the Baud rate of the soft serial port is set to 9600. Variable **cnt** is incremented inside the program loop, converted into string, and is sent to UART every 10 seconds.

```
/*******************************************************
 *              SEND NUMBERS TO RASPBERRY PICO
 *              ==============================
 * This program sends numbers to the Rspberry Pi Pico over
 * the serial link. These numbers are displayed by the Pico
 *
 * Author: Dogan Ibrahim
 * Date  : February, 2020
 * File  : Numbers.c
 *******************************************************/
#include <SoftwareSerial.h>
SoftwareSerial MySerial(2, 3);            // RX, TX

String Temp;
int cnt = 0;
char buffer[5];

void setup()
{
  MySerial.begin(9600);                   // Soft serial speed 9600
}

void loop()
{
  cnt = cnt + 1;                          // Increment cnt
  itoa(cnt, buffer, 10);                  // Convert to string
  MySerial.println(buffer);
  delay(10000);                           // 10 seconds delay
}
```

Figure 7.13: Arduino Uno program: Numbers.c.

7.5 Project 3: Communicating with the Raspberry Pi 4 over the serial link

Description: In this project, we will be using a Raspberry Pi Pico and a Raspberry Pi 4. Our Pico will send the message **Hello from Raspberry Pi Pico** to the RaspberryPi, and the Raspberry Pi will reply with **Hello back**.

Aim: The aim of this project is to show how the Raspberry Pi Pico and Raspberry Pi 4 can communicate over a serial link.

Block diagram: Figure 7.14 shows the block diagram of the project.

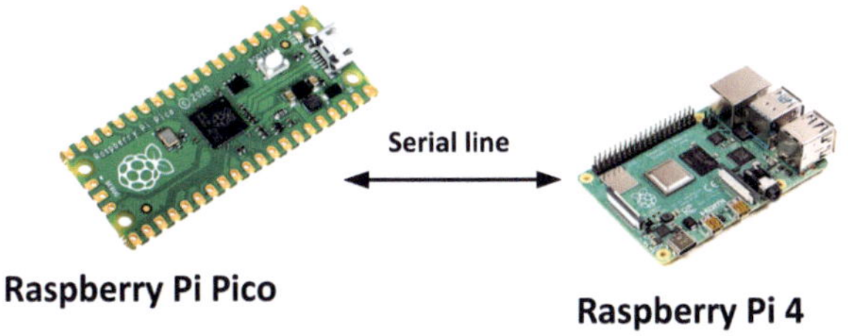

Figure 7.14: Block diagram of the project.

Raspberry Pi serial port

The Raspberry Pis have two built-in UARTs: a PL011 and a mini UART. They are implemented using different hardware blocks, so they have slightly different characteristics. Since both are 3.3 V devices, extra care must be taken when connecting to other serial communication lines operating at higher voltages like +5 V.

On Raspberry Pi models equipped with the Wireless/Bluetooth modules (e.g. Raspberry Pi 3, Zero W, 4, etc), the PL011 UART is by default connected to the Bluetooth module, while the mini UART is the primary UART with the Linux console on it. In all other models, the PL011 is used as the primary UART. By default, **/dev/ttyS0** refers to the mini UART and **/dev/ttAMA0** refers to the PL011. The Linux console uses the primary UART which depends on the Raspberry Pi model used. Also, if enabled, **/dev/serial0** refers to the primary UART (if enabled), and if enabled, **/dev/serial1** refers to the secondary UART.

By default, on the Raspberry Pi 4 the primary UART (**serial0**) is assigned to the Linux console. Using the serial port for other purposes requires this default configuration to be changed. On startup, **systemd** checks the Linux kernel command line for any console entries and will use the console defined therein. To stop this behaviour, the serial console setting needs to be removed from command line. This is easily done as follows:

- start **raspi-config** utility;
- select **Option 5** (Interfacing option);
- select **P6** (serial);
- select **No**;
- select **Yes**;
- select **Finish** and Exit **raspi-config**;
- restart your Raspberry Pi.

In Raspberry Pi 3 and 4, the serial port (**/dev/ttyS0**) is routed to two pins GPIO14 (TXD) and GPIO15 (RXD) on the header. This port is stable and of good quality. Models earlier than model 3 use this port for Bluetooth. Instead, a serial port is created in software (**/dev/ttyS0**).

To search for available serial ports, use the command:

```
pi@raspberrypi:~ $ dmesg | grep tty
```

Circuit diagram: The circuit diagram of the project is shown in Figure 7.15. UART 0 of the Pico (at GP0 and GP1) is connected to the UART of Raspberry Pi 4.

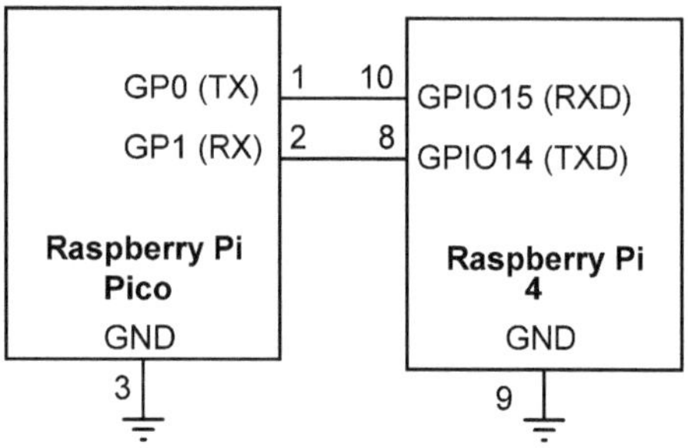

Figure 7.15: Circuit diagram of the project.

Raspberry Pi Pico program listing: Figure 7.16 shows the program listing (Program: **PicotoPi4**) together with the received data. At the beginning of the program, UART 0 is initialized to 9600 Baud. The program loop receives data from the UART using function **readline**. The received data is decoded and displayed on the Thonny string. This is repeated after a 5-second delay.

```
#-----------------------------------------------------------
#        SERIAL LINK WITH RASPBERRY PI 4
#        ===============================
#
# This project sends a message to Raspberry Pi 4 and then
# receives back a message and displays the received message
#
# Author: Dogan Ibrahim
# File  : PicotoPi4.py
# Date  : February 2011
#------------------------------------------------------------
from machine import UART
import utime

uart = UART(0, 9600)

while True:
    uart.write("Hello from Raspberry Pi Pico\n")
    recv = uart.readline()
    enc = recv.decode('utf-8')
    print(enc)
    utime.sleep(5)
```

```
hell
Hello back
Hello back
```

Figure 7.16: Raspberry Pi Pico program: PicotoPi4.

Raspberry Pi 4 program listing: Figure 7.17 shows the Raspberry Pi 4 program listing (Program: **Pi4toPico.py**). The program initializes the serial port, receives a message from the Raspberry Pi Pico, and sends back a different message. The Baud rate is set to 9600.

```
#-----------------------------------------------------------------
#       RASPBERRY PI 4 TO RASPBERRY PI PICO SERIAL COMMS
#       ------------------------------------------------
#
# This program receives a number from the Raspberry Pi Pico,
# increments teh number and sends it back to the Pico
#
# Author: Dogan Ibrahim
# File  : Pi4toPico.py
# Date  : February, 2021
#-----------------------------------------------------------------
import RPi.GPIO as GPIO                   # Import RPi library
from RPLCD.i2c import CharLCD             # Import LCD library
import time                               # Import time library
import serial                             # Import srial
port = "/dev/serial0"                     # Serial port

GPIO.setwarnings(False)

#
# Receive the GPS coordinates and display on the LCD
#
ser = serial.Serial(port,baudrate=9600,timeout=100)

while True:
     data = ser.readline()                # Read a line
     ser.write(b'Hello back\n')
     print(data)
     time.sleep(5)
```

Figure 7.17: Raspberry Pi 4 program: Pi4toPico.py.

Figure 7.18 shows example output from the Raspberry Pi 4 program.

```
b'Hello from Raspberry Pi Pico\n'
b'Hello from Raspberry Pi Pico\n'
b'Hello from Raspberry Pi Pico\n'
b'Hello from Raspberry Pi Pico\n'
b'Hello from Raspberry Pi Pico\n'
b'Hello from Raspberry Pi Pico\n'
b'Hello from Raspberry Pi Pico\n'
b'Hello from Raspberry Pi Pico\n'
```

Figure 7.18: Example output from the Raspberry Pi 4.

Chapter 8 • The I²C Bus Interface

8.1 Overview

The I²C bus is commonly used in microcontroller-based projects. In this Chapter we shall be looking at the use of this bus on the Raspberry Pi Pico. The aim is to make the reader familiar with the I²C bus library functions and to show how they can be used in a real project. Before looking at the details of the project, it is worthwhile to look at the basic principles of the I²C bus.

8.2 The I²C Bus

I²C is one of the most commonly used microcontroller communication protocols for communicating with external devices such as sensors and actuators. The bus is a single-master, multiple-slave network structure capable of operating in standard mode at 100 Kbit/s, at full speed: 400 Kbit/s; in fast mode: 1 Mbit/s; and at high speed: 3.2 Mbit/s. The bus consists of two open-drain wires, SDA and SCL, pulled up with resistors:

SDA: serial data line
SCL: serial clock line

Figure 8.1 shows an I²C bus structure with one master and three slaves.

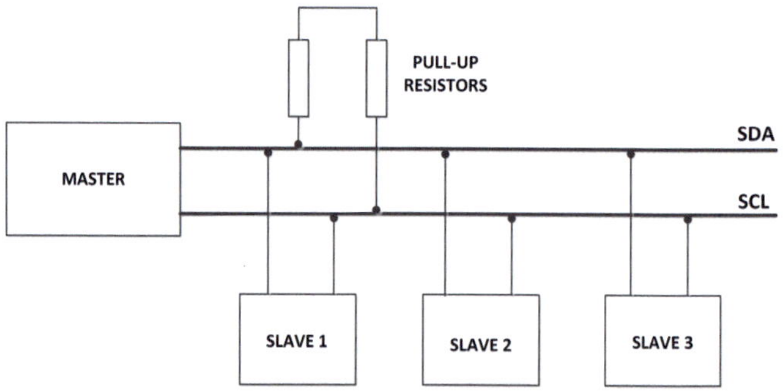

Figure 8.1: I²C bus with one master and three slaves.

Because the I2C bus is based on just two wires, there should be a way to address an individual slave device on the same bus. For this reason, the protocol defines that each slave device provides a unique slave address for the given bus. This address is usually 7-bits wide. When the bus is free, both lines are HIGH. All communication on the bus is initiated and completed by the master which initially sends a START bit, and completes a transaction by sending STOP bit. This alerts all the slaves that some data is coming on the bus and all the slaves listen on the bus. After the start bit, 7 bits of a unique slave address are sent. Each slave device on the bus has its own address and this ensures that only the addressed slave communicates on the bus at any time, to avoid any collisions. The last sent bit is read/write bit such that if this bit is 0, it means that the master wishes to write to the bus (e.g. to a register of a slave). If this bit is a 1, it means that the master wishes to read from the bus (e.g. from the register of a slave). The data is sent on the bus with the MSB bit first. An acknowledgement (ACK) bit takes is suffixed after every byte, allowing the receiver to signal to the transmitter that the byte was received successfully, and another byte may be sent. The ACK bit is sent at the 9th clock pulse.

The communication over the I^2C bus is described in the following sequence.

- The master sends on the bus the address of the slave it wants to communicate with.
- The LSB is the R/W bit which establishes the direction of data transmission, i.e. from mater to slave (R/W = 0), or from slave to master (R/W = 1).
- Requested bytes are sent, each interleaved with an ACK bit, until a stop condition occurs.

Depending on the type of slave device used, some transactions may require separate transaction. For example, the steps to read data from an I^2C compatible memory device are given below.

- Master starts the transaction in write mode (R/W = 0) by sending the slave address on the bus.
- The memory location to be retrieved are then sent as two bytes (assuming 64 Kbit memory).
- The master sends a STOP condition to end the transaction.
- The master starts a new transaction in read mode (R/W = 1) by sending the slave address on the bus.
- The master reads the data from the memory. If reading the memory in sequential format, then more than one byte will be read.
- The master sets a stop condition on the bus.

8.3 I^2C pins of the Raspberry Pi Pico

Raspberry Pi Pico has 2 I^2C pins, named I2C0 and I2C1 (see Figure 8.2). As shown in the image, the I^2C pins are duplicated and are shared with other pins. For example, GP0 (pin 1) is the I2C0 SDA pin and GP1 (pin 1) is the I2C0 SCL pin. Also, GP16 (pin 21) is the I2C0 SDA pin and GP17 (pin 22) is the I^2C SCL pin.

Figure 8.2: Raspberry Pi Pico I²C pins.

The default I²C pins are:

I2C0 SCL	GP9
I2C0 SDA	GP8
I2C1 SCL	GP7
I2C1 SDA	GP6

In the remainder of this Chapter we will be developing projects using the I²C bus.

8.4 Project 1: I²C port expander

Description: A simple project is given in this section to show how the I²C functions can be used in a program. In this project the I²C bus compatible Port Expander chip (MCP23017) is used to give additional 16 I/O ports to the Raspberry Pi Pico. This is useful in some applications where a large number of I/O ports may be required. In this project, an LED is connected to MCP23017 port pin GPA0 (pin 21) and the LED is flashed ON and OFF every second so that the operation of the program can be verified. A 470-ohm current limiting resistor is used in series with the LED.

The aim: The aim of this project is to show how the I²C bus can be used in Raspberry Pi Pico projects.

Block diagram: The block diagram of the project is shown in Figure 8.3.

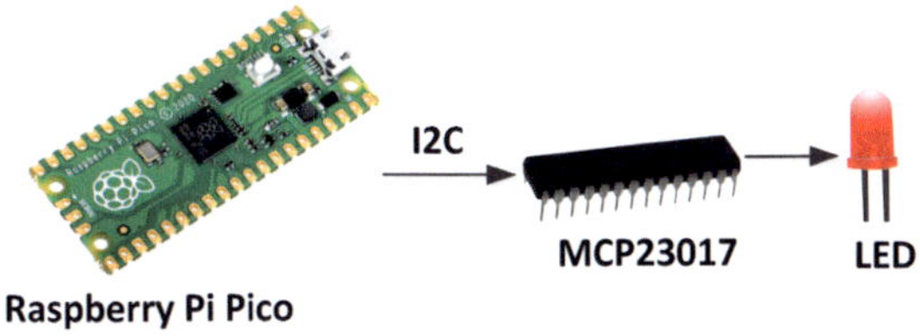

Figure 8.3: Block diagram of the project.

The MCP23017

The MCP23017 is a 28-pin chip with some features listed below. Its pin configuration is shown in Figure 8.4.

- 16 bidirectional I/O ports
- Up to 1.7 MHz operation on I²C bus
- Interrupt capability
- External reset input
- Low standby current
- +1.8 to +5.5 V operation
- 3 address pins, allowing up to 8 devices on the I²C bus
- 28-pin DIL package

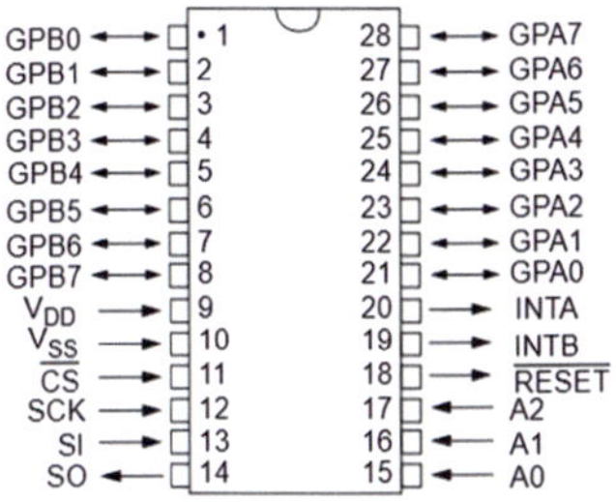

Figure 8.4: Pin configuration of the MCP23017.

The pin descriptions are given in Table 8.1.

Pin	Description
GPA0-GPA7	Port A pins
GPB0-GPB7	Port B pins
VDD	Power supply
VSS	Ground
SDA	I2C data pin
SCL	I2C clock pin
RESET	Reset pin
A0-A2	I2C address pins

Table 8.1: MCP23017 pin descriptions.

The MCP23017 is addressed using pins A0 to A2. Table 8.2 shows the address selection. In this project the address pins are connected to ground, thus the address of the chip is 0x20. The chip address is 7 bits wide with the low bit is set or cleared depending on whether we wish to read data from the chip or write data to the chip respectively. Since in this project we will be writing to the MCP23017, the low bit should be 0, making the chip byte address (also called the **device opcode**) as 0x40.

Table 8.2: Address selection of the MCP23017.

A2	A1	A0	Address
0	0	0	0x40
0	0	1	0x21
0	1	0	0x22
0	1	1	0x23
1	0	0	0x24
1	0	1	0x25
1	1	0	0x26
1	1	1	0x27

The MCP23017 chip has 8 internal registers that can be configured for its operation. The device can either be operated in 16-bit mode or in two 8-bit mode by configuring bit IO-CON.BANK. On power-up this bit is cleared which chooses the two 8-bit mode by default.

The I/O direction of the port pins are controlled with registers IODIRA (at address 0x00) and IODIRB (at address 0x01). Clearing a bit to 0 in these registers makes the corresponding port pin(s) as output(s). Similarly, setting a bit to 1 in these registers make the corresponding port pin(s) input(s). GPIOA and GPIOB register addresses are 0x12 and 0x13 respectively. This is shown in Figure 8.5.

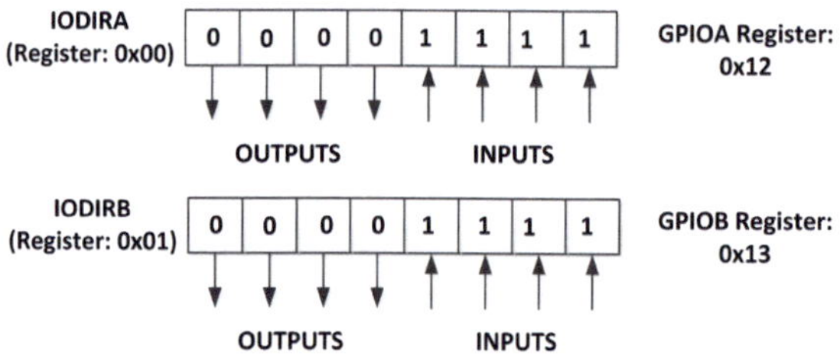

Figure 8.5: Configuring the I/O ports.

Figure 8.6 shows the circuit diagram of the project. Notice that I²C pins of the port expander are connected to pins GP8 (I2C0 SDA) and GP9 (I2C0 SCL) of the Raspberry Pi Pico and are pulled-up using 10-kohm resistors as required by the I²C specifications. The LED is connected to port pin GPA0 of the MCP23017 (pin 21). The address select bits of the MCP23017 are all connected to ground.

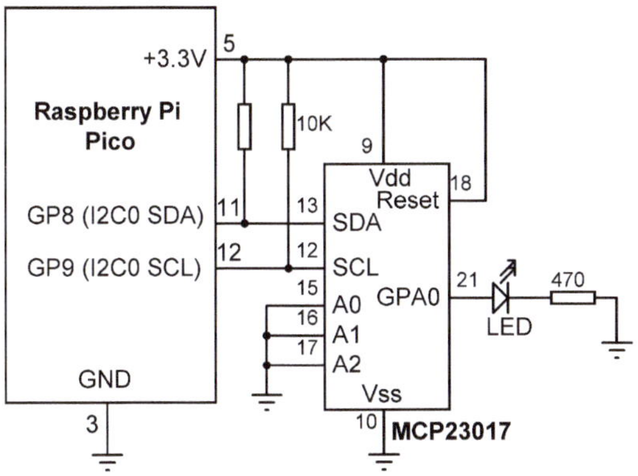

Figure 8.6: Circuit diagram of the project.

More information on the MCP23017 chip can be obtained from the datasheet:

http://docs-europe.electrocomponents.com/webdocs/137e/0900766b8137eed4.pdf

Program listing: Figure 8.7 shows the program listing (Program: **MCP23017**). The Raspberry Pi Pico supports the following I^{2}C functions:

`i2c.scan()`	scan for slave I2C devices
`i2c.writeto()`	write to I2C bus
`i2c.readfrom()`	read from I2C bus
`i2c.writeto_mem()`	write to memory of slave device
`i2c.readfrom_mem()`	read from memory of slave device

Some example I^{2}C operations are:

`print("I2C address=", i2c.scan())`	print the I2C slave addresses on the bus
`i2c.writeto(0x20, b'56')`	write 56 to I2C address 0x20
`i2c.writeto(0x20, bytearray(buff))`	write buffer to I2C address 0x20
`i2c.readfrom(0x20, 3)`	read 3 bytes from I2C address 0x20
`i2c.writeto_mem(0x20, 0x10, b'\x35')`	write 0x35 to memory address 0x10 of the slave whose I2C address is 0x20
`i2c.readfrom_mem(0x20, 0x10, 3)`	read 3 bytes starting from register address 0x10 of slave I2C device whose address is 0x20

At the beginning of the program, the I^2C module is imported to the program and the I^2C interface is defined by specifying the SDA and SCL pin connections to the Pico. Function **i2c.scan()** is called to display the I^2C slave devices on the bus, and the following was displayed:

```
i2c address = [32] which corresponds to hexadecimal 0x20
```

Then the MCP23017 I^2C device address, register **GPIOA** address, and the I/O direction **IODIRA** address are defined. List **conf** stores the **IODIRA** register address and 0 so that MCP23017 PORTA is set to output mode. List **buff1** stores the **GPIOA** register address and what the output should be set to (1 to turn ON the LED). Similarly, **buff2** stores the **GPIOA** register address and what the output should be set to (0 to turn OFF the LED). Inside the main program loop the LED is flashed every second.

```
#-------------------------------------------------------------
#               I2C PORT EXPANDER
#               =================
#
# In this project the MCP23017 port expander chip is used.
# An LED is connected to port pin GPA0 of the port expander
# and this LED is flashed every second
#
# Author: Dogan Ibrahim
# File  : MCP23017.py
# Date  : February 2021
#-------------------------------------------------------------
from machine import Pin,I2C
import utime

i2c = machine.I2C(0, scl=Pin(9), sda=Pin(8), freq=100000)
print("i2c address=",i2c.scan())

Device_Address = 0x20                     # MCP23017 I2C address
MCP_GPIOA_REG = 0x12                      # MCP23017 GPIOA address
MCP_IODIRA_REG = 0                        # MCP23017 IODIRA Address

conf = [MCP_IODIRA_REG, 0]                # Configure as output
buff1 = (MCP_GPIOA_REG, 0)                # Set GPIOA to 0
buff0 = [MCP_GPIOA_REG, 1]                # Set GPIOA to 1

i2c.writeto(Device_Address, bytearray(conf))

while True:
    i2c.writeto(Device_Address, bytearray(buff1))
    utime.sleep(1)
    i2c.writeto(Device_Address, bytearray(buff0))
```

```
    utime.sleep(1)
```

Figure 8.7: Program: MCP23017.

The program can be modified so that the memory functions of i2c are used. The modified program listing (Program: **MCP23017-2**) is shown in Figure 8.8.

```
#----------------------------------------------------------
#              I2C PORT EXPANDER
#              =================
#
# In this project the MCP23017 port expander chip is used.
# An LED is connected to port pin GPA0 of the port expander
# and this LED is flashed every second
#
# This version of the program uses the i2c memory functions
#
# Author: Dogan Ibrahim
# File  : MCP23017-2.py
# Date  : February 2021
#------------------------------------------------------------
from machine import Pin,I2C
import utime

i2c = machine.I2C(0, scl=Pin(9), sda=Pin(8), freq=100000)
print("i2c address=",i2c.scan())

Device_Address = 0x20                # MCP23017 I2C address
MCP_GPIOA_REG = 0x12                 # MCP23017 GPIOA address
MCP_IODIRA_REG = 0                   # MCP23017 IODIRA Address

i2c.writeto_mem(Device_Address, MCP_IODIRA_REG, b'0')

while True:
    i2c.writeto_mem(Device_Address, MCP_GPIOA_REG, b'1')
    utime.sleep(1)
    i2c.writeto_mem(Device_Address, MCP_GPIOA_REG, b'0')
    utime.sleep(1)
```

Figure 8.8: Modified program: MCP23017-2.

8.5 Project 2: EEPROM memory

Description: In this project we will be using the I^{2}C-bus-compatible 24LC256 type EEPROM memory chip and write the characters ABCD to memory locations starting from address 0x1000 of the memory. The data is then read from these locations and displayed on the Thonny screen to confirm that the write/read operation has been successful.

The aim: The aim of this project is to show how an I²C based EEPROM memory can be programmed using the Raspberry Pi Pico.

The 24LC256 memory

The 24LC256 is a 32 K × 8 (256 Kbit) EEPROM memory chip manufactured by Microchip Technology. The chip can be powered from 1.7 V to 5.5 V, with a standby current of 1 μA and a write current of 3 mA. The chip can operate from 100 kHz up to 1 MHz. A hardware write-protect pin is provided to disable writing to the chip. 24LC256 is capable of both random and sequential reads up to a 256 K boundary. The device has page write capability up to 64 bytes of data. The device has 32768 addresses, ranging from 0x0000 to 0x7FFF Figure 8.9 shows the pin layout of the chip.

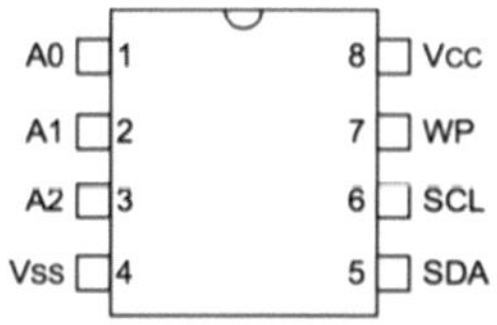

Figure 8.9: Pin layout of the 24LC256.

A0, A1 and A2 are used to set the LSB bits of the device I²C address. As shown below, the upper 4 bits of the device address are fixed at 1010 and the LSB bit is the R/W bit:

1	0	1	0	A2	A1	A0	R/W

For example, if A2 = A1 = A0 = 0 then the I²C address is 0xA0.

Vcc and Vss are the power supply pins.

WP is the write protection pin. If this pin is tied to Ground, writing is enabled. If connected to Vcc then the write operations have no effect.

Circuit diagram

The circuit diagram of the project is shown in Figure 8.10. In this project, I²C pins GP8 (I2C0 SDA) and GP9 (I2C0 SCL) of Raspberry Pi Pico are used. A0, A1 and A2 are connected to ground so that the device address is 0xA0. Also, the write protect pin WP is tied to ground. The SDA and SCL pins are pulled-up using 10-kohm resistors.

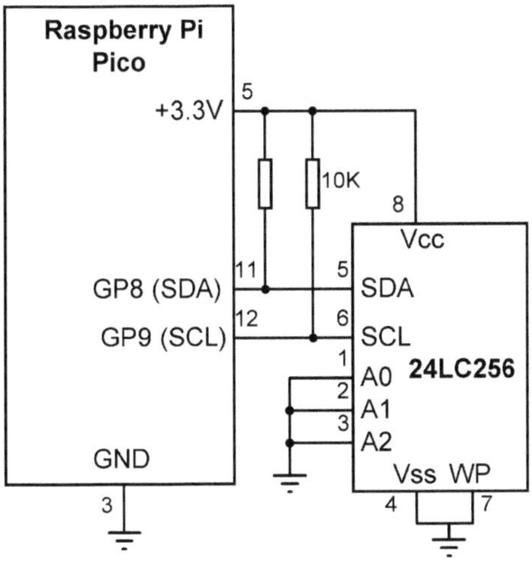

Figure 8.10: circuit diagram of the project.

Before going into details of the memory write and read operations, it is worthwhile to learn how this is done.

Memory-write operation

As an example, assume that we want to write byte 0x25 into memory location 0x0250. Figure 8.11 shows the write steps in detail. First of all, the START bit is sent on the bus, followed by the device address which is assumed to be 0xA0, with the LSB bit set to 0 to indicate that we wish to do a write operation.

The memory address 0x0250 is then split into upper and lower bytes as 0x02 and 0x50 and they are sent sequentially with the higher byte sent first over the bus. Then, the data byte 0x25 is sent (this is called **Byte Writing** since only one byte is written to memory). Notice that we can send multiple bytes (this is called **Page Writing** where up to 64 bytes can be written sequentially. There are 512 pages and each page is 64 bytes long) in the same transaction (an internal address counter is incremented automatically after a byte is sent). The write operation is terminated with the STOP bit. Notice that ACK bit is sent by the EEPROM between the byte transfers.

After a byte write command, the internal address counter will point to the address location following the one that was just written. Page write operations are limited to writing bytes within a single physical page (64 bytes), regardless of the number of bytes actually being written. Physical page boundaries start at addresses that are integer multiples of the page buffer size and end at addresses that are integer multiples of page size –1. If a page write command attempts to write across a physical page boundary, the result is that the data wraps around to the beginning of the current page (overwriting data previously stored there), instead of being written to the next page.

It is, therefore, necessary for the application software to prevent page write operations that would attempt to cross a page boundary (e.g. when writing long strings care should be taken when crossing a page boundary). Some of the page boundaries in bytes are:

Page 1: 0 – 63
Page 2: 64 – 127
Page 3: 128 – 191
Page 4: 192 – 255
Page 5: 256.......

Notice that the data sent the EEPROM is stored in a temporary buffer since a whole page consisting of 64 bytes is refreshed after every write operation. It is therefore important to detect when a write operation has been completed successfully.

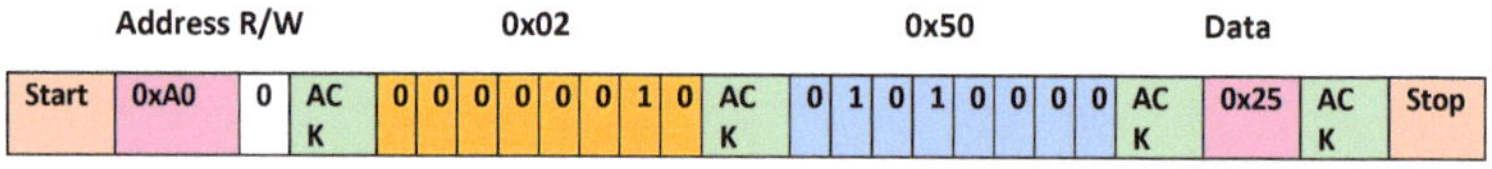

Figure 8.11: Memory Byte Writing operation.

Memory-read operation

Memory-read operations are slightly more complex. There are 3 types of reads: current address read, random read, and sequential read. Random read mode is probably the most commonly used mode where the master can access any memory location in a random manner.

As an example, assume that we want to read the byte at memory location 0x0250 (where 0x25 was stored in Figure 8.11). Figure 8.12 shows the read steps in detail. To perform a **Random Read**, the memory address must be sent first. This is done by an I²C device sending the memory address to the 24LC256 as part of a write operation (R/W bit set to '0'). Once the memory address is sent, the master generates a START condition following the ACK. This terminates the write operation, but not before the internal address counter is set. The master then issues the slave address again, but with the R/W bit set to a 1. The 24LC256 will then issue an ACK and transmit the 8-bit data word. The master will not acknowledge the transfer, though it generates a STOP condition, which causes the EEPROM to discontinue transmission. After a random read command, the internal address counter will point to the address location following the one that was just read.

In **Sequential Read** operation, an internal address pointer is incremented automatically after each read operation. This allows the entire memory contents to be read easily.

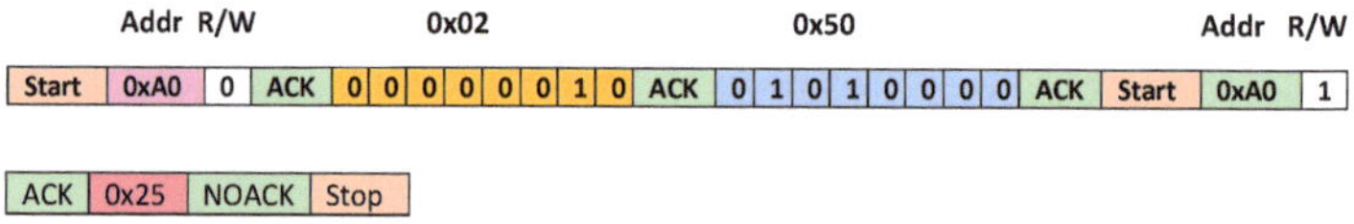

Figure 8.12: Random memory read operation.

Program listing: Figure 8.13 shows the program listing (Program: **EEPROM**). In this program the device address of the EEPROM chip was found to be 80 (hexadecimal 0x50). Inside the main program, a list **wmsg** is defined and is pre-loaded with the data **1357** which is the data to be written to the EEPROM memory. Also, another list called **rmsg** is declared which will be loaded with the data read from the memory chip. The program then calls function **Write** to write the contents of list **wmsg** to the memory chip, starting from address

0x10000. Function **Read** reads 4 bytes of data from the same memory locations and stores them in array **wmsg**. This data is then displayed on the PC screen. **Page writing** is used in this program where the memory address increments automatically after writing or reading a byte of data. **Sequential read** operation is done by the program where the memory address pointer is incremented automatically to point to the next location.

Function: Write

This function has 3 arguments:

memloc: starting memory address where the data will be stored to
data: the data to be stored
addrsize: size of the address

```
def Write(memloc, data,len):
            i2c.writeto_mem(Device_Address, memloc, data, addrsize = 16)
            utime.sleep_ms(10)
```

Function: Read

memloc: This function has two arguments: starting memory address where the data will be read from
len: Number of bytes to read
addrsize: size of the address

```
def Read(memloc, len):
            data = [0]*4
            data = i2c.readfrom_mem(Device_Address, memloc, 4,addrsize=16)
            return(data)
```

```
#-----------------------------------------------------------
#               I2C EEPROM READ/WRITE
#               =====================
#
# In this project a 24LC256 type I2C EEPROM memory chip is
# connected to the Raspberry Pi Pico. The program writes and
# then reads from the memory
#
# Author: Dogan Ibrahim
# File  : EEPROM.py
# Date  : February 2021
#-------------------------------------------------------------
from machine import Pin,I2C
import utime

i2c = machine.I2C(0, scl=Pin(9), sda=Pin(8), freq=100000)
print("i2c address=",i2c.scan())

len = 4
```

```
Device_Address = 0x50                        # EEPROM I2C address

#
# This function reads len bytes starting from specified memory
# address memloc (16 bits)
#
def Read(memloc, len):
    data = [0]*4
    data = i2c.readfrom_mem(Device_Address, memloc, 4,addrsize=16)
    return(data)

#
# This function writes the data to starting from the specified
# memory address memloc (16 bits)
#
def Write(memloc, data,len):
    i2c.writeto_mem(Device_Address, memloc, data, addrsize = 16)
    utime.sleep_ms(10)

wmsg = '1357'                               # Data to be written
rmsg = [0]*len                              # List for return data
Write(0x1000, wmsg, len)                    # Write the data
rmsg = Read(0x1000, len)                    # Read the data

#
# Display the data read starting from address 0x1000
#
print("Data read is: %c%c%c%c\n" %(rmsg[0],rmsg[1],rmsg[2],rmsg[3]))
```

Figure 8.13: Program: EEPROM.

The data displayed by the program was as follows:

i2c address = [80]
Data read is: 1357

8.6 Project 3: TMP102 temperature sensor

Description: In this project, the I^2C-compatible TMP102 temperature sensor chip is used. The ambient temperature is read every second and is displayed on the Thonny screen.

The aim: The aim of this project is to show how the temperature sensor chip TMP102 can be used in a program.

The TMP102

The TMP102 is an I^2C compatible, highly accurate temperature sensor chip with a built-in thermostat with the following basic features:

Supply voltage: 1.4 V to 3.6 V
Supply current: 10 µA
Accuracy: ±0.5 °C
Resolution: 12 bits (0.0625 °C)
Operating range: –40 °C to +125 °C

TMP102 is a 6-pin chip as shown in Figure 8.14. the pin descriptions are:

Pin	Name	Description
1	SCL	I2C line
2	GND	power supply ground
3	ALERT	Over-temperature alert. Open-drain output. Requires a pull-up resistor
4	ADD0	address select
5	V+	power supply
6	SDA	I2C line

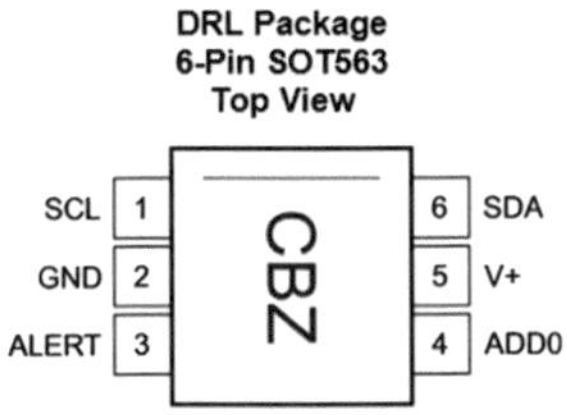

Figure 8.14: TMP102 pin layout.

The TMP102 supports the following operational modes:

- **Continuous conversion**: by default, an internal ADC converts the temperature into digital format with the default conversion rate of 4 Hz, with a conversion time of 26 ms. The conversion rate can be selected using bits **CR1** and **CR0** of the configuration register as: 0.25 Hz, 1 Hz, 4 Hz (default), and 8 Hz. In this project the default 4 Hz is used.
- **Extended mode**: Bit EM of the configuration register selects normal mode (EM = 0), or extended mode (EM = 1). In normal mode (default mode) the converted data is 12 bits. Extended mode is used if the temperature is above 128 °C and the converted data is 13 bits. In this project the normal mode is used.
- **Shutdown mode**: This mode is used to save power where the current consumption is reduced to less than 0.5 µA. The shutdown mode is entered when configuration register bit SD = 1. The default mode is normal operation (SD = 0).
- **One-shot conversion**: Setting configuration register bit OS to 1 selects the one-shot mode which is a single conversion mode. The default mode is continuous conversion (OS = 0).

- **Thermostat mode**: This mode indicates whether to operate in comparator mode (TM = 0) or in interrupt mode (TM = 1). The default is the comparator mode. In comparator mode, the Alert pin is activated when the temperature equals or exceeds the value in the T_{HIGH} register, and remains active until the temperature drops below T_{LOW}. In interrupt mode, the Alert pin is activated when the temperature exceeds T_{HIGH} or goes below T_{LOW} registers. The Alert pin is cleared when the host controller reads the temperature register.

A **Pointer Register** select various registers in the chip as shown in Table 8.1. The upper 6 bits of this register are 0s.

P1	P0	Register Selected
0	0	Temperature register (read only)
0	1	Configuration register
1	0	TLOW register
1	1	THIGH register

Table 8.1: Pointer register bits.

Table 8.2 shows the temperature register bits in normal mode (EM = 0).

BYTE 1:

D7	D6	D5	D4	D3	D2	D1	D0
T11	T10	T9	T8	T7	T7	T5	T4

BYTE 2:

D7	D6	D5	D4	D3	D2	D1	D0
T3	T2	T1	T0	0	0	0	0

Table 8.2: Temperature register bits.

Table 8.3 shows the configuration register bits. The power-up default bit configuration is shown in the Table.

BYTE 1:

D7	D6	D5	D4	D3	D2	D1	D0
OS	**R1**	**R0**	**F1**	**F0**	**POL**	**TM**	**SD**
0	1	1	0	0	0	0	0

BYTE 2:

D7	D6	D5	D4	D3	D2	D1	D0
CR1	**CR0**	**AL**	**EM**	**0**	**0**	**0**	**0**
1	0	1	0	0	0	0	0

Table 8.3: Configuration register bits.

The **Polarity** bit (POL) allows the user to adjust the polarity of the Alert pin output. If set to 0 (default), the Alert pin becomes active low. When set to 1, the Alert pin becomes active-High.

The default device address is 0x48. TMP102 is available as a module (breakout module) as shown in Figure 8.15. The temperature register address is 0x00 and this should be sent after sending the device address. This is then followed with a read command where 2 bytes are read from the TMP102. These 2 bytes contain the temperature data.

The temperature-reading sequence is given below.

- Master sends the device address 0x48 with the R/W set to 0.
- Device responds with ACK.
- Master sends the temperature register address 0x00.
- Device responds with ACK.
- Master resends device address 0x48 with the R/W bit set to 1.
- Master reads upper byte of temperature data.
- Device sends ACK.
- Master reads lower byte of temperature data.
- Device sends ACK.
- Master sends Stop condition on the bus.

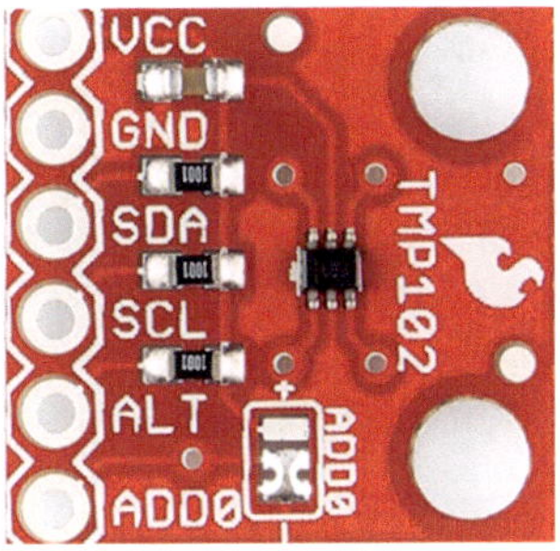

Figure 8.15: TMP102 as a module.

Block diagram: Figure 8.16 shows the block diagram of the project.

Figure 8.16: Block diagram of the project.

Circuit diagram: The circuit diagram of the project is shown in Figure 8.17. On-chip pull-up resistors are available on the TMP102 I²C bus lines, hence there is no need to use external pull-up resistors.

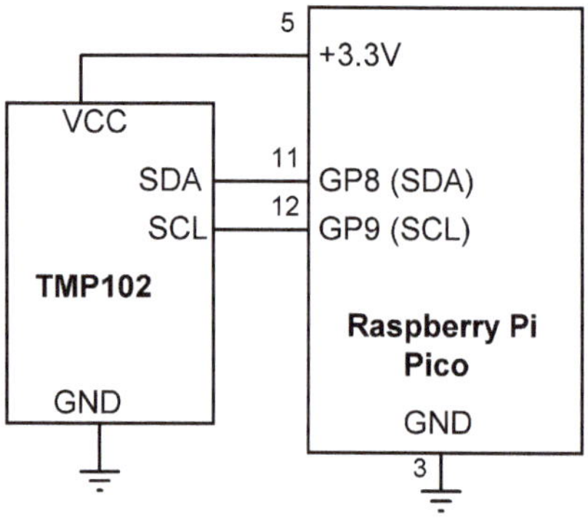

Figure 8.17: Circuit diagram of the project.

Program listing: Figure 8.18 shows the program listing (Program: **TMP102**). At the beginning of the program, the I²C address of TMP102 and the Pointer register addresses are defined. The Pointer register is set to 0 to select the temperature register.

The program runs inside a **while** loop and calls function **Read** every second. **Read** reads the temperature from TMP102, converts it into positive (or negative) degrees Celsius and then returns the reading to the main program. The two bytes read are combined to form the 12-bit temperature data in variable **temp**. If the temperature is negative, then it is in 2's complement form and its complement is taken and 1 is added to find the true negative value. By multiplying **temp** with the LSB we find the temperature in degrees Centigrade. The temperature is displayed on the Thonny screen as a floating point number.

Table 8.4 shows the data output format of the temperature. Let us look at two examples:

Example 1: Measured value = 0011 00100000 = 0x320 = 800 decimal

This is positive temperature, so the temperature is: 800 × 0.0625 = +50 ºC

Example 2: Measured value = 1110 01110000 = 0xE70

This is negative temperature. The complement is 0001 10001111, and adding 1 gives 0001 10010000 = 400 decimal. The temperature works out as: 400 × 0.0625 = 25, i.e. -25 ºC

Temperature	Digital Output (Binary)	Digital Output (Hex)
128	011111111111	7FF
100	011001000000	640
50	001100100000	320
0.25	000000000100	004
-0.25	111111111100	FFC
-25	111001110000	E70
-55	110010010000	C90

Table 8.4 The data output for some temperature readings.

```
#----------------------------------------------------------------
#               TMP102 TEMPERATURE SENSOR
#               =========================
#
# In this project a TMP102 type I2C compatible temperature
# sensor chip is connected to Raspberry Pi Pico. The temperature
# readings are displayed on the Thonny screen.
#
# Author: Dogan Ibrahim
# File  : TMP102.py
# Date  : February 2021
#------------------------------------------------------------------
from machine import Pin,I2C
import utime

i2c = machine.I2C(0, scl=Pin(9), sda=Pin(8), freq=100000)
print("i2c address=",i2c.scan())

Device_Address = 0x48                   # TMP102 I2C address
PointerReg = 0                          # TMP102 register

#
# This function reads the temperature, extracts degrees Celius
# and returns the temperature to the main calling program
#
def Read():
    data = [0, 0]
    LSB = 0.0625
    data = i2c.readfrom_mem(Device_Address, PointerReg, 2)
    temp = (data[0] << 4) | (data[1] >> 4)
```

```
        if temp > 0x7FF:
            temp = (~temp) & 0xFF
            temp = temp + 1
            temperature = -temp * LSB
        else:
            temperature = temp * LSB
        return(temperature)

#
# Main program reads and displays the temperature every second
#
while True:
    Temperature = Read()
    print("Temperature = %+5.2f" %Temperature)
    utime.sleep(1)
```

Figure 8.18: Program: TMP102.c.

Example output from the program is shown in Figure 8.19.

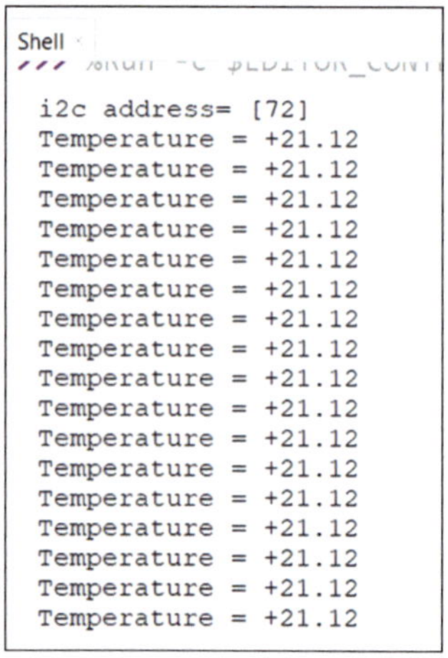
Shell

```
i2c address= [72]
Temperature = +21.12
Temperature = +21.12
Temperature = +21.12
Temperature = +21.12
Temperature = +21.12
Temperature = +21.12
Temperature = +21.12
Temperature = +21.12
Temperature = +21.12
Temperature = +21.12
Temperature = +21.12
Temperature = +21.12
Temperature = +21.12
Temperature = +21.12
Temperature = +21.12
Temperature = +21.12
Temperature = +21.12
```

Figure 8.19: Example output from the program.

8.7 Project 4: BMP280 temperature and atmospheric pressure sensor

Description: In this project the I²C compatible BMP280 module is used to read and display the ambient temperature and atmospheric pressure on the Thonny screen.

The aim: The aim of this project is to show how the BMP280 chip can be used in a program.

The BMP280

The BMP280 (Figure 8.20) is an I²C compatible highly accurate temperature and atmospheric pressure sensor chip having the following basic features:

- Temperature range: –40 to +85ºC
- Pressure range: 300 to 1100 hPa
- Relative pressure accuracy: ±0.12 hPa
- Current consumption: 2.7 µA
- I^2C and SPI interface
- Supply voltage: 1.71 V to 3.6 V
- Footprint 2.0 x 2.5 mm^2
- 8-pin LGA metal package

The BMP280, manufactured by Bosch, is used in many applications, including navigation, temperature and pressure monitoring, elevator and floor detection (altitude measurement), leisure and sports, weather forecast, mobile phones, tablets, GPS devices, flying toys, watches, and so on.

The BMP280 consists of a Piezo-resistive pressure sensing element and a mixed-signal ASIC which performs ADC conversions for the digital interface. The chip can be operated in three power modes: sleep mode, normal mode, and forced mode. The chip is equipped with a built-in digital IIR filter to minimize disturbances in the output.

Interested readers can get detailed information on the BMP280 from the *BMP280 Digital Pressure Sensor* datasheet
(link: https://www.mouser.co.uk/datasheet/2/783/BST_BMP280_DS001-1509562.pdf)

Figure 8.20: BMP280 module.

Block diagram: Figure 8.21 shows the block diagram of the project.

Figure 8.21: Block diagram of the project.

Circuit diagram: The BMP280 can be operated either in I^2C or in SPI mode. In this project we are using the I^2C mode. The circuit diagram of the project is shown in Figure 8.22. I^2C pins GP8 (SDA) and GP9 (SCL) of the Raspberry Pi Pico are connected to the corresponding SDA and SCL pins of the BMP280.

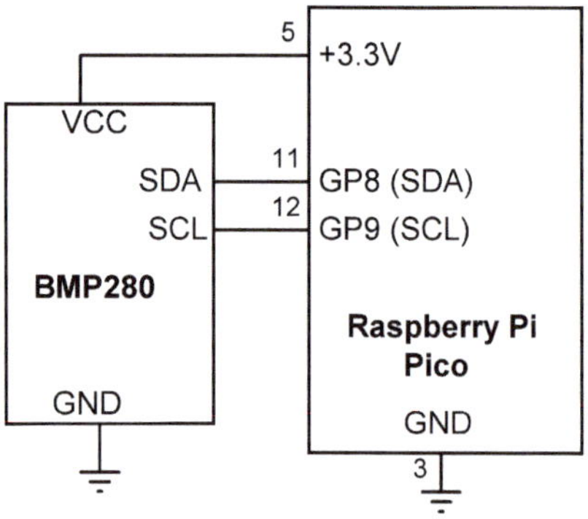

Figure 8.22: Circuit diagram of the project.

Program listing: Programming the BMP280 is a complex process. In this project the program has been adapted by the author to work with the Raspberry Pi Pico. The program can be found at:

https://github.com/ControlEverythingCommunity/BMP280/blob/master/Python/BMP280.py

This program reads the temperature and pressure from the BMP280 chip whose I^{2}C address is 118 (0x76).
Figure 8.23 shows the program listing (Program: **ReadBMP280**) where the temperature and pressure readings are displayed on the Thonny screen. The I^{2}C address is also displayed on the screen.

```
#------------------------------------------------------------
#              BMP280 TEMPERATURE AND PRESSURE SENSOR
#              =======================================
#
# In this project the BMP280 temperature and pressure sensor
# chip is used and the readings are displayed on the screen
# every 5 seconds
#
# Author: Dogan Ibrahim
# File  : ReadBMP280.py
# Date  : February 2021
#--------------------------------------------------------------
from machine import Pin,I2C
import utime
import utime

i2c = machine.I2C(0, scl=Pin(9), sda=Pin(8), freq=100000)
print("i2c address=" ,i2c.scan())


#
```

```
# THis function returns the temperature and pressure readings
# Adapted for the RAspberry Pi Pico from:
#
# https://github.com/ControlEverythingCommunity/
#       BMP280/blob/master/Python/BMP280.py
#
def BMP280():
    # BMP280 address, 0x76(118)
    # Read data back from 0x88(136), 24 bytes
    b1 = i2c.readfrom_mem(0x76, 0x88, 24)

    # Convert the data
    # Temp coefficents
    dig_T1 = b1[1] * 256 + b1[0]
    dig_T2 = b1[3] * 256 + b1[2]
    if dig_T2 > 32767 :
        dig_T2 -= 65536
    dig_T3 = b1[5] * 256 + b1[4]
    if dig_T3 > 32767 :
        dig_T3 -= 65536

# Pressure coefficents
    dig_P1 = b1[7] * 256 + b1[6]
    dig_P2 = b1[9] * 256 + b1[8]
    if dig_P2 > 32767 :
        dig_P2 -= 65536
    dig_P3 = b1[11] * 256 + b1[10]
    if dig_P3 > 32767 :
        dig_P3 -= 65536
    dig_P4 = b1[13] * 256 + b1[12]
    if dig_P4 > 32767 :
        dig_P4 -= 65536
    dig_P5 = b1[15] * 256 + b1[14]
    if dig_P5 > 32767 :
        dig_P5 -= 65536
    dig_P6 = b1[17] * 256 + b1[16]
    if dig_P6 > 32767 :
        dig_P6 -= 65536
    dig_P7 = b1[19] * 256 + b1[18]
    if dig_P7 > 32767 :
        dig_P7 -= 65536
    dig_P8 = b1[21] * 256 + b1[20]
    if dig_P8 > 32767 :
        dig_P8 -= 65536
    dig_P9 = b1[23] * 256 + b1[22]
    if dig_P9 > 32767 :
```

```
        dig_P9 -= 65536

# BMP280 address, 0x76(118)
# Select Control measurement register, 0xF4(244)
#             0x27(39)       Pressure and Temperature Oversampling rate = 1
#                                  Normal mode
    i2c.writeto_mem(0x76, 0xF4, b'\x27')
# BMP280 address, 0x76(118)
# Select Configuration register, 0xF5(245)
#             0xA0(00)       Stand_by time = 1000 ms
    i2c.writeto_mem(0x76, 0xF5, b'\xA0')

    utime.sleep(0.5)

# BMP280 address, 0x76(118)
# Read data back from 0xF7(247), 8 bytes
# Pressure MSB, Pressure LSB, Pressure xLSB, Temperature MSB, Temperature LSB
# Temperature xLSB, Humidity MSB, Humidity LSB
    data = i2c.readfrom_mem(0x76, 0xF7, 8)

# Convert pressure and temperature data to 19-bits
    adc_p = ((data[0] * 65536) + (data[1] * 256) + (data[2] & 0xF0)) / 16
    adc_t = ((data[3] * 65536) + (data[4] * 256) + (data[5] & 0xF0)) / 16

# Temperature offset calculations
    var1 = ((adc_t) / 16384.0 - (dig_T1) / 1024.0) * (dig_T2)
    var2 = (((adc_t) / 131072.0 - (dig_T1) / 8192.0) * ((adc_t)/131072.0 -
(dig_T1)/8192.0)) * (dig_T3)
    t_fine = (var1 + var2)
    cTemp = (var1 + var2) / 5120.0


# Pressure offset calculations
    var1 = (t_fine / 2.0) - 64000.0
    var2 = var1 * var1 * (dig_P6) / 32768.0
    var2 = var2 + var1 * (dig_P5) * 2.0
    var2 = (var2 / 4.0) + ((dig_P4) * 65536.0)
    var1 = ((dig_P3) * var1 * var1 / 524288.0 + ( dig_P2) * var1) / 524288.0
    var1 = (1.0 + var1 / 32768.0) * (dig_P1)
    p = 1048576.0 - adc_p
    p = (p - (var2 / 4096.0)) * 6250.0 / var1
    var1 = (dig_P9) * p * p / 2147483648.0
    var2 = p * (dig_P8) / 32768.0
    pressure = (p + (var1 + var2 + (dig_P7)) / 16.0) / 100
    return(cTemp, pressure)
```

```
#
# Main program, read and siaplay the temperature and pressure
#
while True:
    T,P = BMP280()
    print("Temperature in Celsius : %.2f C" %T)
    print("Pressure : %.2f hPa \n" %P)
    utime.sleep(5)
```

Figure 8.23: Program: ReadBMP280.

Figure 8.24 shows example output from the program.

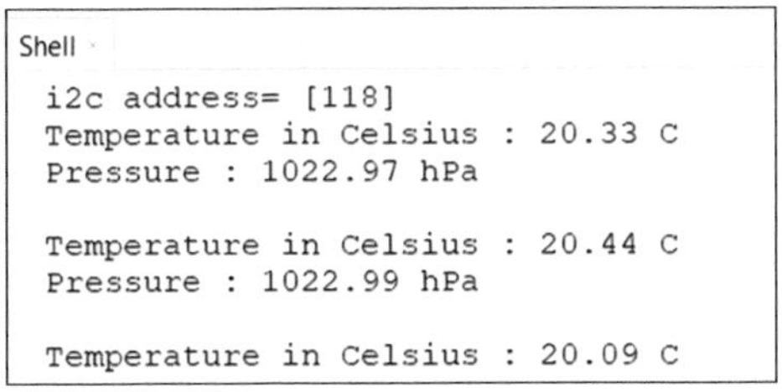

Figure 8.24: Example output from the program.

Building the BMP280 reading program into a module

The BMP280 reading program can be built into a module so that it can be imported at the beginning of the program and used with ease. The steps to follow are given below.

- Use the Thonny to save the function given in Figure 8.25 with the name **bmp280.py** on your Raspberry Pi Pico.

```
import machine
import utime
def BMP280():
    i2c = machine.I2C(0, scl=machine.Pin(9), sda=machine.Pin(8), freq=100000)
    # BMP280 address, 0x76(118)
    # Read data back from 0x88(136), 24 bytes
    b1 = i2c.readfrom_mem(0x76, 0x88, 24)

    # Convert the data
    # Temp coefficents
    dig_T1 = b1[1] * 256 + b1[0]
    dig_T2 = b1[3] * 256 + b1[2]
    if dig_T2 > 32767 :
        dig_T2 -= 65536
    dig_T3 = b1[5] * 256 + b1[4]
    if dig_T3 > 32767 :
        dig_T3 -= 65536
```

```
# Pressure coefficents
    dig_P1 = b1[7] * 256 + b1[6]
    dig_P2 = b1[9] * 256 + b1[8]
    if dig_P2 > 32767 :
        dig_P2 -= 65536
    dig_P3 = b1[11] * 256 + b1[10]
    if dig_P3 > 32767 :
        dig_P3 -= 65536
    dig_P4 = b1[13] * 256 + b1[12]
    if dig_P4 > 32767 :
        dig_P4 -= 65536
    dig_P5 = b1[15] * 256 + b1[14]
    if dig_P5 > 32767 :
        dig_P5 -= 65536
    dig_P6 = b1[17] * 256 + b1[16]
    if dig_P6 > 32767 :
        dig_P6 -= 65536
    dig_P7 = b1[19] * 256 + b1[18]
    if dig_P7 > 32767 :
        dig_P7 -= 65536
    dig_P8 = b1[21] * 256 + b1[20]
    if dig_P8 > 32767 :
        dig_P8 -= 65536
    dig_P9 = b1[23] * 256 + b1[22]
    if dig_P9 > 32767 :
        dig_P9 -= 65536

# BMP280 address, 0x76(118)
# Select Control measurement register, 0xF4(244)
#             0x27(39)       Pressure and Temperature Oversampling rate = 1
#                                  Normal mode
    i2c.writeto_mem(0x76, 0xF4, b'\x27')
# BMP280 address, 0x76(118)
# Select Configuration register, 0xF5(245)
#             0xA0(00)       Stand_by time = 1000 ms
    i2c.writeto_mem(0x76, 0xF5, b'\xA0')

    utime.sleep(0.5)

# BMP280 address, 0x76(118)
# Read data back from 0xF7(247), 8 bytes
# Pressure MSB, Pressure LSB, Pressure xLSB, Temperature MSB, Temperature LSB
# Temperature xLSB, Humidity MSB, Humidity LSB
    data = i2c.readfrom_mem(0x76, 0xF7, 8)
```

```
# Convert pressure and temperature data to 19-bits
    adc_p = ((data[0] * 65536) + (data[1] * 256) + (data[2] & 0xF0)) / 16
    adc_t = ((data[3] * 65536) + (data[4] * 256) + (data[5] & 0xF0)) / 16

# Temperature offset calculations
    var1 = ((adc_t) / 16384.0 - (dig_T1) / 1024.0) * (dig_T2)
    var2 = (((adc_t) / 131072.0 - (dig_T1) / 8192.0) * ((adc_t)/131072.0 -
(dig_T1)/8192.0)) * (dig_T3)
    t_fine = (var1 + var2)
    cTemp = (var1 + var2) / 5120.0


# Pressure offset calculations
    var1 = (t_fine / 2.0) - 64000.0
    var2 = var1 * var1 * (dig_P6) / 32768.0
    var2 = var2 + var1 * (dig_P5) * 2.0
    var2 = (var2 / 4.0) + ((dig_P4) * 65536.0)
    var1 = ((dig_P3) * var1 * var1 / 524288.0 + ( dig_P2) * var1) / 524288.0
    var1 = (1.0 + var1 / 32768.0) * (dig_P1)
    p = 1048576.0 - adc_p
    p = (p - (var2 / 4096.0)) * 6250.0 / var1
    var1 = (dig_P9) * p * p / 2147483648.0
    var2 = p * (dig_P8) / 32768.0
    pressure = (p + (var1 + var2 + (dig_P7)) / 16.0) / 100
    return(cTemp, pressure)
```

Figure 8.25: Function 'bmp280.py'.

- Modify the program **ReadBMP280-2** in Figure 8.23 as shown in Figure 8.26.

```
#-----------------------------------------------------------
#              BMP280 TEMPERATURE AND PRESSURE SENSOR
#              ======================================
#
# In this project the BMP280 temperature and pressure sensor
# is connected to the Raspberry Pi Pico. The temperature and
# pressure readings are displayed every 5 seconds on the
# Thonny screen
#
# In this version of the program the BMP280 code is imported
# as a module
#
# Author: Dogan Ibrahim
# File  : ReadBMP280-2.py
# Date  : February 2021
#-------------------------------------------------------------
```

```
from machine import Pin,I2C
import utime
import bmp280

i2c = machine.I2C(0, scl=Pin(9), sda=Pin(8), freq=100000)
print("i2c address=" ,i2c.scan())

while True:
    T,P = bmp280.BMP280()
    print("Temperature in Celsius : %.2f C" %T)
    print("Pressure : %.2f hPa \n" %P)
    utime.sleep(5)
```

Figure 8.26: Modified program: ReadBMP280-2.

8.8 Project 5: Display BMP280 temperature and atmospheric pressure on an LCD

Description: This project is similar to the previous project, but here the temperature and pressure readings are displayed on the LCD.

Block diagram: Figure 8.27 shows the block diagram of the project.

Figure 8.27: Block diagram of the project.

Circuit diagram: The circuit diagram of the project is shown in Figure 8.28.

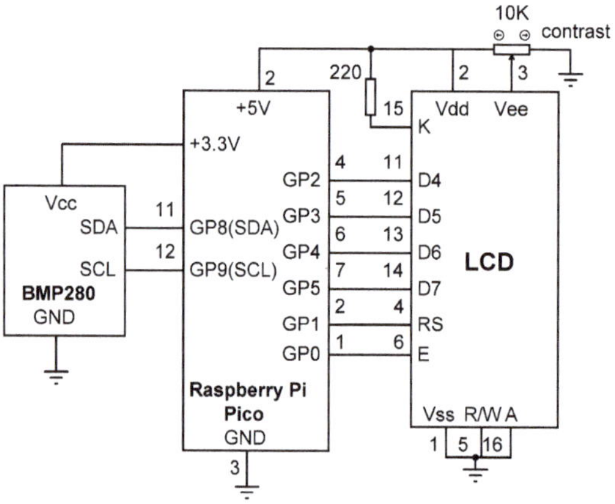

Figure 8.28: Circuit diagram of the project.

Program listing: Figure 8.29 shows the program listing (Program: **TempPres**). At the beginning of the program modules bmp280, utime, I²C, and LCD are imported to the program and the LCD is initialized. Inside the program loop the temperature and pressure readings are displayed on the top and bottom rows of the LCD respectively.

```
#-----------------------------------------------------------
#  DISPLAY BMP280 TEMPERATURE AND PRESSURE READINGS ON LCD
#  =========================================================
#
# In this project a BMP280 temperature and pressure sensor
# module is connected to Raspberry Pi Pico. The readings
# are displayed on LCD
#
# Author: Dogan Ibrahim
# File  : TempPres.py
# Date  : February 2021
#------------------------------------------------------------
from machine import Pin,I2C
import utime
import bmp280
import LCD

LCD.lcd_init()

while True:
    T,P = bmp280.BMP280()                     # Read T and P
    Temp = "T=" + str(T)[:5] + " C"           # Format T
    Press = "P=" + str(P)[:6] + " hPa"        # Format P
    LCD.lcd_clear()                           # Clear LCD
    LCD.lcd_puts(Temp)                        # Display Temperature
    LCD.lcd_goto(0, 1)                        # At 0, 1
    LCD.lcd_puts(Press)                       # Display Pressure
    utime.sleep(5)                            # Wait 5 seconds
```

Figure 8.29: Program: TempPres.

Figure 8.30 shows an example of a pressure reading appearing on the LCD.

Figure 8.30: Example display on the LCD.

Chapter 9 • The SPI Bus Interface

9.1 Overview

In this Chapter we shall be developing projects using the SPI bus (serial Peripheral Interface) with the Raspberry Pi Pico. The SPI bus is commonly a widely used protocol to connect sensors and many other devices to microcontrollers. The SPI bus is a master-slave type bus protocol. In this protocol, one device (the microcontroller) is designated as the master, and one or more other devices (usually sensors) are designated as slaves. In a minimum bus configuration there is one master and only one slave. The master establishes communication with the slaves and controls all the activity on the bus.
Figure 9.1 shows an SPI bus example with one master and 3 slaves. The SPI bus uses 3 signals: clock (SCK), data in (SDI, or RX), and data out (SDO, or TX). SDO of the master is connected to the SDIs of the slaves, and SDOs of the slaves are connected to the SDI of the master. The master generates the SCK signals to enable data to be transferred on the bus. In every clock pulse one bit of data is moved from master to slave, or from slave to master. The communication is only between a master and a slave, and the slaves cannot communicate with each other. It is important to note that only one slave can be active at any time since there is no mechanism to identify the slaves. Thus, slave devices have enable lines (e.g. CS or CE) which are normally controlled by the master. A typical communication sequence between a master and several slaves is given below.

- Master enables slave 1.
- Master sends SCK signals to read or write data to slave 1.
- Master disables slave 1 and enables slave 2.
- Master sends SCK signals to read or write data to slave 2.
- The above process continues as required.

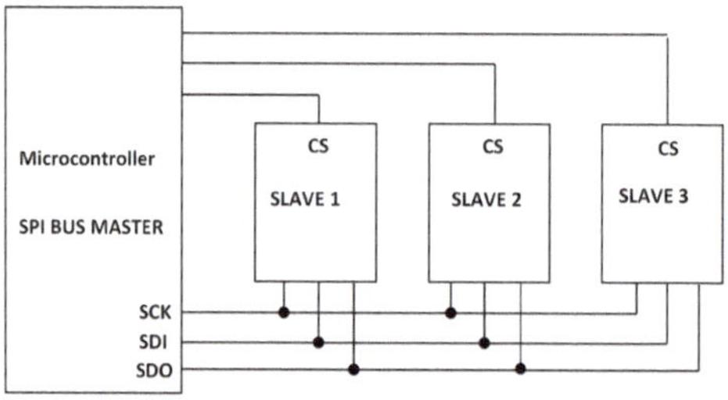

Figure 9.1: SPI bus with one master and 3 slaves.

The SPI signal names are also called MISO (Master in, Slave out), and MOSI (Master out, Slave in). Clock signal SCK is also called SCLK and the CS is also called SSEL. In the SPI projects in this Chapter the Raspberry Pi is the master and one or more slaves are connected to the bus. Transactions over the SPI bus are started by enabling the SCK line. The master then asserts the SSEL line Low so that data transmission can begin. The data transmission involves two registers, one in the master and one in the slave device. Data is shifted out from the master into the slave with the MSB bit first. If more data is to be transferred, then the process is repeated. Data exchange is complete when the master stops sending clock pulses and deselects the slave device.

The master and the slave must agree on the clock polarity and phase on the line, which are known as the **SPI bus modes**. These two settings go by the names 'Clock Polarity' (CPOL) and 'Clock Phase' (CPHA) respectively. CPOL and CPHA can have the following values:

CPOL	Clock-Active State
1	Clock active High
1	Clock active Low

CPHA	Clock Phase
1	Clock out of phase with data
2	Clock in phase with data

The four SPI modes are:

Mode	CPOL	CPHA
0	0	0
1	0	1
2	1	0
3	1	1

When CPOL = 0, the active state of the clock is 1, and its idle state is 0. For CPHA = 0, data is captured on the rising clock, and data is shifted out on the falling clock. For CPHA = 1, data is captured on the falling edge of the clock and gets shifted out on the rising edge of the clock.

When CPOL = 1, the active state of the clock is 0, and its idle state is 1. For CPHA = 0, data is captured on the falling edge of the clock and gets output on the rising edge. For CPHA = 1, data is captured on the rising edge of the clock and gets shifted out on the falling edge.

9.2 Raspberry Pi Pico SPI ports

There are 2 SPI ports on the Raspberry Pi Pico, named SPI0 and SPI1. Figure 9.2 shows the SPI pin configuration.

Figure 9.2: Raspberry Pi Pico SPI pins.

In the remaining sections of this Chapter we will be developing a project using the SPI bus.

9.3 Project 1: SPI Port expander

Description: A simple project is given in this section to show how the SPI functions can be used in a program. This project is very similar to the port expender project in the previous Chapter. In that project the I²C compatible chip MCP23017 was used. In this project, the SPI-bus-compatible port expander chip type MCP23S17 is used to give additional 16 I/O ports to the Raspberry Pi Pico. The operation of the MCP23S17 is identical to the operation of MCP23017, except that the MCP23S17 uses the SPI bus. In this project, an LED is connected to MCP23S17 port pin GPA0 and the LED is flashed ON and OFF every second. A 470-ohm current limiting resistor is used in series with the LED.

The aim: The aim of this project is to show how the SPI bus can be used in Raspberry Pi Pico based projects.

Block diagram: The block diagram of the project is same as in Figure 8.3, but the MCP23017 chip is replaced with the MCP23S17.

The MCP23S17

The MCP23S17 is a 28-pin chip with some interesting features:

- 16 bidirectional I/O ports
- Up to 1.7 MHz operation on I²C bus
- Interrupt capability
- External reset input

- Low standby current
- +1.8 V to +5.5 V operation
- 3 address pins, allowing up to 8 devices to be used on the SPI bus
- 28-pin DIL package

The pin configuration is shown in Figure 9.3, which is same as the pin configuration of MCP23017, but SPI pins are used instead of I²C pins.

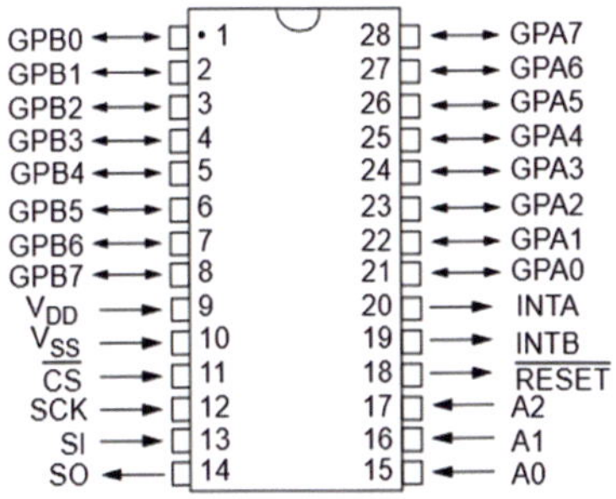

Figure 9.3: Pin configuration of the MCP23S17.

The pin descriptions are given in Table 9.1.

Pin	Description
GPA0-GPA7	Port A pins
GPB0-GPB7	Port B pins
VDD	Power supply
VSS	Ground
SI	SPI MOSI data pin
SCK	SPI clock pin
SO	SPI MISO data pin
CS	SPI SSEL chip enable pin
A0-A2	I2C address pins
RESET	Reset pin
INTA	Interrupt pin
INTB	Interrupt pin

Table 8.1: MCP23S17 pin descriptions.

The MCP23S17 is a slave-SPI device. The slave address contains four upper fixed bits (0100) and three user-defined hardware address bits (pins A2, A1 and A0) with the read/write bit filling out the control byte. These address bits are enabled/disabled by control register IOCON.HAEN. By default, the user address bits are disabled at power-up (i.e. IOCON.HAEN = 0) and A2 = A1 = A0 = 0. and the chip is addressed with 0x40. As such, we can use two MCP23S17 chips on SPI0 by connecting one CS bit to CE0, and the other one to CE1 and addressing both chips with 0x40. By setting bit HAEN to 1, we can change the addresses of the devices in multiple MCP23S17 based applications (e.g. more than 2) by connecting the A2, A1, and A0 accordingly. 16 such chips can be connected (8 to CE0 and 8 to CE1), corresponding to 16 × 16 = 256 I/O ports. Figure 9.4 and Figure 9.5 show the addressing format. The address pins should be externally biased even if disabled.

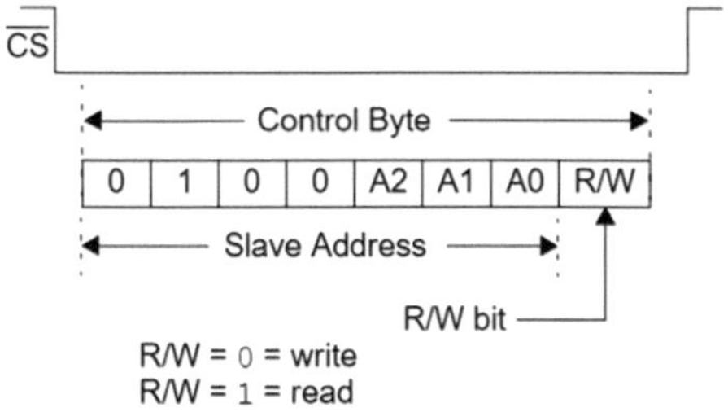

Figure 9.4: MCP23S17 control byte format.

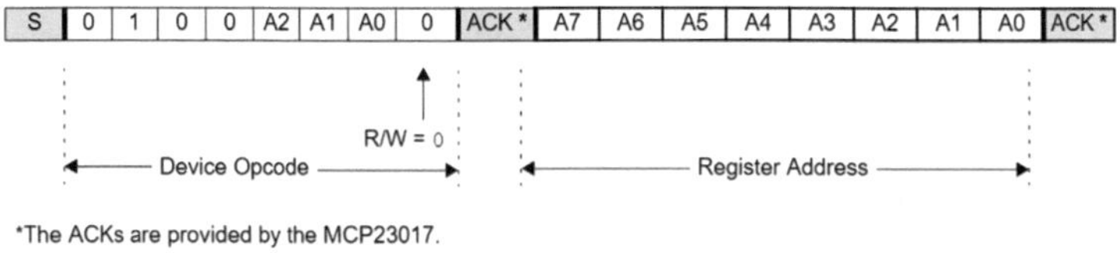

Figure 9.5: MCP23S17 addressing registers.

Like the MCP23017, the MCP23S17 chip has 8 internal registers that can be configured for its operation. The device can either be operated in 16-bit mode or in two 8-bit mode, by configuring bit IOCON.BANK. On power-up this bit is cleared which chooses the two 8-bit mode by default.

The I/O direction of the port pins are controlled with registers IODIRA (at address 0x00) and IODIRB (at address 0x01). Clearing a bit to 0 in these registers makes the corresponding port pin(s) as output(s). Similarly, setting a bit to 1 in these registers make the corresponding port pin(s) input(s). GPIOA and GPIOB register addresses are 0x12 and 0x13 respectively. This is shown in Figure 9.6.

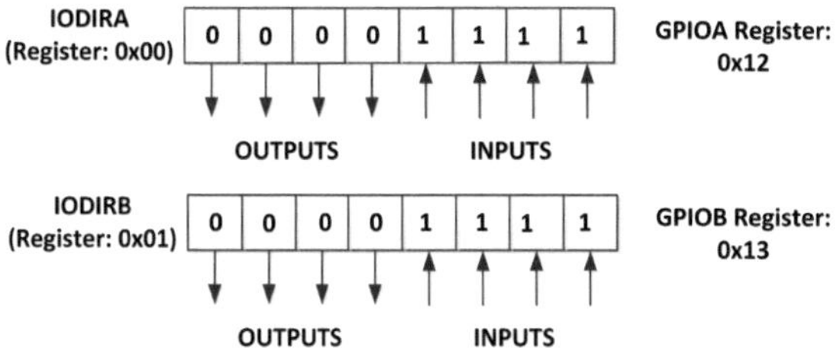

Figure 9.6: Configuring the I/O ports.

Further information on the MCP23S17 chip can be obtained from the Microchip Inc data sheet at the following web site:

http://ww1.microchip.com/downloads/en/DeviceDoc/20001952C.pdf

Circuit diagram: Figure 9.7 shows the circuit diagram of the project. SPI0 pins at GP3 (SPI0 TX) and GP2 (SPI0 SCK) are used to interface to the chip. CS is controlled separately and in this project GP26 is used as the CS pin. SPI0 RX pin is not used in this project since there is no input from the MCP23S17.

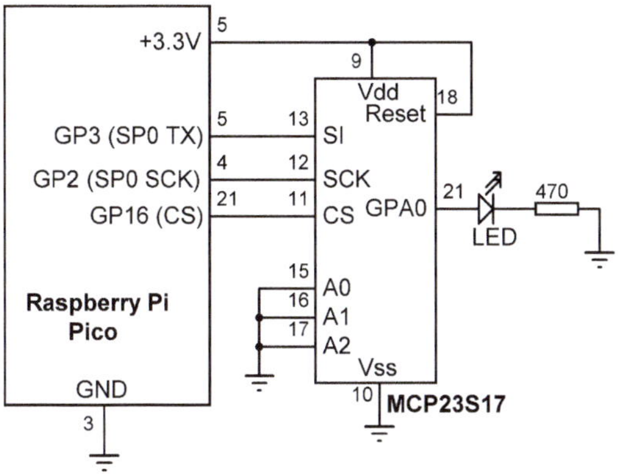

Figure 9.7: Circuit diagram of the project.

Program listing: Figure 9.8 shows the program listing (Program: **MCP23S17**). The programming of the MCP23S17 chip is as follows (notice that not all SPI devices require device addresses):

- send device address (0x40 in this project);
- send register address;
- send register data.

First of all, we have to program the I/O direction register **IODIRA** to 0 so that PORTA pins are outputs. This register has address 0x0. Then, we should program bit 0 of PORTA (pin: GPIOA) where the LED is connected to. The address of register **GPIOA** is 0x12.
At the beginning of the program the SPI interface signals between the Raspberry Pi Pico and MCP23S17 are defined. The required addresses of the MCP23S17 and the **CS** connection are then defined, and CS is initially set to 1 so that the MCP23S17 chip command mode is disabled (CS must be controlled separately).

Function **Configure** configures PORTA as output. Function **Send** sends data to the specified port register (**RegAddr**) so that the required pin is at logic 1 or 0. Data is either 0 or 1. When 1, the LED is turned ON, and when 0 the LED is turned OFF. The main program runs in a loop and calls function **Send** every second to flash the LED.

```
#------------------------------------------------------------
#               SPI BUS PORT EXPANDER
#               =====================
#
# In this project the SPI bus compatible MCP23S17 chip is used
# to add 16 more ports to Raspberry Pi Pico.An LED is connected
# to pin GPA0 of the expander and the LED is flashed every
# second
#
# Author: Dogan Ibrahim
# File  : MCP23S17.py
# Date  : February 2021
#--------------------------------------------------------------
from machine import Pin,SPI
import utime

spi_sck = Pin(2)                        # SCK pin at GP2
spi_tx = Pin(3)                         # TX pin at GP3
spi_rx = Pin(0)                         # RX pin at GP0 (not used)

spi = SPI(0,sck=spi_sck,mosi=spi_tx,miso=spi_rx,baudrate=100000)

Device_Address = 0x40                   # MCP23S17 SPI address
MCP_GPIOA = 0x12                        # MCP23S17 GPIOA address
MCP_IODIRA = 0                          # MCP IODIRA address
CS = Pin(16, Pin.OUT)                   # CS
CS.value(1)                             # Disable chip

#
# This function configures PORTA as output
#
def Configure():
    buff = [0, 0, 0]
    buff[0] = Device_Address
    buff[1] = MCP_IODIRA
    buff[2] = 0
    CS.value(0)
    spi.write(bytearray(buff))
    CS.value(1)

#
# This function sends data to register RegAddr
#
def Send(RegAddr, data):
    buff = [0, 0, 0]
    buff[0] = Device_Address
```

```
    buff[1] = RegAddr
    buff[2] = data
    CS.value(0)
    spi.write(bytearray(buff))
    CS.value(1)

#
# Main program reads and displays the temperature every second
#
while True:
    Configure()

    while True:
        Send(MCP_GPIOA, 1)              # LED ON
        utime.sleep(1)                  # 1 second delay
        Send(MCP_GPIOA, 0)              # LED OFF
        utime.sleep(1)                  # 1 second delay
```

Figure 9.8: Program 'MCP23S17'.

Raspberry Pi Pico supports the following SPI functions:

`spi.read(nbytes)`	read nbytes
`spi.readinto(buffer)`	read into the specified buffer
`spi.write(buffer)`	write buffer contents to the SPI bus
`spi.write_readinto(wbuffer, rbuffer))`	write from wbuffer while reading into rbuffer (both buffers must have the same length)

Default SPI bus settings are:

baud rate:	1,000,000	can be set as required
polarity:	0	can be 0 or 1
phase:	0	can be 0 or 1
bits:	8	should be 8
firstbit:	MSB	can be SPI.MSB or SPI.LSB
SPI0 SCK:	GP6	
SPI0 MOSI	GP7	
SPI0 MISO	GP4	
SPI1 SCK	GP10	
SPI1 MOSI	GP11	
SPI1 MISO	GP8	

sck, **mosi**, and **miso** are the SPI pins and they can be assigned to GPIO pins using the **Pin** functions (see Figure 9.8).

Chapter 10 • Wi-Fi with the Raspberry Pi Pico

10.1 Overview

In this Chapter we shall be developing projects using a Wi-Fi link to establish communication between the Raspberry Pi Pico and a smartphone.

10.2 Project 1: Controlling an LED from a smartphone using Wi-Fi

Description: In this project we will be sending commands over the Wi-Fi link from a mobile phone to control an LED (the LED can be replaced with a relay for example to control an equipment) connected to the Raspberry Pi Pico. Commands must be terminated with a Return (CR/LF or 'newline'). Valid commands include:

LON	Turn LED ON
LOFF	Turn LED OFF

Aim: The aim of this project is to showcase the use the Wi-Fi connectivity on the Raspberry Pi Pico.

Pico Wi-Fi connectivity: The Raspberry Pi Pico has no built-in Wi-Fi module and as such it cannot be connected to a Wi-Fi network without interfacing it to an external Wi-Fi module. Perhaps the easiest and the cheapest way of providing Wi-Fi capability to the Pico is by using an ESP-01 processor board. This is a tiny board (see Figure 10.1), measuring only 2.7 cm × 1.2 cm, and based on the ESP8266 processor chip, and costing around $3 USD. The ESP-01 has the following motivating features:

- Operating voltage: +3.3 V
- Interface: using simple AT commands over serial port/UART
- Integrated TCP/IP protocol stack. 802.11 b/g/n
- No external components required

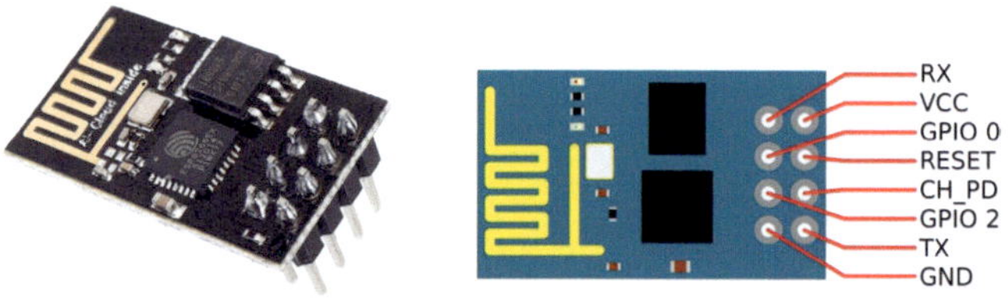

Figure 10.1: ESP-01 processor board.

ESP-01 communicates with the host processor through its TX and RX serial port pin. It is an 8-pin board with pin names as follows:

VCC:	+3.3 V power supply pin
GND:	Power supply ground
GPIO0:	I/O pin. This pin must be connected to +3.3 V for normal operation, and to GND for uploading firmware to the chip
GPIO2:	General purpose I/O pin

RST:	Reset pin. Must be connected to +3.3 V for normal operation
CH_PD:	Enable pin. Must be connected to +3.3 V for normal operation
TX:	Serial output pin
RX:	Serial input pin

The ESP-01's pins are not standard breadboard-compatible, so an adaptor is required if the board is to be attached to a breadboard (see Figure 10.2).

Figure 10.2: ESP-01 breadboard adapter.

Block Diagram: Figure 10.3 shows the project block diagram.

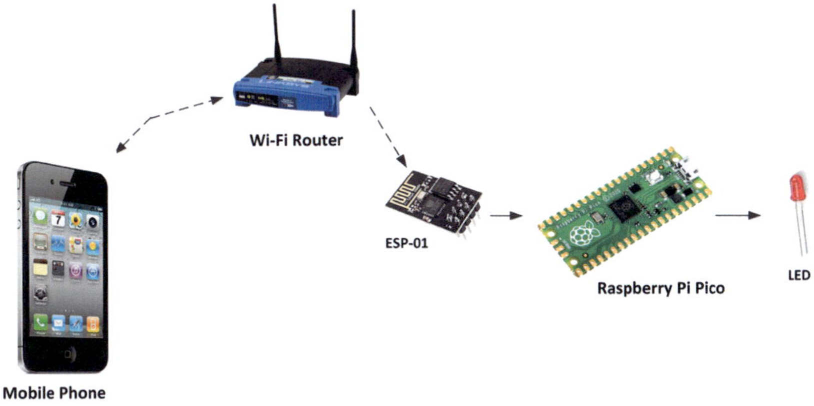

Figure 10.3: Block diagram of the project.

Circuit Diagram: Figure 10.4 shows the circuit diagram of the project. The Raspberry Pi Pico's UART 0 TX and RX pins are used to communicate with the ESP-01.

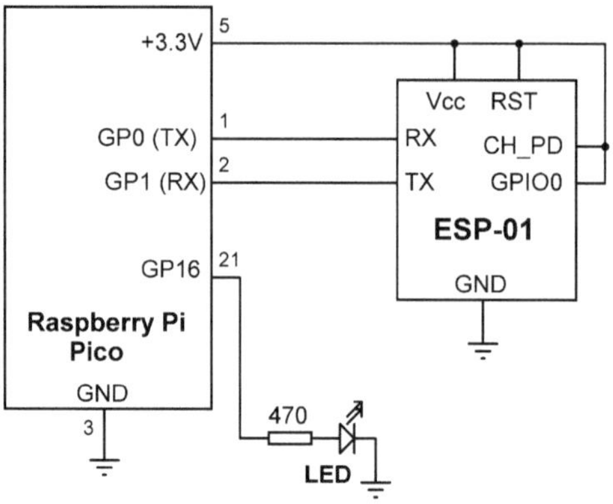

Figure 10.4: Circuit diagram of the project.

Program Listing: Figure 10.5 shows the program listing (program: **Picowifi**). Inside the setup routine serial communication speed is set to 115200 which is the default Baud rate for ESP-01, and the LED is configured as output and turned OFF. Function **ConnectToWiFi** is called to connect to the local Wi-Fi router. AT-style commands are used to configure the ESP-01 to connect to the Wi-Fi router.

The remainder of the program runs in an endless loop formed using a **while** statement. Inside this loop, data is received from the smart mobile phone and the LED is controlled accordingly. Commands **LON** and **LOFF** turn the LED ON and OFF, respectively. Data packets are received from the smartphone using the **readline** function. Function **find** looks for a substring in a string and returns a non-zero value if the substring is found. The **find** function is used because the data received from the mobile device is in the following format: **+IDO,n: data** (e.g. **+IDO,3:LON**) where 0 is the link ID and n is the number of characters received. Using the function **find** we can easily search for the strings **LON** or **LOFF** in the received data packet.

Function **ConnectToWiFi** sends the following commands to the ESP-01 to connect to the Wi-Fi network:

AT+RST	-	reset ESP-01
AT+CWMODE	-	set ESP-01 mode (here it is set to Station mode)
AT+CWJAP	-	set Wi-Fi ssid name and password
AT+CPIMUX	-	set connection mode (here it is set to multiple connection)
AT+CIFSR	-	returns the IP address (not used here)
AT+CIPSTART	-	set TCP or UDP connection mode, destination IP address, and port number (here, UDP is used with port number set to 5000. Destination IP address is set to "0.0.0.0" so that any device can send data as long as port 5000 is used (You can change this to the IP address of your smart phone to receive data only from your phone).

```
#------------------------------------------------------------
#               USING WI-FI
#               ===========
#
# In this project a ESP-01 chip is connected to the Raspberry
# Pi Pico. This chip is used to connect the Pico to the Wi-Fi
#
# Author: Dogan Ibrahim
# File  : Picowifi.py
# Date  : February 2021
#--------------------------------------------------------------
from machine import Pin, UART
import utime
uart = UART(0, baudrate=115200,rx=Pin(1),tx=Pin(0))

LED = Pin(16, Pin.OUT)
LED.value(0)

#
# Send AT commands to ESP-01 to connect to local WI-Fi
#
def ConnectToWiFi():
      uart.write("AT+RST\r\n")
      utime.sleep(5)

      uart.write("AT+CWMODE=1\r\n")
      utime.sleep(1)

      uart.write('''AT+CWJAP="BTHomeSpot-XNH","49345xyzpq"\r\n''')
      utime.sleep(5)

      uart.write("AT+CPIMUX=0\r\n")
      utime.sleep(3)

      uart.write('''AT+CIPSTART="UDP","0.0.0.0",5000,5000,2\r\n''')
      utime.sleep(3)

ConnectToWiFi()

#
# Main program loop
#
while True:
     buf = uart.readline()              # Read data
     dat = buf.decode('UTF-8')          # Decode
     n = dat.find("LON")                # Includes LON?
```

```
if n > 0:
   LED.value(1)                          # LED ON
n = dat.find("LOFF")                     # Includes OFF?
if n > 0:
   LED.value(0)                          # LED OFF
```

Figure 10.5: Program: Picowifi.

Notice that small delays are used after each command. Command **AT+CWJAP** requires a longer delay. The program can easily be modified such that the delays can be removed and the responses from the ESP-01 can be checked. This way, as soon as the correct response is received, the program can continue. You may have to hardware-reset the ESP-01 by powering it down and up again before you run the program.

Testing the program

The program can easily be tested using the **PacketSender** program (see Figure 10.6) on the PC or using a smart phone after installing a UDP app.

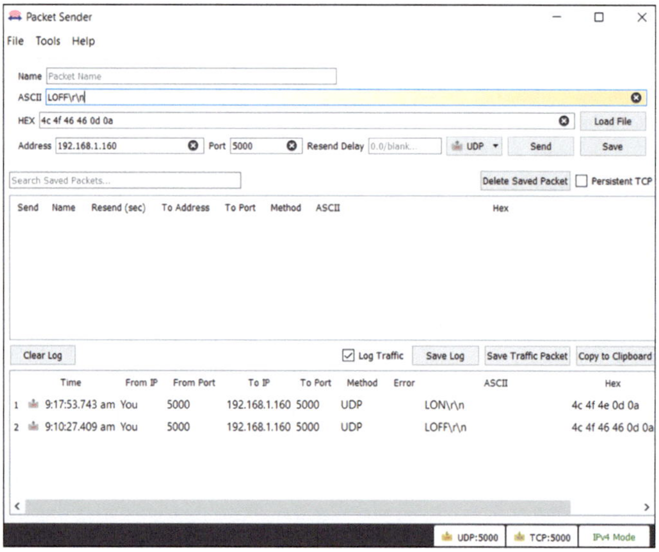

Figure 10.6: Using the PacketSender to test the program.

You should install a **UDP Server** app on your Android mobile phone before starting the test with the smartphone. There are many freely available UDP apps in the **Play Store**. The one installed and used in this project is called the **UDP/TCP Widget** by *K.J.M* as shown in Figure 10.7.

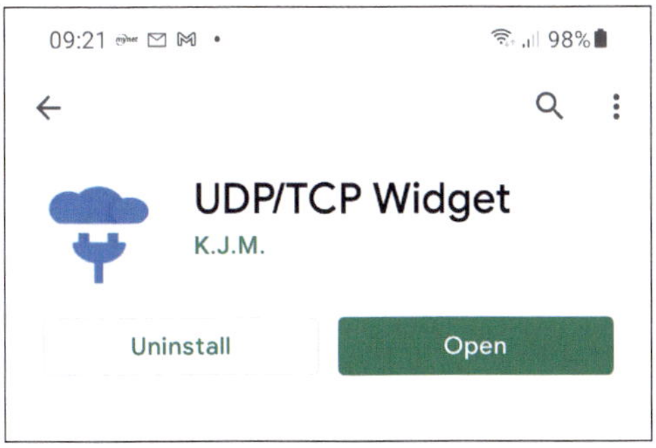

Figure 10.7: UDP/TCP Widget apps for Android.

The steps to test the program are as follows.

- Construct the circuit.
- Download the program to your Raspberry Pi Pico.
- Start the **UDP/TCP Widget** apps on your mobile phone.
- Click the gear symbol and set the Protocol to **UDP**, IP address to the **IP address** of your Raspberry Pi Pico (192.168.1.160 in author's Pico), and set the **Port** to 5000 as shown in Figure 10.8.

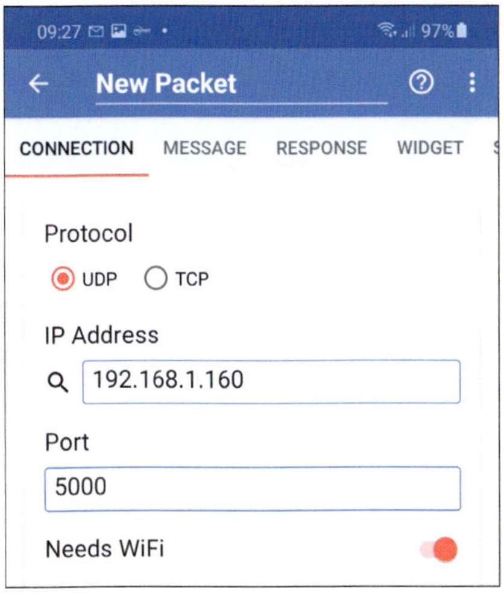

Figure 10.8: Configuring the app.

- Click the **MESSAGE** menu item and select **Text (UTF-8)** as the **Format**, and enter command **LON** to turn ON the LED. Select **LF\n** as the **Terminator** and click the OK symbol (check symbol), as shown in Figure 10.9.
- Now, click the **SEND button** (Figure 10.10) to send the command to the Raspberry Pi Pico. You should see the message **Packet Sent** displayed at the top of your Android screen temporarily.

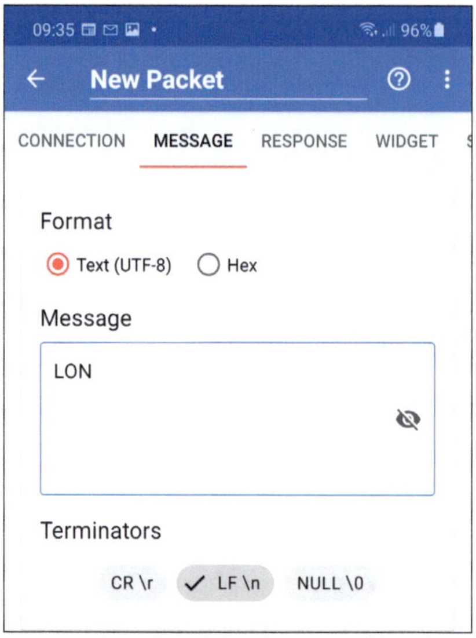

Figure 10.9: Command to turn ON the LED.

Figure 10.10: Click SEND to send the command.

Notice that the IP address of the ESP-01 can be obtained by scanning all the devices on the local Wi-Fi router. For example, the Android app called **Who Uses My WiFi – Network Scanner** by *Phuongpn* can be used to see the IP addresses of all the devices connected to your router. The ESP-01 is listed as shown in Figure 10.11 (IP: **192.168.1.160**), listed with the name **Espressif**.

Figure 10.11: Finding the IP address of the ESP-01.

10.3 Project 2: Displaying the internal temperature on a smartphone using Wi-Fi

Description: In this project we will be reading the internal temperature of the Raspberry Pi Pico and then send this data to a smartphone over a Wi-Fi link.

A request for data is made by the smartphone when it sends the characters **T?** to the Raspberry Pi Pico. This project uses two-way UDP communication to receive and send data.

Aim: The aim of this project is to show how two-way communication can be established with a smartphone over the Wi-Fi link.

Block Diagram: Figure 10.12 shows the block diagram of the project.

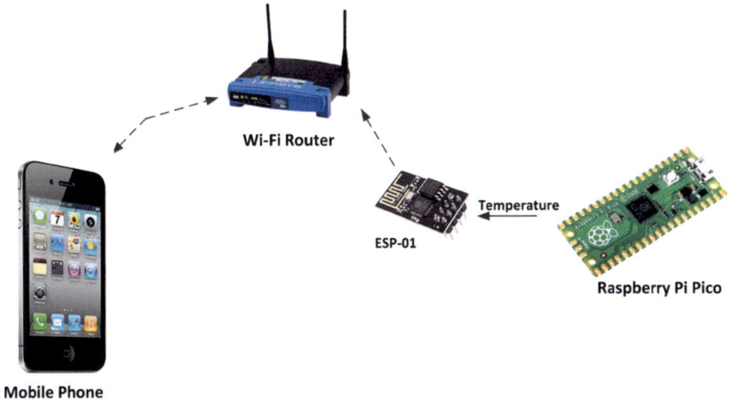

Figure 10.12: Block diagram of the project.

Circuit Diagram: The circuit diagram of the project is same as in Figure 10.4.

Program Listing: The program listing is shown in Figure 10.13 (program: **Temptowifi**). Function **ConnectToWiFi** is called to connect to the local Wi-Fi router as in the previous program. Inside the main program loop, the program waits to receive command **T?** and when this command is received, function **GetTemperature** is called and the Raspberry Pi Pico's internal temperature is read and stored in variable **T** in the main program. String variable **Tstr** stores string **T=** followed by the value of the temperature as a string. The length of this string is stored in variable **Tlen**. Sending data through the Wi-Fi UDP link involves sending command **AT+CIPSEND** to ESP-01, followed by the number of bytes to be sent (i.e. the length of the data). The actual data is then sent after a short delay.

```
#------------------------------------------------------------
#              SEND TEMPERATURE TO SMART PHONE
#              ================================
#
# In this project a ESP-01 chip is connected to the Raspberry
# Pi Pico. Internal temperature of the Raspberry Pi Pico is
# sent to the smart phone
#
# Author: Dogan Ibrahim
# File  : Temptowifi.py
# Date  : February 2021
#--------------------------------------------------------------
from machine import Pin, UART, ADC
import utime
```

```
uart = UART(0, baudrate=115200,rx=Pin(1),tx=Pin(0))

Conv = 3.3 / 65535
AnalogIn = ADC(4)

def GetTemperature():
    V = AnalogIn.read_u16()
    V = V * Conv
    Temp = 27 - (V - 0.706) / 0.001721
    return Temp

#
# Send AT commands to ESP-01 to connect to local WI-Fi
#
def ConnectToWiFi():
      uart.write("AT+RST\r\n")
      utime.sleep(5)

      uart.write("AT+CWMODE=1\r\n")
      utime.sleep(1)

      uart.write('''AT+CWJAP="BTHomeSpot-XNH","49345axyzw"\r\n''')
      utime.sleep(5)

      uart.write("AT+CPIMUX=0\r\n")
      utime.sleep(3)

      uart.write('''AT+CIPSTART="UDP","192.168.1.199",5000,5000,2\r\n''')
      utime.sleep(3)

ConnectToWiFi()

#
# Main program loop. Send the temperature to smart phone
#
while True:
     buf = uart.readline()                         # Read data
     dat = buf.decode('UTF-8')                     # Decode
     n = dat.find("T?")                            # T? received?
     if n > 0:
         T = GetTemperature()                      # Get the temperature
         Tstr = "T=" + str(T)                      # Insert T=
         Tlen = str(len(Tstr))                     # Length
         Dt = "AT+CIPSEND="+Tlen + "\r\n"          # AT command to send
         uart.write(Dt)                            # Send to ESP-01
```

```
    utime.sleep(2)                          # Wait 2 sec
    uart.write(Tstr)                        # Send data
```

Figure 10.13: Program: Temptowifi.

Testing the program

The program can either be tested on a PC using the freely available **PacketSender** program or a smartphone with a UDP app installed. **PacketSender** enables the user to send and received UDP as well as TCP packets from a PC. This program could be very useful during testing of UDP and TCP based programs. Figure 10.14 shows the **PacketSender** program where command **T?** is sent and the temperature is received and displayed. Notice that 192.168.1.199 was the PC IP address during the testing.

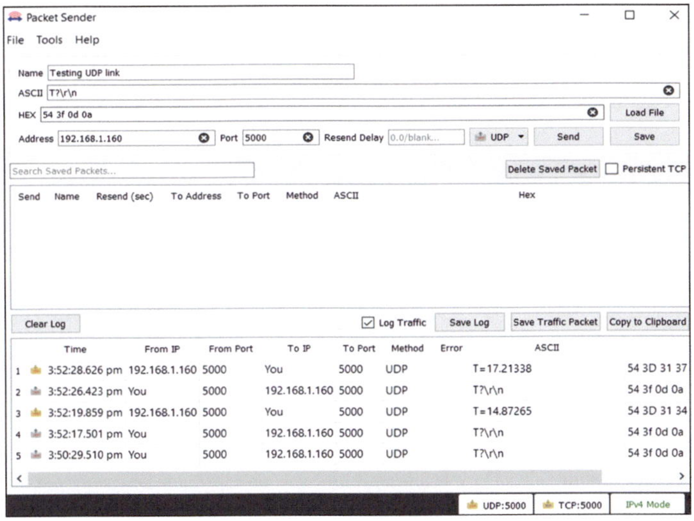

Figure 10.14: Using the PacketSender program.

Alternatively, we can use a suitable UDP client/server program to test the program. One such program for Android-running smartphones is the **TCP/UDP Client** app from *Digit Mund* as shown in Figure 10.15. Figure 10.16 shows the startup screen of this app on an Android smartphone. Enter the Raspberry Pi Pico **IP address**, **Port number**, **Protocol,** and click the menu button **REQUEST**.

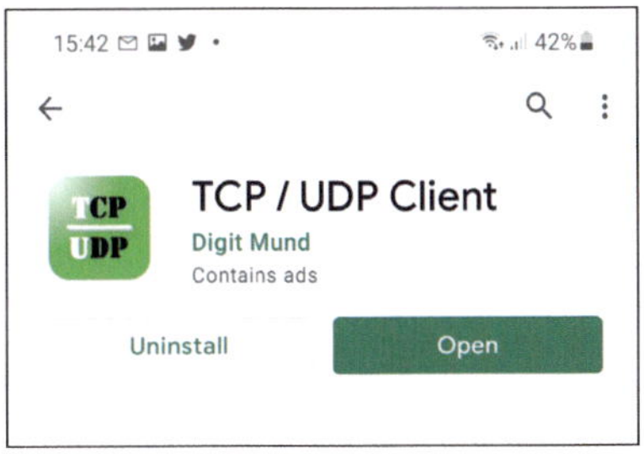

Figure 10.15: UDP app.

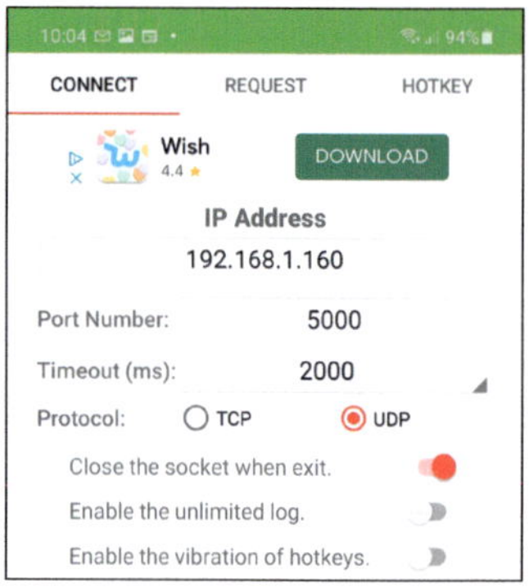

Figure 10.16: Startup screen of the app.

An example run of the program on the app is shown in Figure 10.17, where command **T?** is sent to the Raspberry Pi Pico and the temperature is received and displayed on the Android screen.

Figure 10.17: Example run of the program.

Chapter 11 • Bluetooth with the Raspberry Pi Pico

11.1 Overview

Bluetooth is one of the most popular means of exchanging data wirelessly over short distances. Nowadays, many electronic devices such as smartphones, laptops, iPads, games, gadgets, portable health monitoring devices, and so on, are all equipped with Bluetooth modules. Bluetooth is used by many people to share picture and music files using their smartphones.

Bluetooth is a paired communication protocol where both devices must enable their Bluetooth links and use then use the same key to connect to each other. When the connection is established, the data can be sent both ways. There is no need to worry about line-of-sight between the devices since the communication is based on radio waves, albeit with limited range.

Sometimes the pairing between devices may fail. You should pay attention to the following points for successful pairing between the devices.

- Make sure Bluetooth is turned on at both devices.
- Make your device discoverable. On some devices you may have to click a button to make Bluetooth discoverable.
- Male sure the two devices are close to each other.
- Make sure the devices to be paired are compatible with each other, e.g. their versions are compatible.
- Enter the same pairing code on both devices when asked.

11.2 Raspberry Pi Pico Bluetooth interface

The Raspberry Pi Pico has no built-in Bluetooth module. We have to use an external Bluetooth module to enable the Pico to communicate with other devices via the Bluetooth. One possibility may be to use a Raspberry Pi computer, but a cheaper option may be to use a serial Bluetooth module, such as the HC-06. In the next section we will develop a project and learn how to connect a HC-06 type low-cost Bluetooth module to our Raspberry Pi Pico.

11.3 Project 1: Controlling an LED from your smartphone using Bluetooth

Description: In this project we will be sending commands over the Bluetooth link from a smartphone to control an LED connected to the Raspberry Pi Pico (you could easily replace the LED with a buzzer so that electrical devices can be controlled remotely). In this project, valid commands are:

L1	Turn LED ON
L0	Turn LED OFF

Aim: The aim of this project is to showcase the use of a low-cost serial Bluetooth module with the Raspberry Pi Pico.

The HC-06 Bluetooth module

The HC-06 is a low-cost popular 4-pin, serially controlled module with a pinout as pictured in Figure 11.1.

Figure 11.1: The HC-06 Bluetooth module.

The HC-06 is a serially controlled module with a set of interesting specifications:

- +3.3 V to +6 V operation
- 30 mA unpaired current (10 mA matched current)
- Built-in antenna
- Band: 2.40 GHz – 2.48 GHz
- Power level: +6 dBm
- Default communication: 9600 baud, 8 data bits, no parity, 1 stop bit
- Signal coverage 10 m (30 ft) approx.
- Safety features: authentication and encryption
- Modulation mode: Gaussian frequency-shift keying

Block Diagram: Figure 11.2 shows the block diagram of the project.

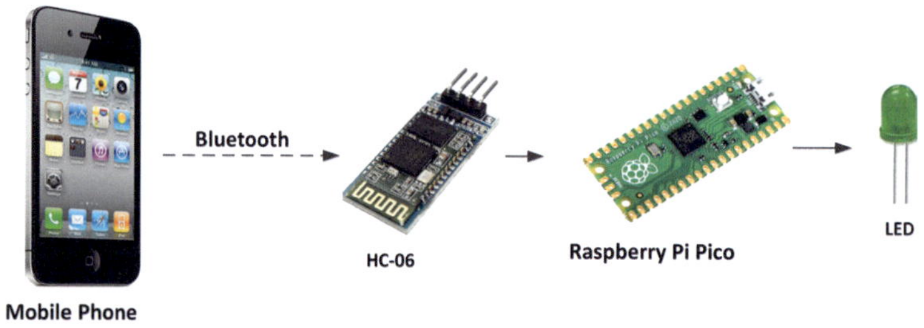

Figure 11.2: Block diagram of the project.

Circuit Diagram: Figure 11.3 shows the project circuit diagram. The RXD and TXD pins of the Bluetooth module are connected to UART 0 pins GP0 (TX) and GP1 (RX) of the Raspberry Pi Pico, respectively. The LED is connected to GP16 (pin 21) through a 470-ohm current-limiting resistor.

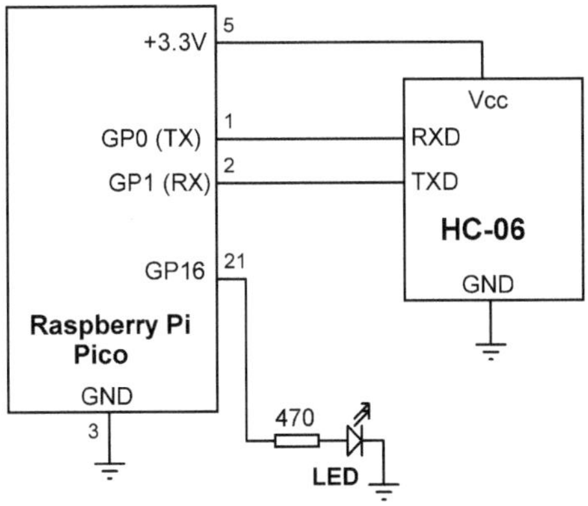

Figure 11.3: Circuit diagram of the project.

Program listing: Check out Figure 11.4 (program: **BlueLED**). At the beginning of the program the hardware UART interface is set to baud rate 9600, which is the default speed of the HC-06. The LED is configured as an output and turned OFF. The remainder of the program runs in an endless loop. Inside this loop data (commands) are received from the Bluetooth device using a function call to **readline**. The data read is stored in list **buf**. The program then controls the LED based on the received command. For example, **L1** turns the LED ON, **L0** turns it OFF, and so on.

```
#------------------------------------------------------------
#               BLUETOOTH COMMUNICATION
#               =======================
#
# In this project a HC-06 type serial Bluetooth module and
# and LED are connected to the Raspberry Pi Pico. The LED
# is controlled by sending commands from a Bluetooth
# compatible smart phone.
#
# Author: Dogan Ibrahim
# File  : BlueLED.py
# Date  : February 2021
#--------------------------------------------------------------
from machine import Pin, UART
import utime

uart = UART(0, baudrate=9600,rx=Pin(1),tx=Pin(0))

LED = Pin(16, Pin.OUT)
LED.value(0)

#
# Main program loop. Receive a command and control the LED
#
```

```
while True:
    buf = uart.readline()                          # Read data
    dat = buf.decode('UTF-8')                      # Decode
    if dat[0] == 'L' and dat[1] == '1':            # L1?
        LED.value(1)                               # LED ON
    elif dat[0] == 'L' and dat[1] == '0':          # L0?
        LED.value(0)                               # LED OFF
```

Figure 11.4: Program: BlueLED.

Testing the program

The program can be tested by using an Android-running smartphone to send commands through a Bluetooth communication interface. There are many freely available Bluetooth communication programs in the Play Store. The one chosen by the author was called the **Bluetooth Controller** by *mightyIT* (it@memighty.com) as shown in Figure 11.5. You should install this app on your Android smartphone so that you can send commands to the development board.

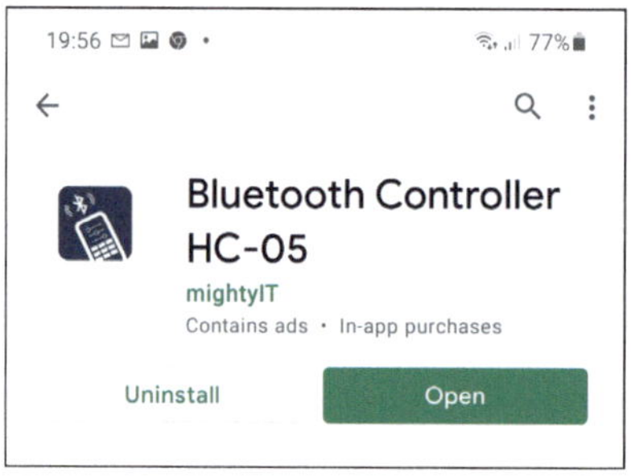

Figure 11.5: Bluetooth Controller app.

The steps to test the application are as given below.

- Construct the project.
- Download the program to your Raspberry Pi Pico.
- Active the **Bluetooth Controller** apps on your mobile phone.
- The app will look for nearby Bluetooth devices. Click on **HC-06** when displayed on the phone screen (you may have to scan for devices).
- You will now be asked to enter the password to pair the phone with the development board. Enter the default password: **1234**.
- Start the Bluetooth apps on your smartphone. Click the semicircle with an arrow located at the top right side of the screen to connect to HC-06.
- You should see a green colour dot at the top right-hand side of the screen when a connection is made to the HC-06. Also, the HC-06 with its address (like HC-06 [98:D3:31:FB:5E:B6]) should be displayed at the top left side of the screen.
- To turn the LED ON, enter command **L1** and click **Send ASCII**. You should see the LED turning ON. Enter command **L0** to turn OFF the LED. Figure 11.6 shows an example screen.

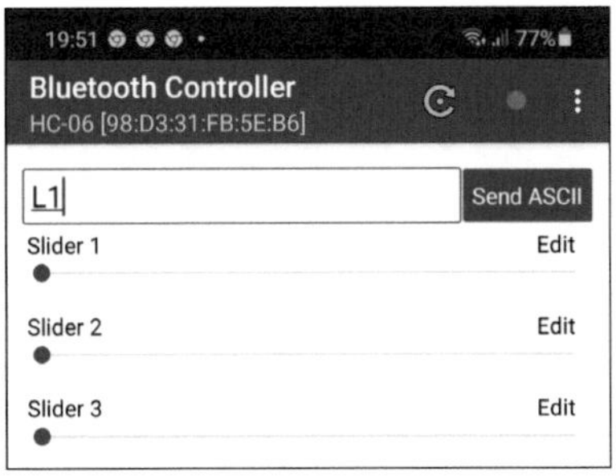

Figure 11.6: Example command to turn the LED ON.

We can modify the program in Figure 11.5 by sending a confirmation to the smartphone when there is change in the LED status. The required modifications are shown below:

```
while True:
    buf = uart.readline()                          # Read data
    dat = buf.decode('UTF-8')                      # Decode
    if dat[0] == 'L' and dat[1] == '1':            # L1?
        LED.value(1)                               # LED ON
        uart.write("LED is ON")                    # Send confirmation
    elif dat[0] == 'L' and dat[1] == '0':          # L0?
        LED.value(0)                               # LED OFF
        uart.write("LED is OFF")                   # Send confirmation
```

For example, as shown in Figure 11.7, the message **LED is ON** is displayed on the screen after the command **L1** is sent.

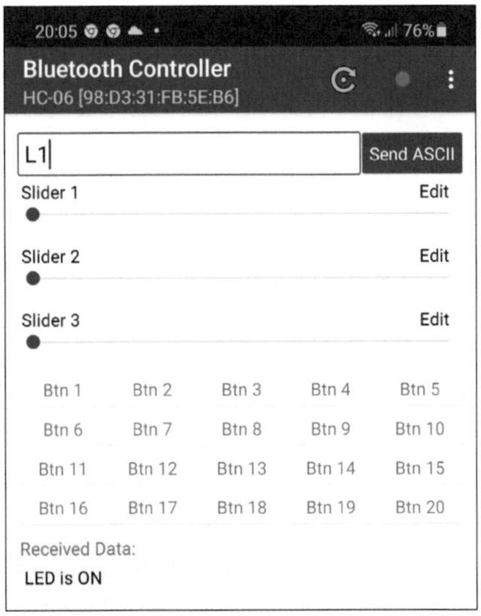

Figure 11.7: Example display with confirmation.

11.4 Project 2: Sending the Raspberry Pi Pico's internal temperature to the smartphone

Description: In this project the internal temperature of the Raspberry Pi Pico is read every 10 seconds and gets sent to a smartphone over a Bluetooth link.

Aim: The aim of this project is to showcase data being sent from the Raspberry Pi Pico to a smartphone at regular intervals.

Block Diagram: Figure 11.8 shows the block diagram of the project.

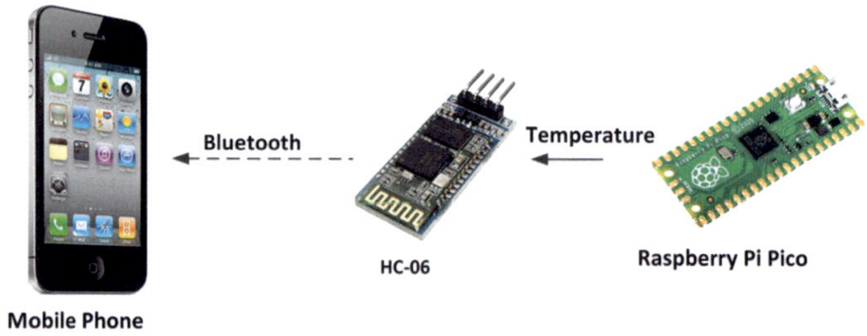

Figure 11.8: Block diagram of the project.

Circuit Diagram: Figure 11.9 shows the project circuit diagram. RXD and TXD pins of the Bluetooth module are connected to UART 0 pins GP0 (TX) and GP1 (RX) of Raspberry Pi Pico respectively.

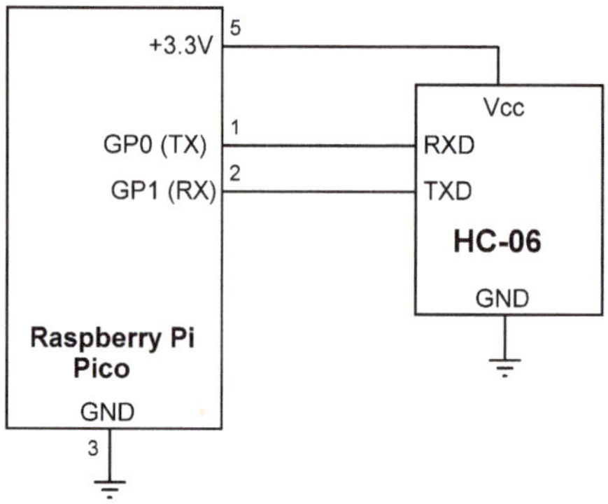

Figure 11.9: Circuit diagram of the project.

Program listing: The program listing of the project is shown in Figure 11.10 (program: **BlueTemp**). At the beginning of the program the hardware UART interface is set to baud rate 9600, which is the default speed of the HC-06 module. The Function **GetTemperature** returns the internal temperature of the Raspberry Pi Pico. Inside the main program loop the temperature is read and sent to the smartphone every 10 seconds. Figure 11.11 shows the temperature displayed on a smartphone using the **Bluetooth Controller** app described in the previous section.

```
#------------------------------------------------------------
#              SEND TEMPERATURE TO SMART PHONE
#              ===============================
#
# In this project a HC-06 type serial Bluetooth module is
# connected to the Raspberry Pi Pico. Internal temperature
# readings are sent to a smart phone every 10 seconds
#
# Author: Dogan Ibrahim
# File  : BlueTemp.py
# Date  : February 2021
#--------------------------------------------------------------
from machine import Pin, UART, ADC
import utime

uart = UART(0, baudrate=9600,rx=Pin(1),tx=Pin(0))

Conv = 3.3 / 65535
AnalogIn = ADC(4)

def GetTemperature():
    V = AnalogIn.read_u16()
    V = V * Conv
    Temp = 27 - (V - 0.706) / 0.001721
    return Temp

#
# Send the temperature to smart phone
#
while True:
     T = GetTemperature()
     Temp = "T=" + str(T) + "\r\n"
     uart.write(Temp)
     utime.sleep(10)
```

Figure 11.10: Program: BlueTemp.

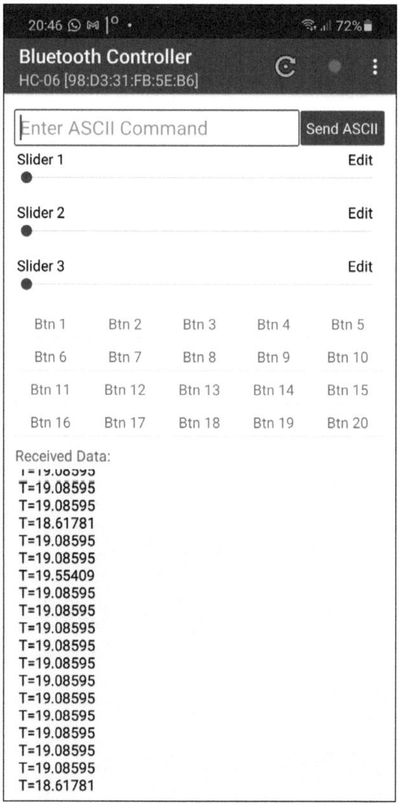

Figure 11.11: Temperature displayed on the smartphone.

Chapter 12 • Using Digital-to-Analogue Converters (DACs)

12.1 Overview

DACs are used to convert digital signals into analogue form. Such converters have many applications in digital signal processing (DSP) and digital control applications. For example, we can generate waveforms by writing programs and then convert these waveforms into analogue forms and output them from our digital computer. We also need DACs if we want to interface a speaker or some other device operating with analogue voltages to our Raspberry Pi Pico.

The Raspberry Pi Pico has no built-in ADC converter and consequently an external DAC chip must be used to output analogue signals. In this Chapter we will be learning how to use a popular DAC (the MCP4921) chip with our Raspberry Pi Pico to generate some simple signal waveforms.

12.2 The MCP4921 DAC

Before using the MCP4921, it is worthwhile to look at its features and operation in some detail. MCP4921 is a 12-bit DAC that operates with the SPI bus interface. Figure 12.1 shows the pin layout of this chip. The basic features include:

- 12-bit operation
- 20 MHz clock support
- 4.5 μs settling time
- external voltage reference input
- 1× or 2× gain, with control
- 2.7 V to 5.5 V supply voltage
- –40 ºC to +125 ºC temperature range

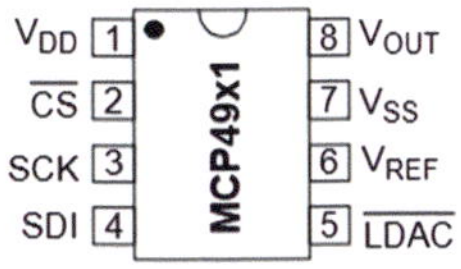

Figure 12.1: Microchip MCP4921 DAC.

For more details, see the information at:
http://ww1.microchip.com/downloads/en/devicedoc/21897b.pdf

The pin descriptions are:

Vdd:	supply voltage
CS:	chip select (Active-Low)
SCK:	SPI clock
SDI:	SPI data in
LDAC:	used to transfer input register data to the output (Active-Low)
Vref	reference input voltage
Vout:	analogue output
Vss:	supply ground

In this project we will be operating the MCP4921 with a gain of 1 (i.e. unity). As a result, with a reference voltage of 3.3 V and 12-bit conversion data, the LSB resolution of the DAC will be 3300 mV / 4096 = 0.8 mV.

12.3 Project 1: Generating squarewave signal with amplitude under +3.3 V

Description: In this project we will be using the DAC to generate a squarewave signal with a frequency of 500 Hz (period = 2 ms), and 50% duty cycle (i.e. ON time = 1 ms, OFF time = 1 ms). The output voltage will be 2 V_{peak} (notice that this could not have been achieved without using a DAC since the output HIGH voltage of a pin is +3.3 V).

Aim: The aim of this project is to show how a DAC chip can be interfaced to a Raspberry Pi Pico.

Block Diagram: Figure 12.2 shows the block diagram of the project.

Figure 12.2: Block diagram of the project.

Circuit Diagram: The circuit diagram of the project is shown in Figure 12.3. Pins GP3 (SPI0 TX) and GP2 (SPIO SCK) are connected to MCP4921 pins SDI and SCK, respectively. The CS of the MCP4921 is controlled separately from GP16 (pin 21). The output of the DAC is connected to the oscilloscope.

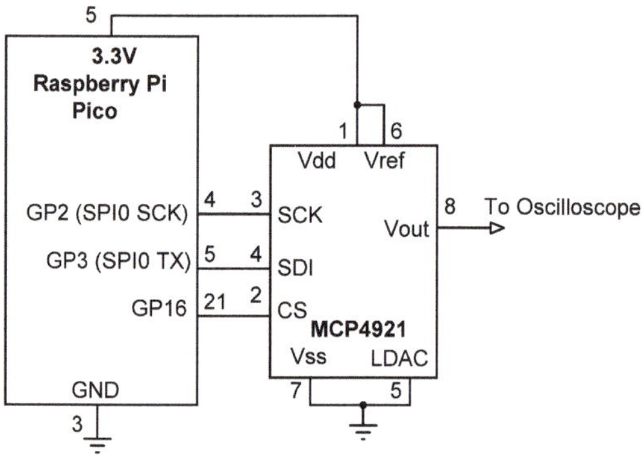

Figure 12.3: Circuit diagram of the project.

Data is written to the DAC in 2 bytes. The lower byte specifies D0:D8 of the digital input data. The upper byte consists of the following bits:

D8:D11	bits D8:D11 of the digital input data
SHDN	1: active (output available), 0: shutdown the device

GA	output gain control. 0: gain is 2×, 1: gain is 1×
BUF	0: input unbuffered, 1: input buffered
A/B	0: write to DACa, 1: Write to DACb (MCP4921 supports only DACa)

In normal operation, we will send the upper byte (D8:D11) of the 12-bit (D0:D11) input data with bits D12 and D13 set to 1 so that the device is active, and the gain is set to 1×. Then we will send the low byte (D0:D7) of the data. This means that 0x30 should be added to the upper byte before sending it to the DAC.

Program listing: Figure 12.4 shows the program listing (program: **Square**). Since we are using a DAC with the reference voltage set to +3.3 V (3300 mV), and 12-bit wide data (i.e. 4096 steps), the required digital value to set the output voltage to 2 V is given by **ONvalue**, where:

ONvalue = 2000 × 4095 / 3300

The OFF value of the signal (**OFFvalue**) is set to 0 V. Function **DAC** configures the DAC so that 2 V is output from it. First the HIGH byte (in **buff[0]**) is put into buffer buff, followed by the LOW byte (in **buff[1]**):

```
buff[0] = (data >> 8) & 0x0F
  buff[0] = buff[0] + 0x30
buff[1] = data & 0xFF
spi.write(bytearray(buff))
```

The durations of the ON and OFF times are set to 1 ms. However, it was found by the experiments that the DAC routine takes some time and because of this, the period and consequently the frequency of the output waveform are not very accurate. The ON and OFF times are slightly bigger than 1 ms. Readers can experiment to adjust the delay to get exactly 1 ms if required.

```
#----------------------------------------------------------
#       GENERATE SQUARE WAVE SIGNAL WITH AMPLITUDE +2V
#       ==============================================
#
# In this project a MCP4921 type DAC chip is connected to the
# Raspberry Pi Pico.The program generates a square wave signal
# with frequency f=500Hz, 50% duty cycle (ON and OFF tiems equal
# and each 1ms), and 2V amplitude
#
# Author: Dogan Ibrahim
# File  : Square.py
# Date  : February 2021
#------------------------------------------------------------
from machine import Pin, SPI
```

```
import utime

spi_sck = Pin(2)                              # SCK pin at GP2
spi_tx = Pin(3)                               # TX pin at GP3
spi_rx = Pin(0)                               # RX pin at GP0 (not used)

spi = SPI(0,sck=spi_sck,mosi=spi_tx,miso=spi_rx,baudrate=100000)

CS = Pin(16, Pin.OUT)                        # CS
CS.value(1)                                  # Disable chip

ONvalue = int(2000 * 4095 / 3300)            # For +2V amplitude
OFFvalue = 0

def DAC(data):
    buff = [0, 0]
    buff[0] = (data >> 8) & 0x0F             # HIGH byte
    buff[0] = buff[0] + 0x30
    buff[1] = data & 0xFF                    # LOW byte
    CS.value(0)                              # Enable MCP4921
    spi.write(bytearray(buff))               # Send to SPI bus
    CS.value(1)                              # DIsable MCP4921

#
# Main program
#
while True:
    DAC(ONvalue)
    utime.sleep_ms(1000)
    DAC(OFFvalue)
    utime.sleep_ms(1000)
```

Figure 12.4: Program: Square.

Figure 12.5 shows the output waveform generated by the program. This waveform was captured using a PCSGU250 type digital oscilloscope. The horizontal axis was set to 1 ms/division and the vertical axis was 1 V/division. The peak output voltage is 2 V as expected.

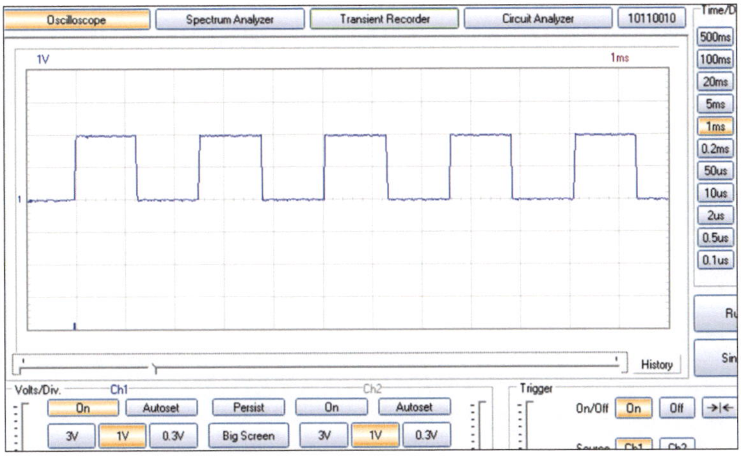

Figure 12.5: Output waveform.

Using timer interrupt for accurate timing

As we have seen in Figure 12.5, the period of the waveform is not exactly 2 ms. In this section we will be using timer interrupts to achieve more accurate timing.

Figure 12.6 shows te new program listing (Program:**Square2**). In this version of the program, a variable called **flag** is used to output the ON and the OFF times alternately. The timer works in the background and calls function DAC 1000 times a second (i.e. 500 ON pulses and 500 OFF pulses).

```
#-----------------------------------------------------------
#       GENERATE SQUARE WAVE SIGNAL WITH AMPLITUDE +2V
#       ==============================================
#
# In this project a MCP4921 type DAC chip is connected to the
# Raspberry Pi Pico.The program generates a square wave signal
# with frequency f=500Hz, 50% duty cycle (ON and OFF tiems equal
# and each 1ms), and 2V amplitude
#
# This version of the program uses timer interrupts
#
# Author: Dogan Ibrahim
# File  : Square2.py
# Date  : February 2021
#-------------------------------------------------------------
from machine import Pin, SPI, Timer
#import utime

spi_sck = Pin(2)                            # SCK pin at GP2
spi_tx = Pin(3)                             # TX pin at GP3
spi_rx = Pin(0)                             # RX pin at GP0 (not used)
```

```
spi = SPI(0,sck=spi_sck,mosi=spi_tx,miso=spi_rx,baudrate=100000)

CS = Pin(16, Pin.OUT)                          # CS
CS.value(1)                                    # Disable chip

ONvalue = int(2000 * 4095 / 3300)              # For +2V amplitude
OFFvalue = 0

tim = Timer()
flag = 0

#
# Timer interrupt service routine
#
def DAC(timer):
    global flag, Onvalue, OFFvalue
    global CS
    buff = [0, 0]
    if flag == 0:
        data = ONvalue
        flag = 1
    else:
        data = OFFvalue
        flag = 0
    buff[0] = (data >> 8) & 0x0F               # HIGH byte
    buff[0] = buff[0] + 0x30
    buff[1] = data & 0xFF                      # LOW byte
    CS.value(0)                                # Enable MCP4921
    spi.write(bytearray(buff))                 # Send to SPI bus
    CS.value(1)                                # DIsable MCP4921

#
# Main program
#
tim.init(freq = 1000, mode = Timer.PERIODIC, callback = DAC)
```

Figure 12.6: Program: Square2.

Figure 12.7 shows the new output. Clearly, the period of the waveform is exactly 2 ms (i.e. frequency of exactly 500 Hz).

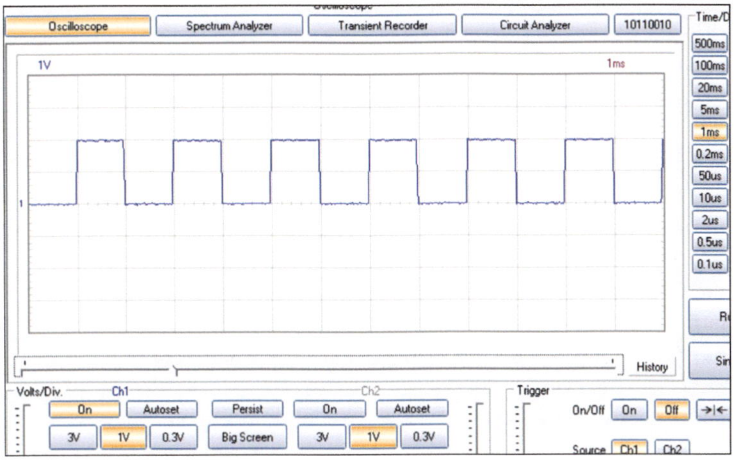

Figure 12.7: Output waveform.

12.4 Project 2: Generating fixed voltages

Description: In this project we will be using the DAC to generate fixed voltages. Voltages with amplitudes 0, 1, 2, and 3 V with 100-ms delay between each voltage will be generated. The block diagram and circuit diagram are as in Figure 12.2 and Figure 12.3, respectively.

Program listing: Figure 12.8 shows the program listing (Program: **FixedV**). Function 'Voltage' converts the voltage into digital value for 12 bits and returns it to the main program.

```
#------------------------------------------------------------
#              GENERATE FIXED VOLTAGES
#              =======================
#
# In this project a MCP4921 type DAC chip is connected to the
# Raspberry Pi Pico.The program generates fixed voltages with
# amplitues 0, 1, and 2V and the delay between each output
# being 100ms
#
# Author: Dogan Ibrahim
# File  : FixedV.py
# Date  : February 2021
#--------------------------------------------------------------
from machine import Pin, SPI
import utime

spi_sck = Pin(2)                           # SCK pin at GP2
spi_tx = Pin(3)                            # TX pin at GP3
spi_rx = Pin(0)                            # RX pin at GP0 (not used)

spi = SPI(0,sck=spi_sck,mosi=spi_tx,miso=spi_rx,baudrate=100000)
```

```
CS = Pin(16, Pin.OUT)                        # CS
CS.value(1)                                  # Disable chip

def Voltage(V):
    Amplitude = int(V * 4095 / 3300)
    return Amplitude

def DAC(data):
    buff = [0, 0]
    buff[0] = (data >> 8) & 0x0F             # HIGH byte
    buff[0] = buff[0] + 0x30
    buff[1] = data & 0xFF                    # LOW byte
    CS.value(0)                              # Enable MCP4921
    spi.write(bytearray(buff))               # Send to SPI bus
    CS.value(1)                              # DIsable MCP4921

#
# Main program
#
while True:
    DAC(Voltage(0))
    utime.sleep_ms(100)
    DAC(Voltage(1000))
    utime.sleep_ms(100)
    DAC(Voltage(2000))
    utime.sleep_ms(100)
    DAC(Voltage(3000))
    utime.sleep_ms(100)
```

Figure 12.8: Program: FixedV.

Figure 12.9 shows the generated output waveform.

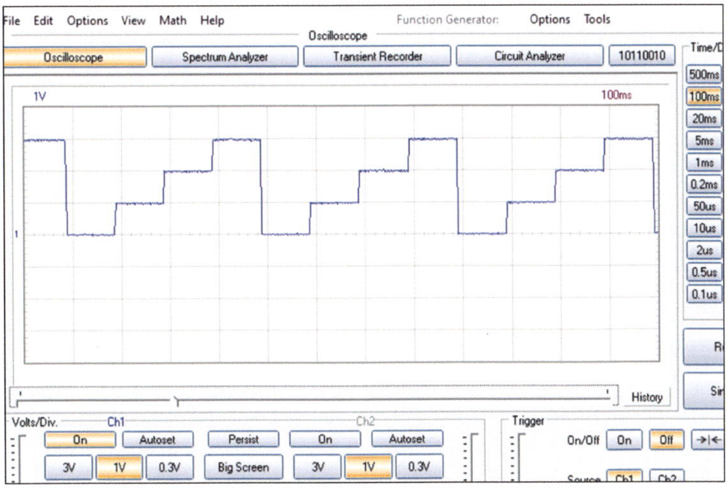

Figure 12.9: Output waveform.

12.5 Project 3: Generating a sawtooth signal

Description: In this project we will be using the DAC to generate a sawtooth-shaped signal with the following specifications:

Peak voltage:	3.3 V
Step width:	2 ms
Number of steps:	10

The block diagram and circuit diagram are as in Figure 12.2 and Figure 12.3, respectively.

Program listing: Figure 12.10 shows the program listing (Program: **Sawtooth**). Function 'Voltage' converts the voltage into digital value for 12 bits and returns it to the main program. Notice that as described earlier, the timing of the generated signal is not very accurate and timer interrupts can be used to generate accurate output.

```
#----------------------------------------------------------
#              GENERATE SAWTOOTH WAVEFORM
#              ==========================
#
# In this project a MCP4921 type DAC chip is connected to the
# Raspberry Pi Pico.The program generates sawtooth waveform
# having 10 steps
#
# Author: Dogan Ibrahim
# File  : Sawtooth.py
# Date  : February 2021
#------------------------------------------------------------
from machine import Pin, SPI
import utime
```

```
spi_sck = Pin(2)                            # SCK pin at GP2
spi_tx = Pin(3)                             # TX pin at GP3
spi_rx = Pin(0)                             # RX pin at GP0 (not used)

spi = SPI(0,sck=spi_sck,mosi=spi_tx,miso=spi_rx,baudrate=100000)

CS = Pin(16, Pin.OUT)                       # CS
CS.value(1)                                 # Disable chip

def Voltage(V):
    Amplitude = int(V * 4095 / 3300)
    return Amplitude

def DAC(data):
    buff = [0, 0]
    buff[0] = (data >> 8) & 0x0F             # HIGH byte
    buff[0] = buff[0] + 0x30
    buff[1] = data & 0xFF                    # LOW byte
    CS.value(0)                              # Enable MCP4921
    spi.write(bytearray(buff))               # Send to SPI bus
    CS.value(1)                              # DIsable MCP4921

#
# Main program
#
k = 0.0
while True:
    DAC(int(Voltage(k*3300)))
    utime.sleep_ms(2)
    k = k + 0.1
    if k == 1.0:
        k = 0.0
```

Figure 12.10: Program: Sawtooth.

Figure 12.11 shows the generated output waveform. Here, the horizontal axis was 10 ms/division, and the vertical axis, 1 V/division.

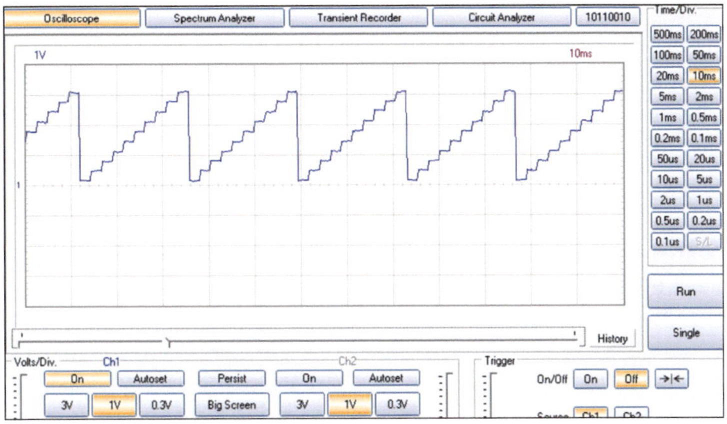

Figure 12.11: Output waveform.

12.6 Project 4: Generating a triangular signal

Description: In this project we will be using the DAC to generate a triangular-shaped signal having 10 steps going up, and 10 steps going down. The step width is set to 1 ms. The block diagram and circuit diagram are as in Figure 12.2 and Figure 12.3, respectively.

Program listing: Figure 12.12 shows the program listing (Program: **Triangle**). Function 'Voltage' converts the voltage into digital value for 12 bits and returns it to the main program.

```
#-----------------------------------------------------------
#              GENERATE TRIANGLE WAVEFORM
#              ==========================
#
# In this project a MCP4921 type DAC chip is connected to the
# Raspberry Pi Pico.The program generates triangle waveform
#
# Author: Dogan Ibrahim
# File  : Triangle.py
# Date  : February 2021
#-------------------------------------------------------------
from machine import Pin, SPI
import utime

spi_sck = Pin(2)                            # SCK pin at GP2
spi_tx = Pin(3)                             # TX pin at GP3
spi_rx = Pin(0)                             # RX pin at GP0 (not used)

spi = SPI(0,sck=spi_sck,mosi=spi_tx,miso=spi_rx,baudrate=100000)

CS = Pin(16, Pin.OUT)                       # CS
CS.value(1)                                 # Disable chip
```

```
def Voltage(V):
    Amplitude = int(V * 4095 / 3300)
    return Amplitude

def DAC(data):
    buff = [0, 0]
    buff[0] = (data >> 8) & 0x0F              # HIGH byte
    buff[0] = buff[0] + 0x30
    buff[1] = data & 0xFF                     # LOW byte
    CS.value(0)                               # Enable MCP4921
    spi.write(bytearray(buff))                # Send to SPI bus
    CS.value(1)                               # DIsable MCP4921

#
# Main program
#
while True:
    k = 0.0
    while k < 1.0:                            # Going up
        DAC(int(Voltage(k*3300)))
        utime.sleep_ms(1)
        k = k + 0.1

    k = 1.0
    while k > 0.0:                            # Going down
        DAC(int(Voltage(k*3300)))
        utime.sleep_ms(1)
        k = k - 0.1
```

Figure 12.12: Program: Triangle.

Figure 12.13 shows the generated output waveform. Notice again that as described earlier, the timing of the generated signal is not very accurate and timer interrupts can be used to generate accurate output.

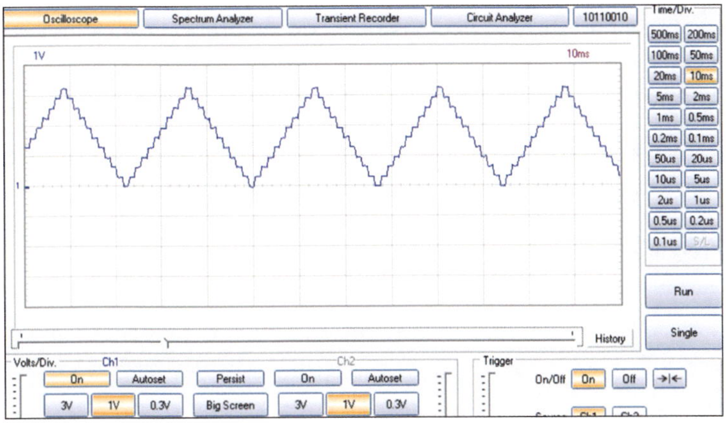

Figure 12.13: Output waveform.

12.7 Project 5: Arbitrary periodic waveform

Description: In this project we will generate an arbitrary-wave, periodic waveform with a period of 20 ms. The details of the waveform are as shown in Figure 12.14.

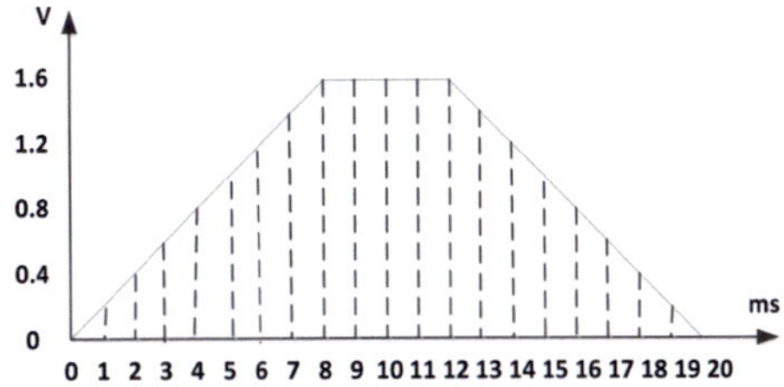

Figure 12.14: The waveform to be generated.

The waveform takes the following values:

Time (ms)	Amplitude (V)	Time (ms)	Amplitude (V)
0	0	11	1.6
1	0.2	12	1.6
2	0.4	13	1.4
3	0.6	14	1.2
4	0.8	15	1.0
5	1.0	16	0.8
6	1.2	17	0.6
7	1.4	18	0.4
8	1.6	19	0.2
9	1.6	20	0.0
10	1.6		

Aim: The aim of this project is to demonstrate how an arbitrary waveform can be generated.
The block diagram and circuit diagram are as in Figure 12.2 and Figure 12.3, respectively.

Program listing: Figure 12.15 shows the program listing (Program: **Arbitrary**). The voltage samples are stored in list Waveform. Inside the main program, a loop runs from 0 to 20 (inclusive), gets the required voltage amplitude at every sample and calls the DAC to generate the required sample.

```
#------------------------------------------------------------
#              GENERATE ARBITRARY WAVEFORM
#              ===========================
#
# In this project a MCP4921 type DAC chip is connected to the
# Raspberry Pi Pico.The program generates an arbitarry waveform
# whose characteristics are defined in the text
#
# Author: Dogan Ibrahim
# File  : Arbitrary.py
# Date  : February 2021
#--------------------------------------------------------------
from machine import Pin, SPI
import utime
import math

spi_sck = Pin(2)                           # SCK pin at GP2
spi_tx = Pin(3)                            # TX pin at GP3
spi_rx = Pin(0)                            # RX pin at GP0 (not used)

spi = SPI(0,sck=spi_sck,mosi=spi_tx,miso=spi_rx,baudrate=100000)

CS = Pin(16, Pin.OUT)                      # CS
CS.value(1)                                # Disable chip

Waveform = [0.0,0.2,0.4,0.6,0.8,1.0,1.2,1.4,1.6,1.6,1.6,1.6,1.6,
                    1.4,1.2,1.0,0.8,0.6,0.4,0.2,0.0]

def Voltage(V):
    Amplitude = int(V * 4095 / 3.3)
    return Amplitude

def DAC(data):
    buff = [0, 0]
    buff[0] = (data >> 8) & 0x0F            # HIGH byte
    buff[0] = buff[0] + 0x30
    buff[1] = data & 0xFF                   # LOW byte
```

```
        CS.value(0)                           # Enable MCP4921
        spi.write(bytearray(buff))            # Send to SPI bus
        CS.value(1)                           # DIsable MCP4921

#
# Main program
#
while True:
    for k in range(21):
        DAC(int(4095*Waveform[k]/3.3))
        utime.sleep_ms(1)
```

Figure 12.15: Program: Arbitrary.

Figure 12.16 shows the generated output waveform. Notice again that as described earlier, the timing of the generated signal is not very accurate and timer interrupts can be used to generate accurate output.

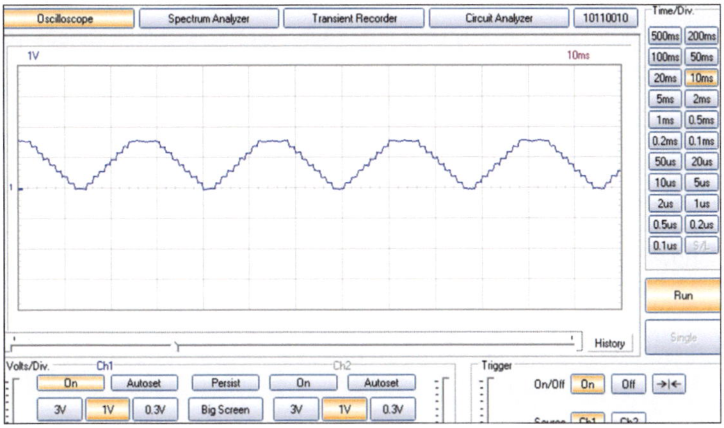

Figure 12.16: Output waveform.

12.8 Project 6: Generating a sinewave

Description: In this project we will generate a sinewave-shaped signal using the trigonometric function *sin*. The generated sine wave should have the peak-to-peak amplitude of 1.4 V, a frequency of 50 Hz, and an offset of 1 V.
The block diagram and circuit diagram are as in Figure 12.2 and Figure 12.3, respectively.

Program listing: Since the required frequency is 50 Hz, the period is 20 ms or 20,000 μs. If we assume that the sinewave will consist of 100 samples, then each sample must be output at 20,000 / 100 = 200 μs.

The sine function has the following format:

Offset + PeaktoPeak / 2 × sin(2 × π × Count / *T*)

where, ***T*** is the period of the waveform and is equal to 100 samples. **Count** is a variable that ranges from 0 to 100 and is incremented by 1, **PeaktoPeak** is the peak-to-peak amplitude, and Offset is the DC offset (this is necessary because the sinewave has negative values, but the DAC only outputs positive values and therefore we have to shift the sinewave up by a DC offset).
The sum of Offset and Amplitude voltage must not be greater than +3.3 V, being the maximum output voltage the DAC can deliver, hence:

Offset + PeaktoPeak <= +3.3 V

The actual required DC offset is equal to:

Required DC offset = Offset – PeaktoPeak / 2.

Therefore, Offset in the above formula is calculated as:

Offset = Required DC offset + PeaktoPeak / 2

The sinewave is divided into 100 samples and each sample is output at 200 μs intervals. The sine formula can be written as follows:

Required DC offset + PeaktoPEak / 2 + PeaktoPeak / 2 × sin(0.0628 × Count)

Therefore, at each sample, we will calculate and output the above value to the DAC.

Figure 12.17 shows the program listing (Program: **Sine**). At the beginning of the program the peak-to-peak amplitude and the offset are defined and converted into digital values for the DAC. The sine values are calculated outside the program loop and stored in list **sins** in order to save time. Inside the main program the sine samples are sent to the DAC and are then output.

```
#------------------------------------------------------------
#               GENERATE SINE WAVEFORM
#               ======================
#
# In this project a MCP4921 type DAC chip is connected to the
# Raspberry Pi Pico.The program generates a sine waveform with
# the specifications given in the text
#
# Author: Dogan Ibrahim
# File  : Sine.py
# Date  : February 2021
#--------------------------------------------------------------
from machine import Pin, SPI
import utime
import math
```

```
spi_sck = Pin(2)                                         # SCK pin at GP2
spi_tx = Pin(3)                                          # TX pin at GP3
spi_rx = Pin(0)                                          # RX pin at GP0 (not
used)

spi = SPI(0,sck=spi_sck,mosi=spi_tx,miso=spi_rx,baudrate=100000)

CS = Pin(16, Pin.OUT)                                    # CS
CS.value(1)                                              # Disable chip

R = 0.0628
T = 100
Conv = 4095.0 / 3.3
PeaktoPeak = 1.4 * Conv                                  # 1.4V
ReqDCoffset = 1.0 * Conv                                 # 1.6V

def DAC(data):
    buff = [0, 0]
    buff[0] = (data >> 8) & 0x0F                         # HIGH byte
    buff[0] = buff[0] + 0x30
    buff[1] = data & 0xFF                                # LOW byte
    CS.value(0)                                          # Enable MCP4921
    spi.write(bytearray(buff))                           # Send to SPI bus
    CS.value(1)                                          # DIsable MCP4921

#
# Main program
#
sins=[0]*101

for i in range (101):
    sins[i] = ReqDCoffset+PeaktoPeak/2 + PeaktoPeak/2 * math.sin(R*i)

while True:
    for k in range(101):
        value = sins[k]
        DAC(int(value))
        utime.sleep_us(200)
```

Figure 12.17: Program: Sine.

Figure 12.18 shows the generated output waveform. Here, the horizontal axis was 20 ms/division, and the vertical axis was 1 V/division. The offset and the peak-to-peak amplitude of the waveform are correct, but as described earlier the timing of the generated signal is not very accurate and timer interrupts can be used to generate accurate output.

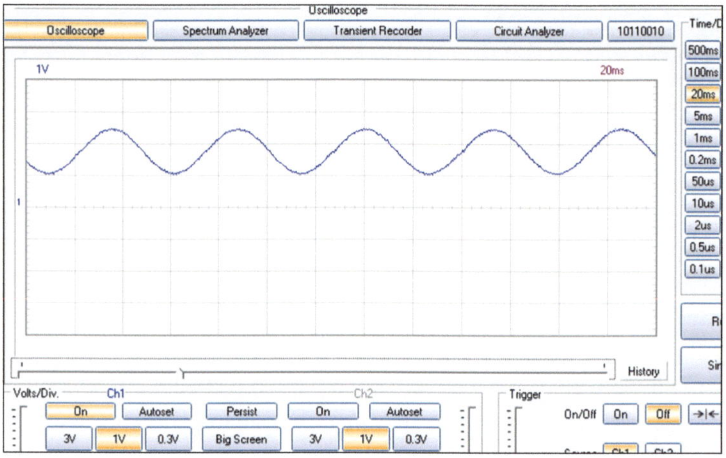

Figure 12.18: Output waveform.

12.9 Project 7: Generating an accurate sinewave signal using timer interrupts

Description: In this project we will generate an accurate sinewave signal using timer interrupts. Here, the required peak-to-peak amplitude is 1.4 V, the required offset is 1 V, and the required frequency is 50 Hz (period = 20 ms). In this project, we will take 50 samples instead of 100, so that the duration of each sample is 400 µs. In the program, a timer interrupt is configured with the callback function of **DAC** and frequency of 2500 Hz (i.e. 400 µs for each call). Inside function DAC, the data samples are indexed by variable **k** which is incremented at each interrupt. These samples are then output by the DAC.

Program listing: Figure 12.19 shows the program listing (Program: **Sineint**).

```
#----------------------------------------------------------
#              GENERATE SINE WAVEFORM
#              ======================
#
# In this project a MCP4921 type DAC chip is connected to the
# Raspberry Pi Pico.The program generates a sine waveform with
# the specifications given in the text
#
# This program uses timer interrupts for accurate timings
#
# Author: Dogan Ibrahim
# File  : Sineint.py
# Date  : February 2021
#------------------------------------------------------------
from machine import Pin, SPI, Timer
import utime
import math
```

```
tim = Timer()
spi_sck = Pin(2)                                # SCK pin at GP2
spi_tx = Pin(3)                                 # TX pin at GP3
spi_rx = Pin(0)                                 # RX pin at GP0 (not used)

spi = SPI(0,sck=spi_sck,mosi=spi_tx,miso=spi_rx,baudrate=100000)

CS = Pin(16, Pin.OUT)                           # CS
CS.value(1)                                     # Disable chip

R = 2 * 3.14159/50
T = 100
Conv = 4095.0 / 3.3
PeaktoPeak = 1.4 * Conv                         # 1.4V
ReqDCoffset = 1.0 * Conv                        # 1.6V
k = 0

def DAC(timer):
    global k, CS, sins
    buff = [0, 0]
    k = k + 1
    if k == 50:
      k = 0
    data = int(sins[k])
    buff[0] = (data >> 8) & 0x0F               # HIGH byte
    buff[0] = buff[0] + 0x30
    buff[1] = data & 0xFF                      # LOW byte
    CS.value(0)                                # Enable MCP4921
    spi.write(bytearray(buff))                 # Send to SPI bus
    CS.value(1)                                # DIsable MCP4921

#
# Main program
#
sins=[0]*101

for i in range (101):
    sins[i] = ReqDCoffset+PeaktoPeak/2 + PeaktoPeak/2 * math.sin(R*i)

tim.init(freq=2500, mode = Timer.PERIODIC, callback = DAC)
```

Figure 12.19: Program: Sineint.

Figure 12.20 shows the output waveform. Here, the horizontal axis was10 ms/division and the vertical axis was 1 V/division. Clearly, the period of the waveform is exactly 20 s as required, the offset is 1 V and the peak-to-peak amplitude is 1.4 V.

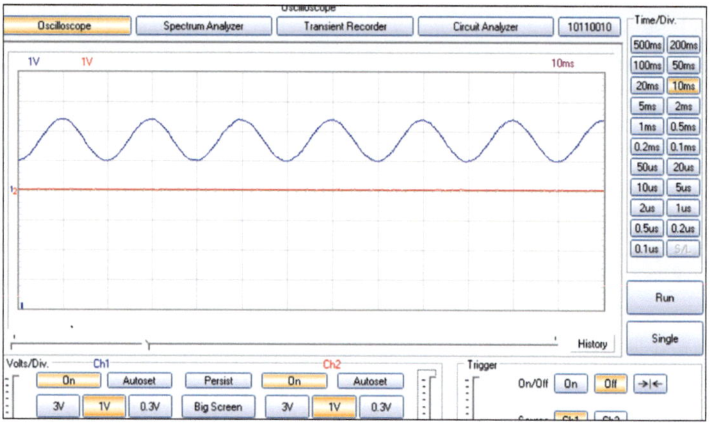

Figure 12.20: Output waveform.

Chapter 13 • Automatic Program Execution after the Raspberry Pi Pico Boots

There may be applications where we may want to start a program automatically after the Raspberry Pi Pico boots. Perhaps the easiest way to learn how this is done is to give a very simple example. The program shown in Figure 13.1 flashes an LED connected to port pin GP6 every second. We will configure the Raspberry Pi Pico so that the LED starts flashing immediately after the Pico boots.

```
#------------------------------------------------------------
#       RUNNING A PROGRAM AUTOMATICALLY AFTER REBOOT
#       ===========================================
#
# In some applications we may want to run a program
# automatically after reboot.This is done easily by saving
# the program with the name "main.py". This very simple
# program flashes an LED connected to GP16 automatically
# after the Raspberry Pi Pico boots.
#
# Author: Dogan Ibrahim
# File  : main.py
# Date  : February 2021
#--------------------------------------------------------------
from machine import Pin
import utime

LED = Pin(16, Pin.OUT)                    # LED at pin 16

while True:                               # Do Forever
    LED.value(1)                          # LED ON
    utime.sleep(1)                        # Wait 1 second
    LED.value(0)                          # LED OFF
    utime.sleep(1)                        # Wait 1 second
```

Figure 13.1: Simple program to flash an LED.

The steps to execute are as follows.

- Give a name to your program and run it to make sure that there are no errors, and it runs as expected (in this case, the LED flashes every second).
- Stop the program by clicking menu item **Run** in Thonny, followed by **Stop/Restart backend**.
- Click **File** followed by **Save as**, then click **Raspberry Pi Pico** (Figure 13.2) to save the file in the Raspberry Pi Pico memory.

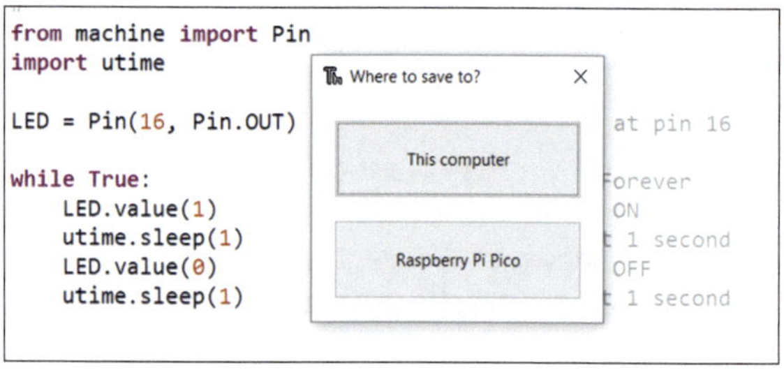

Figure 13.2: Click Raspberry Pi Pico to save file.

- Enter the filename as **main.py** and click **OK**.
- Confirm that the file is saved correctly. Click **File** followed by **Open** and click **Raspberry Pi Pico**. You should see file with the name 'main.py' listed (Figure 13.3). You may have to scroll down.

Figure 13.3: File 'main.py'.

- Reboot your Raspberry Pi Pico and you should see the LED flashing as soon as the Pico boots.
- You can stop the program out of Thonny by clicking **Run**, followed by **Stop/ Restart backend**.
- You should either remove or rename file **main.py** if you do not want it to start automatically.

That's it! From now on, you can make your Raspberry Pi Pico auto-execute a suitable program, immediately after booting.

Appendix A • Bill of Components

Electronic Components & Modules

- Through-hole / leaded parts only
- 8× red LED
- 8× 470Ω resistor
- 2× pushbutton
- 1× RGB LED
- 2× 2-digit 7-segment LED display (e.g. DC56-11EWA)
- 4× NPN transistor (any, small-signal), e.g. BC548, BC108
- 1× LCD
- 1× 10kΩ potentiometer
- 1× 220Ω resistor
- 1× buzzer
- 1× HC-SR04 ultrasonic sensor
- 2× TMP36 temperature sensor
- 1× 1kΩ resistor
- 1× 2kΩ resistor
- 1× 3.3V relay
- 1× LDR
- 2× 10kΩ resistor
- 1× KY-013
- 1× KY-021
- 1× KY-034
- 1× diode (e.g. 1N4148)
- 1× IRL540 MOSFET
- 1× small, brushed DC motor
- 1× 2.2kΩ resistor
- 1× MCP23017
- 1× MCP23S17
- 1× BMP280 module
- 1× 24LC256 EEPROM
- 1× HC-06 Bluetooth module
- 1× MCP4921 DAC
- 1× breadboard
- 10× jumper wires (male-male, various lengths)
- 1× microUSB cable

Processor Boards & SBCs:

- 1× Raspberry Pi Pico
- 1× ESP-01 *
- 1× Arduino UNO *
- 1× Raspberry Pi 4 *

* For the advanced communications projects only.

Index